AVID
READER
PRESS

A SANE PERSON'S GUIDE TO TAKING BACK THE BIBLE FROM FUNDAMENTALISTS, FASCISTS, AND FLOCK-FLEECING FRAUDS

JOHN FUGELSANG

AVID READER PRESS

NEW YORK AMSTERDAM/ANTWERP LONDON TORONTO SYDNEY/MELBOURNE NEW DELHI

Avid Reader Press
An Imprint of Simon & Schuster, LLC
1230 Avenue of the Americas
New York, NY 10020

First Avid Reader Press hardcover edition August 2025

Manufactured in the United States of America

7 9 10 8

Library of Congress Control Number: 2025938762

ISBN 978-1-6680-6689-8
ISBN 978-1-6680-6691-1 (ebook)

For my mother and father;
also known as

Peggy *and* Jack;

also known as

Sister Damien *and* Brother Boniface.

And I'm sorry for all the profanity.

Jesus was:

A peaceful, radically nonviolent revolutionary
Who wasn't American and never spoke English
Who hung around lepers, hookers, and crooks
Never sought tax cuts for rich Nazarenes
Was anti-wealth and anti–death penalty
Anti–public prayer, too (Matthew 6:5)
Never asked lepers for a co-pay
Never called poor people "lazy"
Never even slightly antigay
Never mentioned abortion
Supported paying taxes
And was a long-haired
Community-organizing
Authority-questioning
Anti-slut-shaming
Brown-skinned
Palestinian
Unarmed
Homeless
Jew

. . . but only if you believe what's actually in the Bible.

I’ve come to view Jesus
the way I’ve come to view Elvis.
I love the guy, but some of the fan clubs terrify me.

Contents

“Why do you call me, ‘Lord, Lord,’ and do not do what I say?”

Jesus, Luke 6:46

An Introduction

I'm here because two people broke a promise to God.

My mother was born during the Depression in the Blue Ridge Mountains of Virginia. Her name was Mary Margaret, but she always went by Peggy, and she entered the convent directly out of high school. Her prom date had asked her that night if she would marry him. She politely declined, gently informing the poor boy that she'd already made plans to marry someone else.

At age eighteen, while other kids were still enjoying the 1950s, she joined the Daughters of Wisdom order. She ceased to be Mary Margaret and received her new name, Sister Damien. This was before the movie *The Omen* was released, but you can imagine the jokes she would've had to live with had things worked out differently.

The convent put her through nursing school and then sent her to Africa, first to work with lepers, and then at a village hospital in Malawi.

But before they sent her overseas to begin her new life, they briefly assigned her to Holy Family Hospital in Brooklyn, New York.

My father had been born in Brooklyn just a few months before her, and had become a Franciscan brother a year after graduating high school. He'd been working as a butcher at the Brooklyn fish market, and after losing half a finger, celibacy probably seemed like a step up. Upon entering the brotherhood, he ceased being Jack and became Brother Boniface. As a brother, he taught history to Catholic boys at St. Francis Prep, coached basketball, wore the robe and rope belt, and walked among the people like the Lost Jedi of Flatbush.

My father, the brother, met my mother, the sister, when he entered Holy

Family for tuberculosis treatment. By all accounts, he was instantly smitten by this quiet, Southern girl in a nun's habit, a woman he knew he couldn't have, and had promised God he would never want.

She was reserved and came from the segregated South; he was all Brooklyn charm and passionate about civil rights in ways her Southern father was not. He was exactly one foot taller than her, and their strong Southern and Brooklyn regionalisms did not suggest any potential compatibility.

But they became friends, and when the convent sent Sister Damien to Malawi, Brother Boniface took it upon himself to write her letters—many letters—to innocently keep her informed of what was going on in the states—civil rights, Vietnam, and US politics.

Her village had no TV or radio, so his letters became the de facto newspaper for the entire convent. Her Mother Superior would open his envelopes and read them aloud; Damien was often the last to read her own mail.

Eventually, she returned—briefly—to the US. After ten years of hiding his feelings, poorly, my father eventually convinced her to leave the convent and go on a date.

They were married two months later, in the chapel at Fort Story Army base in Virginia Beach. They soon settled on Long Island and tried to raise us to be progressive, free-thinking, sexually repressed Catholics.

Which is why I would eventually turn to stand-up comedy, as I could never afford the therapy I so deeply required.

SON OF A NUN

My brothers and I were raised in Bohemia, Long Island, listed in the *Guinness Book* under "Most Ironic Town Name." If you knew what "bohemian" meant, you were probably the town bohemian. We were an *extremely* Catholic family. I'm pretty sure we had open-casket reunions.

Lots of kids had to go to church twice a year. A few had to go every Sunday and give something up for Lent. We attended Catholic Mass every Sunday and every single holy day, even when that meant church *after school.* Skipping church was not an option—ever, for any reason—except extreme illness or if you were dying. And if it looked like you might die on a Sunday, then you'd still have to get to five o'clock Mass on Saturday night.

We learned all the Bible stories that kids are usually taught: Adam and Eve in the garden, Noah building the ark, Moses parting the Red Sea. The slaughter of the Midianites, where God commands Moses to kill all the men and nonvirgin women—but keep all the virgin girls—didn't make its way into any of our illustrated children's Bibles.

My dad was a lector, CCD (like Sunday school, except rarely on Sundays and seldom in schools) teacher, and eucharistic minister at church; my Uncle Louis in Brooklyn was a Catholic deacon; my brother an altar boy. And when my mother became head nurse at a convent nursing home for her former order, there was a steady multicultural flow of elderly nuns in and out of our house.

We said grace before every dinner and our prayers before bedtime.

Whereas some kids were taught piano, my parents got me *organ lessons*.

And to the best of my knowledge, I was the only child in Bohemia, Long Island, to have been baptized in his parents' living room by a priest his mother had known in the jungles of Africa.

And I was taught—relentlessly—that Christianity was about the things Jesus prioritized: Service to others. Forgiveness. Caring for the poor, the sick, the stranger, the prisoner. Fighting injustice with nonviolence, like Dr. King and Gandhi. Standing up for the less fortunate, like Dorothy Day and Catholic Charities. Love. Empathy. Compassion. And go wash your hands, we're leaving for Mass in five minutes.

My parents presented as Republicans, identified as Independents, and lived like closeted Democrats.

Like most dads, mine was liberal in some ways and conservative in others. He maintained the same severely short haircut regardless of what decade he was in, flew the US flag outside our home, and believed God was love. His overall parenting strategy was to guarantee that I'd be way too liberal to ever fit in with Christians and far too Christian to ever blend with liberals.

And almost every therapist I've ever been able to afford has agreed that his plan worked perfectly.

When I was very young, my father pulled me out of bed late one night to watch Jimmy Carter sign the Camp David Accords between Israel and Egypt. He couldn't believe an American Christian had helped bring peace to part of the Middle East, and he wanted his kid to witness Christian, Jew, and Muslim embracing each other.

I was too sleepy and confused to even understand what I was seeing. Moshe Dayan had an eyepatch, which was cool, I guess. My father's face convinced me of the moment's significance. I had never seen him so happy. To him, this was everything Christianity—and America—could and should be.

I was lucky to grow up around large Catholic families in both Brooklyn and the South—and to have eventually married into a very sane Protestant family. I've been blessed with relations who've been White, Black, and Latino; gay and transgender; cops and convicts; military members, teachers, chefs, immigrants, DREAMers, and firefighters; hardcore right-wingers, reasonable Libertarians, compassionate lefties, and the happily politically apathetic. I've had Muslim cousins, Jewish in-laws, an atheist brother, and an ex-nun mother. I don't get to hate *anybody.*

Big families meant many reunions, many conservative relatives, many cans of beer. My dad would often debate loved ones on politics and scripture, in the same gregarious Brooklynite way he'd debated for years with his Franciscan housemates. It exasperated my Southern mom, but everyone mostly loved each other, despite any differences in voting habits.

I think many of us remember an America when family could disagree over politics while still generally getting along. Maybe yours still can.

And I swear, it all seemed quite normal at the time.

I had no idea growing up what *Roe v. Wade* was, nor did I know that the issue of abortion was splitting and redefining American Christianity. But when the Christian Coalition and the Moral Majority decided to make abortion their central political issue—half a decade after *Roe v. Wade,* by the way—the American church would never be the same.

In the eighties and nineties, my father the social studies teacher always kept the news on. Being that this was during the rise of the Moral Majority and Christian right, I was exposed to many interviews with white men who were introduced as "Christian leaders."

But these Christians didn't talk about helping the poor, welcoming the stranger, or fighting injustice. They never mentioned the evils of racism. They didn't quote scripture to justify the need for all of us to take care of the least of us.

If you watched American TV news in the late twentieth century, you received a steady diet of Jerry Falwell, Pat Robertson, and all manner of ex-segregationists and blow-dried televangelists, all ranting about welfare queens, feminists, and AIDS patients.

These right-wing Christian media stars preached the virtue of forcing poor pregnant women to give birth against their will, that they might experience substantially greater poverty and greater risk to their health. They warned us that any government programs that actually helped the poor were "communist." They expressed outrage at protests *against* racism, while never denouncing actual racism. They always punched down—always attacking the poor, the addicts, the migrants at the border, and a gay minority they assured me the Bible condemned, somewhere.

Millions of American Christians were media-fed this version of Christianity. White supremacist. Pro-apartheid. Anti-labor. Zero teachings of Jesus. Offering only condemnation and propaganda, always seeking more power, and always needing more cash.

Watching TV news was the first time I became aware of Christianity as a political force in my country, but it was a Christianity I couldn't understand. I didn't have the words to express it, but it was awkward to be told I was the same religion as these men.

These were the fundamentalists, the power-hungry grifters who took advantage of the fact that most people don't know the Bible all that well. They were charlatans, frauds, hypocrites, and villains. And they made for great TV.

Within a decade, Christianity in US media culture would become synonymous with the criminalize-abortion movement and condemning gay people. And the fact that attacking abortion and gay people has (checks notes) *nothing* to do with the ministry and teachings of Jesus has never gotten in the way of the right-wing agenda. And apparently, the media's still never been told.

My parents generally felt that some people had abortions too casually, but they would never vote for any politician who would take that right away. They never joined a political party but also never voted Republican (for "Jesus-based reasons"). Years later, my mother would tell me about hospitals pre-*Roe*, saying most nuns she'd worked with as nurses vigorously supported giving women the choice.

But by the 1990s, if you told another young person you were "Christian," they often presumed that you despised gay people and feminists and thought the government should force rape victims to be pregnant by their attacker.

BEHOLD, THE "SMALL C CHRISTIANS"

Now, some of my atheist friends like to say that religion is responsible for all the world's hate, violence, sexism, homophobia, war, and oppression. In a 2018 *US News and World Report* survey of more than twenty-one thousand people from all regions of the world, the majority of respondents identified religion as the "primary source of most global conflict today." And I can certainly understand why they feel that way.

But they're mistaken.

The primary driver of most global conflict, oppression of women, suppression of science, persecution of gay people, and abuse of power is not religion. It's the *extreme fundamentalist* wings of all the world's religions that provide all these dramas for the rest of humanity.

The overwhelming majority of progressive, moderate, and even conservative Christians, Jews, and Muslims are getting along just fine, right now, in all corners of the earth—just trying to make their way through life and leave a better world for their kids.

Of course, people from different backgrounds peacefully coexisting, working together, and building families, businesses, and communities in a drama-free way doesn't attract much media attention. But the violent lunatics and bigots? They get the eyeballs and clicks, so they still get the coverage.

In recent decades, the US has witnessed fundamentalist Christianity publicly mutating into Christian nationalism: the belief that God intended America to be a Christian nation and that a "true" American should be Christian, too. These hopeless romantics fervently believe the Bible *must* be prioritized in both your government and your day-to-day life.

Well, *their* interpretation of the Bible, that is.

This powerful, profoundly white, well-funded, and growing movement seeks to impose a very narrow religious identity on our entire nation. And it all serves a deeply inspiring vision, where America gets to be a second-rate theocracy, like Iran, guided by ultraconservative values that just so happen to put their group first.

"Christian nationalism" is also becoming an umbrella term for all kinds of right-wing zealotry:

- The fundamentalists, who use faith as a cover for power and control.
- The spiritual bullies, convinced that they get to be as cruel and judgmental as they want because they already know for a fact they're going to heaven.
- The Apocalypse worshippers, whose Bible is pretty much just Revelation duct-taped to a Left-Behind Book.
- Pious politicians who brag they've accepted Jesus as their savior, while actually only accepting him as their mascot.
- The Strapped Bro-Dudes for Jesus, worshiping a jacked-up, gun-toting, ass-kicking Alpha Christ, who doesn't actually appear in the Jesus parts of the Bible.
- The Christian supremacists, who always believe violence is morally acceptable if it's *their* side doing it.
- The Holy Haters, convinced that God despises the same people they do, including LGBTQ people, immigrants, academics,

Muslims, Jews, the poor, foreigners in general, environmentalists, science believers, people who support women's reproductive rights, people who think gun safety laws could maybe help save a few lives, racial minorities, liberals, organized labor, feminists, atheists, and/or anyone else they think God put here by accident.

While many of these movements overlap, the general shared goal is societal control, under the guise of "defending Christianity." They don't care about Jesus's teachings or commandments. They're not really concerned with "freedom of religion." Their mission is earthly power, in the form of a Christian nation that's controlled by their specific, Jesus-free take on the Bible.

These groups are aggressively shaping our political discourse, cultural norms, and legislative priorities. They don't like that they can't control women anymore, and they're terrified of becoming a minority in a country they believe they own.

And our meanest Christians tend to piously and publicly worship Jesus as their King, because that's considerably easier than following his inconvenient teachings.

- They fight for legislation that neglects the poor and vulnerable, defunding social welfare programs and criminalizing homelessness.
- They do this while prioritizing tax cuts for the wealthy, exacerbating poverty and inequality but never alleviating suffering.
- They weaponize scripture they themselves don't follow against minorities they dislike.
- They preach nationalism over global compassion.
- And they often frame anyone who disagrees as "enemies of God."

It's a gospel of control over caring, power over humility, and judgment over mercy. They won't fight for the words of Jesus, but they're profoundly committed to stuff they *believe* he said.

For many of our right-wing friends and neighbors, Jesus is three things—the manger, the miracles, and the cross—but never the three years he spent teaching, reforming, and explaining what a "Christian nation" would actually need to do to earn that label.

Jesus modeled servant leadership, washing his disciples' feet and teaching that the greatest among his followers should be the servant of all (John 13:1–17, Matthew 20:26–28). He was *not* about total right-wing domination of the school board.

Many Americans can remember being raised in a Christianity that focused on love, forgiveness, and service—the values of the biblical Jesus, whom Christians are generally supposed to follow, above the other parts of the Bible. And yet millions of bewildered Americans have grown up to find this religion of peace and empathy has been hijacked by a right-wing movement that uses Jesus's name, waves him over their heads like a prop, and legislates against his actual teachings.

And if there's one thing the Bible shows us, it's that authoritarian government, aligned with some extreme conservative religious fundamentalists, literally killed Jesus.

Also, Some of Them Like to Kill People

From the 2012 Oak Creek, Wisconsin, Sikh temple shooting to the 2015 Charleston church shooting; from the 2017 Charlottesville Unite the Right rally to the 2018 Tree of Life Congregation synagogue shooting; to the US Capitol attack of January 6, 2021—all acts of violence committed by right-wing men who proclaimed themselves Christian.

Any Christian individual or group who advocates, engages in, or justifies violence directly rejects Jesus's unglamorous, deeply unsexy teachings of non-retaliation and love. Jesus blessed the peacemakers (Matthew 5:9) and taught reconciliation (Matthew 5:23–24). His true followers are instructed to live in peace with everyone (Romans 12:18). He quite famously challenged his followers to love their enemies and to care for those who are different from them.

But Christian nationalists and white supremacists have shown what religious zealotry and authoritarian propaganda can do in a country that has over one hundred guns for every person.

ALWAYS IN POWER, ALWAYS UNDER SIEGE

In contemporary America, you'll hear a steady refrain from the pulpits of preachers and the podiums of politicians: "Christianity is under attack." Christians still constitute the majority and wield significant cultural and political influence, mind you, but that's never stopped a narrative of systemic oppression.

This talking point, which pairs nicely with shrieking claims of persecution, warns of an encroaching secular agenda that seeks to destroy "traditional Christian values" and turn our families into transgender atheist groomer communists who listen to hip-hop and use paper straws.

Politicians use the "Christianity under attack" rhetoric to secure votes and consolidate power. By framing themselves as warriors in a spiritual battle, they thirstily pander to a sense of tribal loyalty among a certain kind of Christian voter.

Televangelists and megachurch pastors have long capitalized on the victimhood narrative to solicit donations and build obscene personal wealth. And polarizing cultural wedge issues are historically one of the slickest ways to redirect attention away from real social and economic problems.

Examples of "Christianity under attack" have included First Amendment restrictions on public prayer in government settings, restrictions *against* anti-LGBTQ discrimination, and resistance to teaching creationism in public school science class. Nothing that threatens Christian religious practice—just conservative religious domination.

Donald Trump never even tried to sell himself as an actual Christian to earn blind evangelical obedience. Rather, he easily attracted voters sympathetic to Christian nationalist ideas by branding himself as a defender of "Christians under siege." Which is to say he pandered to and played up the persecution complex:

> "I will tell you, Christianity is under tremendous siege, whether we want to talk about it or we don't want to talk about it. . . . And we're going to reverse that trend big league."
>
> January 30, 2016, campaign event in Dubuque

Christianity *is* under attack—but by divisive right-wing fundamentalists who publicly worship Jesus while fighting against, voting against, and legislating against his actual commandments.

Help the poor? No.

Care for the sick? No.

Turn the other cheek? No.

Render one's taxes? No, sucker.

Be kind to the incarcerated? Hell no.

Welcome the stranger? Bitch, please.

Modern right-wing Christians have been suckered into an anti-Christian trap of aligning with power, instead of challenging it. But conservative power was what Jesus stood up *to*—not *for*—time and time again:

- The authoritarians among the religious leaders, drunk on their own eminence.
- The wealthy, worshiping their own stature and possessions while denying the suffering of the poor.
- The capitalists in the temple, greedily exploiting poor believers.
- The imperial government of Rome, whose hunger for power led to its own collapse.

Religion, like all institutions of man, is inherently flawed, but irony will never let you down.

THE MOST IMPORTANT PART

Shakespeare tells us that even "the devil can recite Scripture for his purpose." And from the very beginnings of the American experiment, Christianity has been used to justify all manner of evils, from slavery to ethnic cleansing to preemptive war.

Historically, American Christians of both major political parties have used a Bible to justify the slaughter of Indigenous people, the enslavement of African people, the labor exploitation of Asian people, ignoring the suffering of European Jewish people, cruelty to gay people, the indiscriminate detention and torture of Muslim people, and of course, pushing perpetual second-class citizenship on female people.

But there's another side to this.

Because for nearly every great injustice perpetrated throughout history by authoritarian Christianity, liberal and moderate Christians—and many conservatives, too—have fought back. Progressive Christians helped lead the battle to abolish slavery. They've opposed imperialism, segregation, and science denial; fought for humane conditions for the American worker and for an end to child labor.

Throughout history, Christian reform movements have dared to critically engage authority with scripture and tradition, supporting compassion, social justice, and human rights, as Jesus did. And I'm sorry, but they really do listen to better music.

Decent Christians—including moderates and sane conservatives—along with righteous atheists, agnostics, and many people of other religions, have *always* had to band together to beat back the batshit-crazy Christians.

St. Francis of Assisi left the Crusades and preached against war. The Reverend Dr. Martin Luther King Jr., a Baptist, used the scriptures to shame white America out of the mutually destructive American apartheid of segregation. And millions of liberal Christians have, very gradually, helped many conservative loved ones beyond a whole lot of homophobia.

It's sadly not a coincidence that some of the most historically bigoted and segregated parts of this American Land have also been known as the "Bible Belt." And if there's one thing I've learned, it's that nobody hates like a Christian who's just been told their hate isn't Christian.

Liberal and moderate Jesus-following Christians—and their allies—have the power to stand up to right-wing Christianity and call its adherents out on their own terms, using the very book fundamentalists wave around so bombastically.

Never forget that the first-ever protest by a white person in this hemisphere against slavery and human rights abuses was against Columbus himself, led by his ship's own Catholic priest, Bartolomé de Las Casas. There's an inspiring true heritage of authentic Christianity, and it's almost always manifested itself in resistance to Christian authoritarianism.

SEPARATION OF CHURCH AND HATE

This is a book about what Christianity started out as, what it became, and why it's still worth fighting for. It's about the grotesque mutation that is Christian nationalism and how fundamentalism has always been the opposite of Jesus, even though it gets most of the TV airtime. And it'll show how the best of Christianity has always pushed back against the worst of it.

This book is *not* an attack on God, Jesus, or Christianity. It's not designed to ridicule people of faith or mock belief.

It's not another atheist manifesto, and it won't try to convince you that religious people are superstitious or dumb.

It's also not going to ask you to believe in miracles or divinity, or to take all of the Bible as literal fact. Most Christians don't.

It doesn't denigrate the idea of organized religion, and it won't mock the life or teachings of Jesus.

It's designed to help you use the Bible when engaging with the Christian fundamentalist in your life, at your job, or, if you must, in your social media feed.

It's a guide to everything the haters got wrong. It focuses on Christianity through the teachings of Jesus, known to some as the "red letters" of the

Bible. And it'll show that if you're debating an authoritarian Christian on almost any subject that divides us, Jesus probably has your back.

Whether you're a believer, agnostic, or atheist, whatever you think about politics, you're going to have to deal with these people at some point. They want to control the level of freedom in US society based on how they pick and choose from the Bible.

It's going to be increasingly vital to dismantle their supernatural authority by elegantly pointing out that they don't really follow this Bible they claim to base their lives on. And you'll be surprised at how good it feels, too.

You may find yourself unable to escape a particular person like this in your life, and that person may delight in projecting authoritarianism or hate as some kind of spiritual piety.

But there are two things to remember: Much of the time, these people don't really know the Bible all that well. And they're 100 percent counting on *you* not knowing the Bible all that well.

For all of our lives, fundamentalists have used the Bible to manipulate their way into our government, all over our school boards, and onto our airwaves. If they're going to stand in your house and claim to represent Jesus, you're allowed to prove if they really mean it.

The extreme right uses Jesus's name as camouflage. This is a guide to camouflage removal.

A FEW HELPFUL DISCLAIMERS

First, I am not a clergy member, nor a professional academic or theologian. This means I will not be using the word "exegesis" at all in this book, beyond this sentence.

But I do know many wonderful scholars and clergy, gracious and learned people with all the spiritual and academic depth I lack, and they have charitably allowed me to ask them about a few theological specifics above my pay grade.

I am but a friendly guy on a barstool, tugging on your coat about what's actually in the Bible. But I promise: What I lack in credentials, I make up for in name-dropping.

As a comedian, I've long known that taking on toxic Christianity is not a commercially viable subject matter. But like many, I got tired of seeing my parents' faith used to merge Jesus and meanness. Against the strenuous wishes of many wise agents and managers, I began talking about Christianity onstage.

And everywhere I've performed, spoken, or broadcast, I've been amazed at the massive numbers of truly good people I've met, of every conceivable background, who were raised Christian but now feel alienated from the domination and cruelty of so many churches.

Now, I won't be claiming to be anything resembling a great Christian. Tragically far from it. I'm happy to run through an extensive list of sins and shortcomings for you.

But Jesus taught me the joy of calling out pious religious frauds, and I'd like to show you how rewarding it can be.

I generally trust people who are seeking the truth; I tend to be wary of those who claim they've found it. When I cite specific scripture, I strongly encourage you to doubt me—and research what the Bible really says. I won't ask you to believe anything I can't prove, so you'll know I'm not selling you religion.

A few more things before we begin:

- This book covers many topics and you're welcome to create your own adventure and skip around. Because the teachings and commandments of Jesus are relevant to many of our modern debates, some quotes and parables are cited more than once, in different chapters.
- Throughout the book, I frequently refer to the Torah as "the Old Testament." I'm sorry if you're offended by the term; it's the simplest shorthand for talking to Christians, and I'm a simple person.
- Also, I won't be capitalizing the *H* in "He" or "Him" every time I talk about Jesus. I tried it, but it started to feel a bit too much after a while.

- I'll still capitalize the *H* when referring to God, so you'll know I'm not trying to be disrespectful. I know how certain right-wing folks are sensitive about pronouns.
- Most cited verses are from the NIV Bible, but I do go full King James for some of the gorier moments.
- And please know, nice conservative Christians, that this book is *not about you*—it's about those extreme right-wing hateful Christians. I come from two large, rather conservative American Christian families. And while I may disagree politically on some issues with our conservative Christian brethren, I've always found most to be quite lovely, and often more liberal with kindness than many, well, liberals.

  But nice conservative Christians are going to have to deal with these haters too, so I thank you for making it this far. There will be much in this book that conservatives will disagree with; I'll try to be as polite as I can. Parts are quite silly, and I'm sorry for that. The point is, intrepid conservative friends, while we may disagree, I know you won't hate me with a violent bloodlust over it.
- And let me point out that nowhere in this book will I suggest that the Democratic party is somehow the party of Jesus on a policy level. Far from it. I've never belonged to a political party, and I'm happy to hear you out about big money in politics, Wall Street donors and lobbyist culture, lip service to climate action, how our representatives don't fight hard enough for single-payer healthcare, universal basic income, unions, paid family leave, etc. I'm all ears.

  But while Democrats fall painfully short in many ways, their party policies on healthcare, social safety nets, immigration, gun safety, women's equality, gay rights, and antiracism are *light-years closer* to the teachings of Jesus than Trump-era Republicanism, which remains the brazen, junk-wagging opposite of JC's actual words.
- Atheist friends—thank you for making it this far. And I get it—we're arguing over a book that was written by Bronze Age goat

herders who thought the earth was flat, etc., etc. I know. And I agree with you that religion should have no power over our governance, but here we are. Nonbelievers will also have to deal with fundamentalist Christians; perhaps you already do, perhaps they're the family you still love. I can confirm that calling them superstitious cult members or saying they're brainwashed to believe in myths doesn't work. The hardcore ones will just double down and say you're on the side of Satan.

- But I find that if we positively engage folks like this on what's actually in the Bible, something else can happen. They may get defensive, but they might appreciate that you took the time to engage them on scripture itself. You'll have an easier time convincing them that Jesus wasn't an immigrant-hating homophobe by talking about *what Jesus himself taught* than if you just call them an immigrant-hating homophobe.
- And again, I'm not asking anyone to take anything in the Bible as literal fact. But if you plan on debating the fundamentalist Christian in your life, it helps to know the specifics of who said what and to ask questions rather than seek conflict.
- Also, I tend to be too irreverent when I should be serious, and can sometimes be way too churchy when it's time for a joke. Sorry in advance; I promise to feel guilt over it.

Finally, some surveys will tell you how the fastest-growing religious demographic in America is Mormonism. Some say Islam. More recent ones say "no affiliation."

I would argue there's a large and growing religious group we don't acknowledge—people who were raised religious but now consider themselves "spiritual" because they're turned off by the cruelties and hypocrisies of organized authoritarian religion.

Spiritual people use religion to become better people. Fundamentalists use religion to pretend they're better than other people.

Human hate has been around a lot longer than religion. It's natural and at times we all fall prey to it, but religion didn't create hate—hate found voice in religion.

The right has turned a movement based on compassion and love into a mean, self-worshiping tax-free clique. The intolerance of right-wing Christianity is what's driving young people away from religion. It's not because our youth are controlled by Satan, although the fundamentalists might be.

They've got a First Amendment right to twist scripture to their liking. You've got a First Amendment right to call them out for it.

It's time to take the Bible back from the hypocrites.

And remember—if your church isn't telling you to love your enemies but keeps telling you who your enemies are, you're not really in a church.

AN INCONVENIENT RADICAL JEW

"The politics of Jesus and the politics of God are that people should be fed, that people have access to life, that people should be treated equally and justly."

Rev. James M. Lawson Jr.

Let's talk about this Jesus whom our right-wing Christian friends speak of so frequently and loudly.

Whether you consider him to have been the divine Son of God, a highly evolved teacher and healer, a philosopher and political dissident, a total work of first-century fiction, a jacked-up apocalyptic sword-of-fire bro-dude, or the "original hippie" version, Jesus remains one of the most influential and revolutionary figures in civilization, spirituality, literature, and/or recorded history.

He's also probably the most misunderstood.

According to the Bible we've grown up with, Yeshua bar Yosef was born in the Roman-occupied Palestine of first-century Judea. As a child growing up on Long Island, I could relate to this, as I also lived among many Italians and Jews.

The local religious authorities of Jesus's day were given a tiny bit of power by the empire that ruled their land. Jesus challenged the authority of some of those religious leaders, devoted himself to what some might call a crusade of social justice for the oppressed, and was ultimately executed by the imperial occupiers.

And those of us who've been raised Christian are traditionally taught this story as small children, before we can appreciate what any of that means.

Jesus's public career as a traveling preacher and healer lasted only three years—less than Nirvana and the Smiths, slightly longer than Cream and the Sex Pistols, and about as long as the Jimi Hendrix Experience. He was only one of many radical preachers of the time, and traveled with twelve men and several women—at least three.

You might think that this would mean there were actually fifteen apostles. But women aren't counted as people in the Bible, so any female apostles were officially decreed by the early church to have been sacred-adjacent groupies.

His sermons often involved bold reinterpretation of the Jewish law of the Torah, prioritizing its spiritual and moral elements—not necessarily obedience to rules and rituals. In Matthew 22:37–40, he taught that the essence of the law could be summarized in commands to love God and love your neighbor. He essentially reduced the Ten Commandments down to two, which today would get him banned from the Louisiana public school system.

To our knowledge, Jesus never wrote anything down, but some of our most familiar expressions come from his sermons and parables. "Salt of the earth," "turn the other cheek," "Good Samaritan," "pearls before swine," "wolf in sheep's clothing." And with better management he could've trademarked some of those. If the early church leaders had just claimed the IP for the entire Cross brand, they could've raked it in and maybe not have had to pillage quite so much.

Jesus lived in a politically turbulent time under military occupation. And while he did not advocate for *violent* rebellion, his teachings and actions were seen as politically subversive. Like so many outspoken individuals of all religions who've fought for decency and justice—Gandhi, Dr. Martin Luther King, Medgar Evers, Viola Liuzzo, Anwar Sadat, Yitzhak Rabin—he was killed by authoritarians who didn't want change.

He was anti-violence—with a temper—and when they finally came for him, he didn't fight back, even though his arms-bearing friends were ready to defend him. He was the most famous innocent brown-skinned man ever to be wrongly executed by the state, and he was deliberately killed in the most painful and humiliating of ways.

Franciscan Father Richard Rohr has called him "this naked, bleeding loser." Bob Dylan sang of him as "the one who came and died a criminal's death." He was poor. He owned no property. And at the time he died, he was extremely unpopular.

In short, he's not the kind of guy who typically inspires great religions.

Yet somehow, out of all the many Jewish splinter sects to spring up in Roman-occupied Judea of two thousand years ago, his group caught on. Within three hundred years his movement became the state religion of the very empire that executed him. Christianity went from a tiny apocalyptic Jewish cult to a conquering religion—outlasting even the Roman Empire.

Unbelievable atrocities and countless charities have been done in his name. His church was founded by radical revolutionaries and devolved into conservative bureaucracies.

As of this writing, approximately 2.4 billion people believe in him, across a wide spectrum of sects, ideologies, and traditions. Five and a half billion people don't believe in his divinity, or even his existence.

ABOUT THOSE MIRACLES

Miracles and legends have a significant place in Christian tradition, often serving as demonstrations of Jesus's divine authority. They inspire awe and reinforce belief in God's power; they're also usually the best moments in any of the many Jesus movies they make kids watch.

The stories in the Bible tell of him healing the blind, exorcising demons, and raising the dead. Miracles became an essential part of Jesus's live appearances, because you get a lot further with "love your enemies" *and* healing a blind guy than you do with just "love your enemies."

And of course, we can't prove any of the miracles ever happened. These stories are rooted in a time and context far removed from our own, recorded decades after Jesus's life. Christians take his divinity as a matter of faith, and millions draw inspiration and strength from belief in Jesus's divinity.

But because miracles rely on faith rather than evidence, citing them for other people to live by never works out too well.

In focusing on what cannot be proven, many Christians fall into the trap of a Christianity that's more about defending the supernatural than embodying the moral teachings of Jesus. It's not the miracles driving people away from religion, it's the Christians who don't live by Jesus's words about how we're supposed to treat each other.

THOSE ACTUAL TEACHINGS

> "The application of Jesus' teaching to his social world is also seen in the fact that his movement was the peace party within Palestine."
>
> Marcus Borg, *Jesus: A New Vision*

Jesus began his preaching career at age thirty, and right away you could see the man had a gift. He knew when to speak in parable and metaphor to convey his truths and freshen things up, making complex spiritual concepts more accessible to a wider crowd—including people who weren't highly educated.

By using familiar imagery and narrative—as in the parables of the good shepherd, the lost sheep, and the light under a bushel—he could reach people of all backgrounds without ever having to resort to lowbrow material. Storytelling instead of sermonizing made it easier for people to remember the points he'd make. Speaking in parables also allowed Jesus to convey a message *indirectly,* thereby avoiding confrontation with religious or political authorities who might oppose him. (For comedians, this is called satire, and is also somewhat tricky to pull off commercially.)

Jesus's wisdom is in the principles that cut across religious and secular boundaries: calls to love your enemies, to care for the poor and marginalized.

These teachings don't require belief in supernatural events to be meaningful. Any skeptic can still recognize the wisdom in "Do unto others as you would have them do unto you" or the revolutionary ethic behind "Blessed are the meek, for they shall inherit the earth."

By prioritizing Jesus's teachings, Christianity can emphasize principles that unite, without relying on coerced belief in two-thousand-year-old supernatural accounts to win people over.

- He asked people to freely share everything they had and turn the other cheek, to deliberately break all ancient cycles of hate and suffering.
- He broke social and religious taboos by associating with outcasts and sinners, like tax collectors, prostitutes, and despised foreign Samaritans. He treated them all with compassion, directing his anger instead toward economic injustice and exploitation (Luke 4:18–19, Luke 6:20–21).
- In Mark 12:17, he supports paying taxes for the government to redistribute.
- In Matthew 26:52, he forbids his disciples from using their weapons.
- In John 8, he opposes the legal death penalty.
- And if any politician called for what Jesus commands in Matthew 25, he'd be labeled an open-borders socialist.

Jesus disdained wealth and earthly power, and challenged traditional laws of his own faith. He rejected earthly materialism, renounced the idea of revenge, and commanded us to welcome the stranger.

I know, right? Just like Donald Trump.

Really. Jesus Warned You About These People.

In Matthew 6:5, Jesus denounces public displays of religious piety that are performed so others can see, rather than out of genuine devotion.

"And when you pray, do not be like the hypocrites, for they love to pray standing in the synagogues and on the street corners to be seen by others."

In the following verse (Matthew 6:6), Jesus unveils the "Our Father" prayer for the first time. But first, he makes it very clear *that prayer is supposed to be done in private*: "But when you pray, go into your room, close the door, and pray to your Father, who is unseen. Then your Father, who sees what is done in secret, will reward you."

This reinforces the idea that prayer is a personal and humble communion with God, not one's thirsty public audition for America's Next Top Christian.

THAT SERMON ON THAT MOUNT

Jesus lays down a spiritual manifesto of social justice, compassion, and ethics in his most famous appearance; it's like his Woodstock.

The Sermon places humility over *any* sense of spiritual superiority. It challenges social and religious norms and calls for us to reject vengeance (even when someone desperately deserves it).

Love Your Enemies (Matthew 5:43–48): Jesus challenges his followers to love and pray for those who persecute them. And he says this to an oppressed people living under foreign military occupation in their own Holy Land. Talk about a tough room.

Do Not Judge (Matthew 7:1–5): He cautions against hypocritical judgment, telling followers to first examine their own faults before pointing out the faults of others (y'know, like all those thoughtful folks on Fox News). Jesus commands the *opposite* of putting your religion on top—teaching the virtues of humility, self-awareness, and a nonjudgmental attitude toward others. Zero judgments for *any* groups.

The Golden Rule (Matthew 7:12) teaches his followers to treat others as they would like to be treated. Which covers all cruelty, exploitation, domination, and discrimination. He makes it very clear that anyone who claims to follow him doesn't get to hate anybody, ever, for any reason, no matter what.

And get a load of these BEATITUDES.

Jesus opens the Sermon with a series of blessings that represent his foundational teachings and core values. Each line begins with the word "blessed," which can also be translated as "happy," "fortunate," or even "lucky." Jesus pronounces his blessings upon specific groups of people. He focuses on the poor and marginalized; he praises nonviolence and peacemaking, radical love, mercy, and inclusion; and he pretty much takes down the status quo.

1. "Blessed are the poor in spirit, for theirs is the kingdom of heaven."
2. "Blessed are those who mourn, for they will be comforted."
3. "Blessed are the meek, for they will inherit the earth."
4. "Blessed are those who hunger and thirst for righteousness, for they will be filled."
5. "Blessed are the merciful, for they will be shown mercy."
6. "Blessed are the pure in heart, for they will see God."
7. "Blessed are the peacemakers, for they will be called children of God."
8. "Blessed are those who are persecuted because of righteousness, for theirs is the kingdom of heaven."

Imagine the hecklers: "Meh, I didn't trudge all the way up Mount of Beatitudes just to hear some virtue signaling from Woke Jesus."

The Beatitudes are Jesus's own guide for ethical conduct in Christian life. And you'll *never* see a right-wing Christian politician or group fight to post these words on a classroom or courtroom wall.

Rev. Dr. Susan Thistlethwaite is Professor of Theology Emerita at Chicago Theological Seminary, and one of the wisest, no-nonsense clergy I've ever met. As she puts it, "Jesus's teachings were codified under oppressive Roman rule where the supreme Roman ruler was literally a god. The ministry of Jesus is clearly a rejection of the state as religiously sanctified (i.e., today's Christian Nationalism). The Sermon on the Mount is Jesus's central teaching, and it does not dictate what you must believe but what is blessed (good in the sight of God). In fact, I think you can legitimately say Jesus announced the Kingdom of God was arriving and the Kingdom of Caesar would be ending. He was likely crucified for that."

FIVE BASIC JESUS FACTS THAT SUNDAY SCHOOL MISSED

1. We created him in our own image.

Jesus was a first-century Jew from the Middle East; given that the people of Judea at the time were predominantly of Semitic descent, he would've shared many characteristics typical of that region—like olive skin, dark hair, and brown eyes. Which means Jesus probably could never have been cast as Jesus in any movie of the twentieth century.

Historically, Western art has often depicted him as a tall, fair-skinned, blue-eyed, light-haired man, influenced more by European aesthetics than history, geography, or reality. Since the first paintings of White Jesus, and the first illustrated Bibles of the 1800s, these depictions have imprinted on Christians a widespread, deeply inaccurate image. Depictions of a Eurocentric Yeshua reinforced centuries of white supremacy by promoting a Jesus who aligns with white European standards of authority (and Caucasian good looks).

This whitewashing of Jesus has always marginalized people of color by directly associating divinity—and ultimate moral authority—with whiteness. And long hair, divinely untouched by humidity.

Movies and TV have imprinted this idea even more deeply into the public consciousness. Max von Sydow gives a beautiful performance in *The Greatest Story Ever Told* (1965) portraying a white Christ, in the Middle East, speaking English with a Swedish accent. In *Jesus of Nazareth* (1977), Robert Powell portrays our Lord as a serene, blue-eyed Shakespearean Xanax user. And say what you want about Mel Gibson's *The Passion of the Christ* (2004), but Jim Caviezel was the first actor to wear colored contacts so his Jesus wouldn't have blue eyes.

Throughout centuries of American colonialism and slavery up to segregation and beyond, images of White Jesus helped justify the subjugation and mistreatment of nonwhite peoples. Caucasian Jesus assured countless generations that Euro-looking people were superior; all the inherent internalized racism for nonwhite folks was just part of the package.

2. Jesus was very proudly Jewish.

You might have an uncle who needs to be reminded of this every now and then.

Jesus of Nazareth was a Torah-observant, radical reform Jewish teacher. His early followers were 100 percent Jews. The first drafts of his story were written by Jews.

The Gospel of Matthew begins with a long genealogy tracing Jesus's lineage from King David and Abraham all the way to Joseph. This genealogy includes forty unique "begats." Here's the full bloodline. I'm including all these names for you to remember the next time you see a painting of a white, blue-eyed Jesus.

1. Abraham begat Isaac
2. Isaac begat Jacob
3. Jacob begat Judah and his brothers
4. Judah begat Perez by Tamar
5. Perez begat Hezron
6. Hezron begat Ram
7. Ram begat Amminadab

8. Amminadab begat Nahshon
9. Nahshon begat Salmon
10. Salmon begat Boaz by Rahab
11. Boaz begat Obed by Ruth
12. Obed begat Jesse
13. Jesse begat David the king

(King David committed adultery with Bathsheba and schemed the death of her husband, so the bloodline gets pretty sexy around this part.)

14. David begat Solomon by Bathsheba
15. Solomon begat Rehoboam
16. Rehoboam begat Abijah
17. Abijah begat Asa
18. Asa begat Jehoshaphat
19. Jehoshaphat begat Joram

(Okay, I must confess; after Jehoshaphat is where it kinda starts to drag. I'll skip to post-Babylonian exile).

Jeconiah begat Shealtiel
Shealtiel begat Zerubbabel
Zerubbabel begat Abihud
Abihud begat Eliakim
Eliakim begat Azor
Azor begat Zadok
Zadok begat Achim
Achim begat Elihud
Elihud begat Eleazar
Eleazar begat Matthan
Matthan begat Jacob
Jacob begat Joseph, the husband of Mary, of whom was born Jesus, the star of the book.

I read this as a child and was baffled. I phonetically sounded out all those names to appreciate the true lineage of Jewish royalty, from King David all the way to Joseph, Jesus's father. This was to establish Jesus's legal right to the throne of David in accordance with Jewish custom and legal tradition. He's set up as the fulfillment of the prophecy: God's anointed one—the Messiah.

Except, of course, if one believes that Jesus is the Son of God, then all that genealogy leads to Joseph not even being Jesus's biological dad. Which makes this the greatest story of an overachieving adopted kid, ever.

3. Yes, Jesus was a liberal.

Before some of you get mad, please understand—I'm going by the dictionary definition of the word "liberalism," not the many modern definitions churned out by assorted media.

> liberalism: "A political philosophy based on belief in progress and stressing the essential goodness of the human race, freedom for the individual from arbitrary authority, and protection and promotion of political and civil liberties."
>
> *Merriam-Webster Dictionary*

Jesus consistently sided with underdogs and championed the little people, not the privileged and powerful. Broad-minded, tolerant, and way too inclusive for the ultraconservatives of his day, the Nazarene modeled generosity and selflessness, and told his followers to share their resources and prioritize the well-being of other people over personal gain.

I realize I've now made Jesus sound like one of those insufferable donation-seeking libs with a clipboard, harassing all the nice people outside of Whole Foods.

But wait . . .

4. He's kind of conservative, too.

(Not right-wing—conservative.)

Wait, what? In what way was *this* guy conservative? Yes, he's got radical inclusivity, all that social justice, and critique of religious hypocrisy. But there's also his abiding respect for Jewish law and tradition, emphasis on personal responsibility, acknowledgment of secular authority, and defense of many traditional values. He challenged and reformed, but *did not reject or denigrate,* the laws of Judaism he claimed to fulfill.

He was observant and attended synagogue, celebrated Passover, and kept the Sabbath sacred. He upheld traditional values such as family, marriage, and fidelity. Some of you may be old enough to remember the Republican party prioritizing the same.

Trump defenders may be intrigued to know that while Jesus *never once* condemned abortions, immigrants, or gay people, he was seriously not a fan of adultery, and spoke out against the divorce laws of Moses because he thought it should be harder for men to dump their wives.

You could even make the argument that the Sermon on the Mount is him being more conservative. Jewish law says not to commit adultery, but Jesus goes beyond and tells men to not even look at a woman lustfully, two thousand years before Me Too.

Jewish law says "don't kill," but Jesus takes it further and says to not even get *mad* at people who deserve it.

We've all known conservatives who were capable of being inclusive. Right-wing people, not so much. But Jesus was a revolutionary, and calling out the ultraconservative hypocrites among the religious authorities is part of what led to his death.

5. Yes, Jesus seriously called out conservative religious hypocrites.

The Pharisees were the traditional religious authorities of Jewish society in Jesus's day. There was great diversity within their ranks, and not all of them opposed Jesus. Some, like Nicodemus, were sympathetic to his teachings

(John 3:1–21), and Jesus is often depicted hanging out with them socially. Many believe Jesus may himself have been a Pharisee.

But some ultraconservative Pharisees preached a meticulous observance of the law in daily life, including dietary rules, purity laws, Sabbath observance, and tithing. They constantly reminded the faithful that holiness was achieved through total obedience. And because their purity laws made them holier than everyone else, they often excluded certain undesirables (sinners, tax collectors, prostitutes, and sick people) from full participation in religious life.

Jesus, on the other hand, reached out to all those people and brought them to the party. He was a lightning rod and the greatest debunker of religious hierarchies and traditions in the entire Bible.

In Mark 7:6–13, Jesus criticizes some of the Pharisees and scribes for focusing on ritual purity while neglecting the heart of God's law.

"These people honor me with their lips, but their hearts are far from me. They worship me in vain; their teachings are merely human rules."

That's Jesus, calling out religious authorities who put man-made dogma over love for each other. He repeatedly points out how devotion to the letter of the law can overlook the spirit and intent of the law, bringing it back to love and compassion for all—especially the least of us.

In the parable of the Good Samaritan (Luke 10:25–37), Jesus goes out of his way to make the hero a despised foreigner who shows care and mercy *after* a priest refused to show compassion, deliberately making a religious authority a villain in his most popular story.

The Sacred Diss Tracks of Matthew 23

Matthew 23 is a scathing rebuke to a group of Pharisees and teachers of the law, telling them off for their hypocrisy and legalism. Jesus accused them of pushing a self-promoting appearance of righteousness while neglecting justice and mercy. I can personally assure you that in the twenty-first century, calling out right-wing Christian authorities in Jesus's particular tone can get one swiftly banned from most cable news appearances.

Verse 13: "Woe to you, teachers of the law and Pharisees, you hypocrites! You shut the door of the kingdom of heaven in people's faces. You yourselves do not enter, nor will you let those enter who are trying to."

Verse 15: "Woe to you, teachers of the law and Pharisees, you hypocrites! You travel over land and sea to win a single convert, and when you have succeeded, you make them twice as much a child of hell as you are."

And this wasn't on social media where he could hide his name and face. Jesus goes on to call them out for their little micro-taxes on everything:

Verse 23: "You give a tenth of your spices—mint, dill, and cumin. But you have neglected the more important matters of the law—justice, mercy and faithfulness. You should have practiced the latter, without neglecting the former."

Verse 24: "You blind guides! You strain out a gnat but swallow a camel." (The gnat and the camel were considered the smallest and largest of the "unclean" animals.)

Jesus isn't done telling these people off yet. This is like when you realize the Kendrick attack on Drake is only halfway through.

Verse 27: "You are like whitewashed tombs, which look beautiful on the outside but on the inside are full of the bones of the dead and everything unclean."

Verse 28: "In the same way, on the outside you appear to people as righteous but on the inside you are full of hypocrisy and wickedness."

Stephen Schwartz turned this into an angry Broadway show tune, brilliantly, in "Alas for You" from *Godspell.*

ABOUT THOSE PHARISEES

While millions have moved beyond the programming of blaming all Jews for killing Jesus, we're still very programmed to equate all of the Pharisees with cruel authoritarian fundamentalists.

Now, some of the ultraorthodox among the Pharisees weren't fans of new interpretations of their law, which means they weren't fans of Jesus, who enjoyed challenging their interpretations to their faces—often publicly, often in front of crowds. These men condemned him for blasphemy, and imperial Rome executed him for sedition.

Again, we're talking about a minority of the religious authorities, but you'll notice how the Pharisees are *always* the only bad guys in all the Jesus movies. The Romans usually feel just awful about having to torture and execute this poor fella, while cinematic Pharisees delight in Jesus's suffering. Pontius Pilate practically gives Jesus a foot massage in *The Passion of the Christ.* And in some of the more famous Hollywood Jesus movies, the sinister Pharisees also tend to be the only Jewish characters who actually *look* Jewish.

Today, "Pharisees" is often a casual euphemism for any villainous religious hypocrites, thereby lumping together the entire group in dangerously stereotypical ways.

I asked Rabbi Danya Ruttenberg, author of *Surprised by God: How I Learned to Stop Worrying and Love Religion,* about historic Pharisees. She said: "The Pharisees were a more democratizing group which followed not only the Written Torah but also the Oral Torah, the oral tradition of Jewish law. . . . Famously, these sages spent a lot of time debating the particulars of Jewish law—and through the process of playing out their disagreements, sharpened one another's thinking. This is a thing in Rabbinic tradition. It's part of the culture."

The rabbi continued: "My suspicion is that when non-Jews read the interactions between Jesus and the Pharisees in the Gospels . . . they may see ferocious rebuke and fearsome condemnation. I read the Gospels and assume that Jesus and the Pharisees . . . are sometimes engaged in earnest debate, sometimes jabbing in jest, sometimes just . . . living in community, and disagreement? But that those debates have rules and parameters that are agreed-upon and upheld by all parties—there's no excoriation; they're just throwing down, like we do."

THE TOP 3 RIGHT-WING ARGUMENTS ABOUT JESUS

CLAIM 1: "Sure, Jesus said to take care of the poor—but that's the job of Christians and churches. He didn't say the government should do it."

You'll notice that the people most convinced that America's a "Christian nation" are the same folks who don't think it's government's job to take care of the poor. But please know—when somebody proclaims, "Jesus says *we're* supposed to do those things, not the government," you are hearing the right-wing argument for rejecting Jesus's teachings in the voting booth.

Laws and policies can be designed to address systemic inequalities. This includes laws to fight poverty, discrimination, and injustice; laws that fight for all members of society to be treated fairly and with dignity; laws that fight for the least of us.

Of course, a society has to want that.

MATTHEW 25: JESUS GOES GLOBAL

If the Sermon on the Mount was Jesus's Woodstock, Matthew 25 is his Live Aid. Not as famous as Woodstock, but much bigger in scope. (The Crusades were Christianity's Altamont, but that's another book.)

The parable of Matthew 25:31–46 is known as the Judgment of the

Nations, since Jesus explains exactly how the nations of earth will gather before him to be judged based on how they treated certain people.

If you'd like some apocalypse sprinkled on top, it's also known as the Final Judgment, because Jesus explains, very directly, how individuals will be forever judged based on their actions during their lives.

If all this sounds a little too dark, it's also known as the parable of the sheep and the goats. It's got all the main themes of Jesus's teachings: compassion, justice, fighting for the marginalized. It's Jesus giving his ultimate marching orders, the sort of story you'd think vociferous Christians would be a bit more focused on.

In the parable, Jesus describes a scene at the end of the world:

"When the Son of Man comes in his glory, and all the angels with him, he will sit on his glorious throne. All the nations will be gathered before him, and he will separate the people one from another as a shepherd separates the sheep from the goats. He will put the sheep on his right and the goats on his left."

You've probably guessed that this is not going to end well for the goats. But this is important—Jesus gives a clear mandate to all people and nations.

"Then the King will say to those on his right, 'Come, you who are blessed by my Father; take your inheritance, the kingdom prepared for you since the creation of the world. For I was hungry and you gave me something to eat, I was thirsty and you gave me something to drink, I was a stranger and you invited me in, I needed clothes and you clothed me, I was sick and you looked after me, I was in prison and you came to visit me.'

"Then the righteous will answer him, 'Lord, when did we see you hungry and feed you, or thirsty and give you something to drink? When did we see you a stranger and invite you in, or needing clothes and clothe you? When did we see you sick or in prison and go to visit you?'

"The King will reply, 'Truly I tell you, whatever you did for one of the least of these brothers and sisters of mine, you did for me.'"

Then, Jesus addresses those who *don't* think societies should care for poor and sick people, or incarcerated people, or immigrants. This part is like Jesus's memo to the Heritage Foundation.

"Then he will say to those on his left, 'Depart from me, you who are cursed, into the eternal fire prepared for the devil and his angels. For I was hungry, and you gave me nothing to eat, I was thirsty and you gave me nothing to drink, I was a stranger and you did not invite me in, I needed clothes and you did not clothe me, I was sick and in prison and you did not look after me.'

"They also will answer, 'Lord, when did we see you hungry or thirsty or a stranger or needing clothes or sick or in prison, and did not help you?'

"He will reply, 'Truly I tell you, whatever you did not do for one of the least of these, you did not do for me.'

"Then they will go away to eternal punishment, but the righteous to eternal life."

It's a happy story. I always wondered what the vibe in the room was like when Jesus finished that one.

But that's it. That's what Christianity was supposed to be about. Not banning abortion, blocking care for trans kids, hating Muslims, fighting for tax cuts, or making people believe in a talking snake.

Jesus asserts that his true followers are the people and societies who care for the poor, the sick, the marginalized, the immigrants, and the incarcerated. And he tells you who his fake followers are—the ones who are openly religious but indifferent to the poor, the sick, the marginalized, the immigrants, and the incarcerated, the lowest of the low. How we treat them is how we treat him.

I mean, we could end the book right here. You've got things to do. But there's more.

Jesus emphasizes that nations will be judged based on their actions and treatment of the vulnerable—*not their religious affiliations or beliefs*. He's not just commanding individuals—he's calling on societies to commit to compassion, mercy, and kindness on a policy level. This means that Christians living in a democracy have the option to vote for—or against—Jesus's very direct instructions.

Note that he doesn't care how pious you are, how often you go to church, or how much money you donate. You get zero points with Jesus for being religiously observant. He's giving instructions on exactly what a Christian nation should do, which is why conservative politicians *never* talk about it.

CLAIM 2: "Scripture is scripture, and it's all equal, and Christians have to follow all of it equally."

This common right-wing argument, usually deployed by someone who wants to identify as "Christian" while picking and choosing random Old Testament passages, is generally used to justify cruelty to queer people (we'll cover those specifics in chapter 5).

Welcome to Leviticus, the third book of the Bible and the Holy Grail of scriptural picking and choosing. If the Ten Commandments are God's simple contract, think of Leviticus as God's six-hundred-plus terms and conditions. It's okay, nobody reads them all.

Leviticus is made up of the Priestly Code and the Holiness Code, early precursors to the modern Bro-Code, and they list an extensive number of behaviors, purification rules, and rituals for the newly freed Hebrew slaves, who had no idea getting out of Egypt was going to take forty years. That's who it's written for.

The "Levitical laws" were essential regulations for a deeply religious and desperately nomadic tribe hoping to survive without a home in the desert. It's a guide to staying devout while also keeping your tribe's numbers up in a Bronze Age wilderness with no refrigerators, antibiotics, or Wi-Fi access.

It lays down the kosher dietary rules any good modern Christian home lives by: Only eat animals with split hooves that chew cud (like cattle); don't eat any animals with split hooves that don't chew cud (like pigs). And seriously don't eat any animals without split hooves that do chew cud (like camels). Oh, and try to avoid eating unclean detestable things that fly, like eagles and bats. So far, it seems like a pretty easy book to follow.

Leviticus has many beautiful passages—and quite a few laws that might seem archaic or barbaric to humans of the twenty-first century. It's a book that's attributed to Moses, doesn't apply to Jesus followers, and whose rules are almost universally ignored by Christians—unless they want to punch down against a gay minority they dislike.

Now it's extremely normal for people to pick and choose the parts of the Bible they want to believe. It's called "selective interpretation," which sounds quite more academic than "smorgasbord Gentiles."

Many Christians passionately cling to the antigay parts of Leviticus, but they don't exactly live by the rest of Leviticus, which also forbids tattoos, wearing mixed fabrics, working on Saturdays, and eating shellfish.

These are Christians desperate to find a way around Jesus to discriminate. This is like the nuclear reactor core of Christian hypocrisy.

THE NEW COVENANT (AKA HOMOPHOBE KRYPTONITE)

It's going to get churchy for a few paragraphs, please bear with me.

Of all the revolutionary acts of Jesus, the concept of a "New Covenant" is central to understanding his teachings, and why Christians get to eat pork chops.

The Abrahamic Covenant, described in the Book of Genesis, represents God's promises to Abraham and his descendants. It's like a treaty between a great power and a lesser power. God will protect them, and they'll be His people. Jewish law is part of this covenant; it's all about the right way to worship, and how to treat each other.

According to Christian belief, radical Jewish reformer Jesus brings about a New Covenant through his life, teachings, death, and resurrection, "fulfilling" and *superseding* the Abrahamic Covenant. In Catholic Mass, they call it "the blood of the new and everlasting Covenant. It will be shed for you, and for all, so that sins may be forgiven."

The New Covenant is the whole theological framework for Jesus's radical reform teachings. For Christians, it's the fulfillment of God's promises, again, but this time through a divine Jewish carpenter who's emphasizing inner transformation, love, and redemption. It stresses the forgiveness of sins and reconciliation with God through Jesus's very famous sacrifice.

It's the starting point for the Christian movement, and essential to understanding why people who claim to be Jesus fans don't get to use Leviticus quotes to justify their antigay hang-ups, ever.

The concept of a New Covenant was also a great selling point for Christianity in its early beta testing days. The previous covenant had all these strict dietary rules to follow. Jesus shows up saying, "How 'bout you guys eat whatever you want, as long as you just love your neighbor? And enough with the burnt offerings, my dad hates the barbecue smell." This was like a spiritual cheat day.

The New Covenant established by Jesus marks a massive shift from the religious law and customs Jesus was raised with, to a different kind of faith-based user experience. It's Jesus's software update, from Law 1.0 to Love 1.0. Calling oneself "Christian" is to accept the new terms and conditions.

Levitical laws don't apply to Christ followers. They are laws specifically given to the Israelites fleeing Egypt.

The Apostle Paul also clarified that Christians are no longer under the Old Testament law, because Jesus is the culmination of the law (Romans 10:4).

And that's why you get to enjoy that bacon, my Gentile friend.

CLAIM 3: NO! The Old Testament law still governs Christians because "Jesus did not come to abolish the law."

Now, you don't think these homophobic Christians are going to drop their gay hang-ups just because hippie Jesus brought a so-called New Covenant, do you? They've got a New Testament way to get around this New Covenant talk, just like they got around not really following Leviticus.

In Matthew 5:17, during the Sermon on the Mount, Jesus addresses the crowd's understanding of the Mosaic Law, saying, "Do not think that I have come to abolish the Law or the Prophets; I have not come to abolish them but to fulfill them."

Right-wing Christians argue that "Jesus came to fulfill the law, not abolish it," because to them, that means Leviticus is still active and in play. "You'll take my homophobia when you pry it from my cold dead hands, Jesus." (Oh, but they'd still like to have bacon, tattoos, and to not have to stone certain rich men to death for adultery.)

It's unfortunately necessary to briefly delve into the nuances of what "fulfilling the law" means in the context of Jesus's teachings. I promise it's worth it.

HOW TO FULFILL THE LAW WITHOUT ACTUALLY ABOLISHING IT

So when Jesus said, "I came not to abolish the law, but to fulfill it," he was referring to the establishment of this New Covenant. "Fulfilling the law" means that Jesus has completed its purpose and brought its requirements to their intended culmination. With this New Covenant, the emphasis shifts to love, grace, and compassion (John 13:34).

And Jesus did this—to his great peril—by *claiming authority to interpret the law directly*. He has this phrase he uses all the time, and it never occurred to me as a kid how revolutionary it was.

"You have heard that it was said. . . . But I tell you . . . "

It's all over the Sermon on the Mount. It's innocuous and seemingly just a speech device, and the closest Jesus ever gets to a catchphrase. But this is how he presents his teachings as both a fulfillment *and* a deeper understanding of the law.

Matthew 5:21–22: "You have heard that it was said to the people long ago, 'You shall not murder, and anyone who murders will be subject to judgment.' But I tell you that anyone who is angry with a brother or sister will be subject to judgment."

Matthew 5:27–28: "You have heard that it was said, 'You shall not commit adultery.' But I tell you that anyone who looks at a woman lustfully has already committed adultery with her in his heart."

Matthew 5:38–39: "You have heard that it was said, 'Eye for eye, and tooth for tooth.' But I tell you, do not resist an evil person. If anyone slaps you on the right cheek, turn to them the other cheek also."

Matthew 5:43–44: "You have heard that it was said, 'Love your neighbor and hate your enemy.' But I tell you, love your enemies and pray for those who persecute you."

In every instance that Jesus proclaims, "But I tell you," he's declaring that he is *fulfilling* the Old Testament law and laying down his new spiritual rules.

On a performance level, "You have heard it said . . . but I tell you" is a great crowd work device. He's like Travolta in *Get Shorty*: "I'm the guy tellin' you how it is."

Not only are Christians supposed to prioritize following Jesus's words above the other parts of the Bible, that's also quite literally why this religion got its name.

By the way, once you point out to the homophobes that they don't believe in or follow Leviticus, and that Leviticus doesn't apply because Jesus brought a New Covenant, it's very likely they still won't give up. Expect a desperate pivot at this point to the Holy Trinity, where they will argue that Jesus is God, which means he's eternal, which means Jesus was present in the Old Testament as well—so all those homophobic laws are his, too.

They're willing to deny the origin of the Christian faith—that it's not traditional Judaism—just to be mean to trans kids.

I was raised on the Trinity, and I'm not here to knock it; of all the biblical concepts that aren't actually mentioned in the Bible, it's one of the most beautiful.

But if your homophobe insists that Christ was present in the Old Testament, and that means Leviticus is actually one of Christ's teachings, just ask them, "And this was during history's BC period, correct?"

You'll also hear fundamentalists try to get around Jesus by claiming "all scripture is 'God breathed.'" We'll get into that in the next chapter, about Paul, who wrote that.

Oh, one more thing about Jesus?

He never, in his lifetime, that we know of, met Paul.

PAUL, JESUS'S PR MAN, WHO IS NOT JESUS

"A person doesn't have to be a Paul-hater. He was doing the best he could.... How would Paul have known that scratching out letters to help sort out the challenges and problems of the early church were somehow going to be turned into the infallible Word of God for all humankind. That's on us, not him. Paul did the best he could given the circumstances and where he was at in his own spiritual journey and evolution."

Jim Palmer, founder of the Center for Non-Religious Spirituality

Remember that time Jesus said, "If you don't work, you don't eat?" Or when he condemned gay people? That's in the New Testament, right?

Or when Jesus gave a list of all the people who can *never* get to heaven?

And when Jesus taught women to be silent, and submit to their husbands?

Many of our friends, neighbors, coworkers, and loved ones clearly remember Jesus saying those exact words in the Bible, somewheres.

Alas, Jesus said none of these things. It was all Paul, founder of modern Christianity; the church's first spin doctor, and the guy who right wingers quote alarmingly more often than Jesus.

. . .

For the first few centuries after Jesus it wasn't easy being a Christian. At best, your conservative Jewish loved ones would be disappointed in you for joining a cult; at worst, the Romans could turn you into lion food.

As a radical reform Jewish movement, early Christian communities faced persecution and harassment from both the empire and those ultraconservative Pharisees, all trying to snuff out this spark before it could spread.

One of the most zealous haters of early Christianity was a man who seemed almost genetically designed to persecute Christians: an ultraorthodox Pharisee who was *also* a Roman citizen, and, on top of that, a dick.

Meet Saul of Tarsus, first mentioned as a witness to the stoning of Stephen, the first Christian martyr, in Acts 7:58–8:1. Saul supported Stephen's execution and led many efforts to arrest and imprison Christians. He reviled the Jesus followers as a dangerous sect that threatened traditional beliefs and practices.

Saul would later become Paul, missionary to the Gentiles, one of the most significant figures in early Christianity—and one of the most contradictory. If Jesus was the game-changing rock star, Paul was his hardworking, deeply uptight, conservative PR guy.

Most of the sexual hang-ups of the New Testament come from Paul, who believed the world would end in his lifetime and generally felt that everyone should be celibate like him.

Everything that passes for homophobia and misogyny in the New Testament comes from Paul—*not* Jesus. For better or for worse, he is the person most responsible for organized Christianity as we know it.

THE PERSECUTOR WHO TRANSITIONED TO PREACHER

Saul was born into a Jewish family in the city of Tarsus in Cilicia (modern-day Turkey). He was of the tribe of Benjamin, a respected lineage within the Jewish community. This also made him a Roman citizen by birth.

Saul's dual identity gave him many special privileges and protections within the empire—*much* more privilege than the surviving Jewish apostles, whose early efforts to establish a church were hampered by guys like Saul stoning them to death.

Saul was trained as a Pharisee and aggressively rejected the reforms of Jesus. And as Jesus's movement began to grow following his execution, Saul got permission from some of the high priests to hunt down and arrest Christians. And clearly, the man loved his work. He was like a bounty hunter who'd have been willing to do it for free. Saul had such a gift for persecuting Christians, they began sending him on missions outside Jerusalem to other cities, like Damascus.

According to Acts 9:1–19, while Saul was traveling to Damascus to arrest Christians, a bright light suddenly flashed around him, and he fell to the ground. He heard the voice of Jesus asking, "Saul, Saul, why do you persecute me?"

At least he *assumed* it was Jesus's voice. Again, these guys had never actually met in real life.

Blinded by the light, Saul was led into Damascus, where he remained blind for three days. Meanwhile Jesus appeared in another vision to a Christian named Ananias, telling him to go visit Saul. Gave him the address and everything. Ananias was a bit confused, because this was Jesus showing up like a Force ghost, asking him to go assist a known murderer of Christians. But he went to the house Jesus gave him, laid his hands on Saul, and restored his sight.

Saul was then baptized, renounced his violent ways, took a new name, and pledged himself to spreading the teachings of Jesus. From pharisee to fanboy.

We don't know why he changed his Hebrew name of "Saul" to the Latin name "Paul," but it was probably a strategic rebrand to better relate to the Greco-Roman world of the Gentiles where he'd do most of his preaching, recruiting, and organizing. A name like Paul would make things easier with a non-Jewish crowd.

I personally never thought Saul needed to change his name. I've known some great Jewish comics who changed their last names to appeal to a wider Gentile audience and I didn't think they needed to, but hey, that's just me.

There was no way that Saul/Paul could have known that one day, bigots and incels would quote *him* instead of Jesus to justify their hatred of women and gay people.

But I get ahead of myself.

KEEP THE TIP

Christianity began as a Jewish sect, reading Jewish Torah scrolls and practicing Jewish religious traditions. Jesus never actually stopped being Jewish. And while Jesus's ministry was primarily focused toward the Jewish people, Paul thought outside the tribe.

As a Roman citizen, Paul could travel more freely throughout the empire, which made his many missionary journeys far easier and allowed him to focus on spreading this Jewish splinter-sect of Jesus to non-Jews throughout Roman territory.

He was a born-again kid with a dream, and he traveled across Asia Minor, Greece, and Rome, setting up Christian communities in part by selling them on how un-Jewish it all really was.

Unlike the Jerusalem-based Christian leadership, Paul's background as a Pharisee and Roman citizen allowed him to bridge cultural gaps and reach a bigger audience—which he did by preaching universal salvation through Christ's sacrifice. Well, that, and he assured the Gentiles they wouldn't have to keep kosher or get circumcised.

His pitch went something like this: "Yes, it's *like* Judaism, but God forgives you for *everything*, and there's ham; plus you can keep your foreskin."

Paul's version caught on and spread rapidly throughout the diverse Roman Empire. It didn't hurt that his movement had little competition for Judea's Top Christian Sect, given that the apostles were still getting murdered by his old buddies back home.

By three hundred years in, Jewish dietary laws had been abandoned. It was now totally kosher to no longer be kosher, and Jesus's Jewish sect had become something very different.

And so it was that Paul took over Christianity and redefined what the religion would be. It's like if Ronnie Wood joined the Rolling Stones in 1975, then the other guys all got killed in a plane crash, and Ronnie just kept the band's name to himself for his solo career.

THE EPISTLE APOSTLE

As you probably know, Paul wrote *a lot* of letters. Many were written to the early Christian communities about their specific challenges in setting up a religion. People like the Romans, Corinthians, Galatians, Ephesians, Philippians, Colossians, Thessalonians—all first-century people whose spiritual concerns were exactly like ours today.

And while Paul upheld many of Jesus's teachings, Christ was more of the *ideas* man. Paul was the outside consultant who conceived all the theological models and organizational structures, did much of the original hiring, and pretty much ran the startup.

There are many debates among theologians about which of Paul's letters were written by him and which were clearly not. These debates are fascinating, and you can really go down a rabbit hole researching them, and they're rather irrelevant to what we're doing here. For the purposes of this book, Paul is Paul. Mostly.

Paul's a bit edgier than Jesus in ways that make him more attractive to a certain kind of right-wing believer. While the Gospel teachings emphasize love, compassion, and inclusivity, Paul's personal opinions about women and sexuality just couldn't help but bleed through in his writings. Which means that over the last two thousand years, many Christians have been taught to prioritize certain passages from Paul's letters that suit their personal biases over Jesus's irritating orders to love everyone.

Paul's Greatest Hits

In 1 Corinthians 14:34–35, Paul announces, "Women should remain silent in the churches. They are not allowed to speak, but must be in submission, as the law says. If they want to inquire about something, they should ask their own husbands at home; for it is disgraceful for a woman to speak in the church."

In Ephesians 5:22–24, "Wives, submit yourselves to your own husbands as you do to the Lord. For the husband is the head of the wife as Christ is the head of the church, his body, of which he is the Savior. Now as the church submits to Christ, so also wives should submit to their husbands in everything."

In 1 Timothy 2:11–12, "A woman should learn in quietness and full submission. I do not permit a woman to teach or to assume authority over a man; she must be quiet."

Now this may shock you, but Paul also had hang-ups about guys who hook up with guys, as covered in chapter 5. These passages have been used by conservative Christians for centuries to justify persecution and opposition to women and LGBTQ rights. They're also, as we will see, not *actually* about gay people as we know them.

But are you starting to see why the right-wing guys really like Paul?

Paul wrote in a patriarchal society where women had limited rights and roles. His letters reflect the norms of his time—and to be fair, some argue that he was much more progressive for his time than it might seem. He actually worked with many women in his ministry—with a high level of respect and acknowledgment of their contributions—which does seem inconsistent with his more misogynist bullshit. In Romans 16, Paul commends several women for their roles in the early church, including Phoebe, who is described as a deacon.

So, Paul is literally both a sexist *and* feminist. He commands women to not speak, but makes them deacons. In Corinthians he says women are to be obedient, while three chapters earlier he says women are to pray and proselytize, as long as they wear a veil.

Was Paul tailoring his writing to appease different crowds? Or—more likely—have scribes just rewritten so much of this over the last two thousand years that we have no idea what Paul thought, or which words are actually his?

The good news is that it really doesn't matter, because Paul is not God or Jesus, though many would like him to be. And again, Paul's letters were all very specific to the issues of the day. Most scholars argue that his teachings should be understood within that context, not necessarily forced onto our modern dilemmas.

At least his letter to the Galatians is still authentic. There, Paul expresses frustration with those who insist that Gentile Christians must be circumcised to be saved, stating, "As for those agitators, I wish they would go the whole way and emasculate themselves!" (Galatians 5:12). That's not just Paul rejecting the idea that circumcision is needed for salvation. It's also the only time in the Bible that anyone makes a joke about cutting off one's own dick.

Thanks, Paul.

Jesus v. Paul—the Original Remote Coworkers

Jesus was a Jewish teacher who ministered primarily to Jewish audiences in first-century Palestine, while Paul was a Pharisee and persecutor of early Christians before his conversion. Paul's background and conservative religious orientation shaped his perspectives just a bit differently from Jesus's. Let's explore.

- Jesus never stopped being Jewish, while Paul dove all-in on a new religion that could attract the non-Jews.
- Jesus specifically says that anyone can get to heaven: "Whoever

comes to me I will never drive away" (John 6:37). Paul frequently lists specific groups of people who can't (1 Corinthians 6:9–10).

- Jesus had a quite decentralized ministry focused on self-transformation, personal relationship with God, radical love, forgiveness, and social justice. Paul was deeply focused on creating hierarchy, doctrines, order, and structure within an organized church (1 Timothy 3:1–7, Titus 1:5–9).
- Jesus led a small, grassroots Jewish movement; Paul turned it into a formalized global religion. These men had different goals.
- Jesus stressed doing good works: "If you want to enter life, keep the commandments" (Matthew 19:17). Actions like loving others and helping the poor were central to his message. But Paul focused on faith in Jesus as the means to salvation: "For it is by grace you have been saved, through faith . . . not by works" (Ephesians 2:8–9). Jesus was about good deeds; Paul was about good observance.
- Jesus held women in high regard and was uncommonly open in his interactions with them. Paul's instructions on women's roles in church gatherings (1 Corinthians 14:34–35, 1 Timothy 2:11–15) are considerably more restrictive and uptight.
- Whereas Jesus's teachings focused on love and forgiveness with no judgments, Paul lays out many structured and conservative ethical rules to early Christians on sexual morality, marriage, and social conduct (1 Corinthians 6:9–20, Ephesians 5:22–6:9).
- Like most Christians, Paul was a flawed human and not, in fact, Jesus. Paul put his hang-ups into the work, and Jesus's movement inherited them.

Different denominations and theologians have interpreted these teachings in various ways, often trying to harmonize them into some coherent theological framework. All too often, however, it's led to Paul being a top ingredient in modern Christianity's All You Can Cherry-Pick Buffet.

"GOD-BREATHED"

Jesus doesn't really allow his followers to get away with homophobia and misogyny the way Paul does. So a particular kind of right-wing Christian is—and for a long time has been—keenly invested in finding detours around Jesus.

So how have they managed to give Paul's *letters about Jesus* the same spiritual authority as the *actual words of Jesus*?

The same way people always have, by taking random lines of the Bible out of context.

When Paul wrote to his protégé, Timothy, and said, "All Scripture is God-breathed," in 2 Timothy 3:16, he was referring to the Hebrew scriptures—the Torah, the Prophets, and the Writings.

Paul—and this is very important—was *not talking about himself.*

In saying "God-breathed," Paul was emphasizing that these Jewish scriptures were all inspired by God, conveying divine truth and authority. He was not talking about his *own* letters that *discussed* scripture as being *the* scripture he was talking about.

At the time Paul wrote this letter (likely in the mid-first century AD), the New Testament didn't exist. As *Star Wars* fans like to say, "It wasn't canon yet."

It wasn't until three hundred years later, in the fourth century AD, that the New Testament canon was formally established—and Paul's letters were chosen to be included as part of the formal Bible.

It was only then that Paul's letters about scripture being "God-breathed" came to refer to *his own letters*. His commentary about Christians and scripture *became* official Christian scripture. This human decision has led to sixteen hundred years of people citing Paul talking *about* God to prove Paul is speaking *for* God.

It's like saying Roger Ebert's review of *The Godfather* is now officially part of *The Godfather*'s script.

Ever since, Paul's letters have been cited by Christians as proof that it's okay to be misogynist or homophobic, regardless of Jesus's words.

Because, hey—"it's in the Bible."

• • •

Despite his often contentious views, Paul's letters also include passages that have inspired and comforted many throughout the centuries. His writings on love, unity, peace, and virtuous living are often cited for their beauty and depth of insight.

1 Corinthians 13:4–7 is often quoted in weddings for its eloquent description of love:

"Love is patient, love is kind. It does not envy, it does not boast, it is not proud. It does not dishonor others, it is not self-seeking, it is not easily angered, it keeps no record of wrongs. Love does not delight in evil but rejoices with the truth. It always protects, always trusts, always hopes, always perseveres."

Paul also advocated for economic equality within the Christian community, urging wealthier believers to provide for the needs of the poor.

"At the present time your plenty will supply what they need, so that in turn their plenty will supply what you need. The goal is equality" (2 Corinthians 8:14).

Prosperity gospel teachings tend to dramatically avoid this one. It's important to remember that Paul has quotes the fundamentalists ignore, too.

While Roman citizenship did provide Paul with some legal protections, it didn't save him from arrest, beatings, or imprisonment. He eventually faced the same persecution he once dished out. Ultimately, we're told that Paul was executed in Rome under Emperor Nero, around AD 64 or 67, indicating that even Roman citizenship didn't give him immunity forever.

According to the New Testament, only about twenty or so people, mostly those of lower-class origins, went on to share Jesus's message after his death. But within years, millions had converted. Christianity spread by word of mouth incredibly quickly; the rate of conversion was remarkable, with something like a 3–4 percent conversion rate per decade.

But after Rome co-opted Christianity, things didn't really proceed according to Jesus's plan.

In the early fourth century, Emperor Constantine converted to

Christianity, ended the persecution of Christians, and set up the Council of Nicaea to formulate a unified organized religion—one creed, to rule them all.

In 380 AD, Emperor Theodosius I made Christianity the official state religion of Rome. Because there's cultural appropriation, and there's taking over the fan club of a guy you killed.

Under Rome, Christianity transitioned from a persecuted little faith into a force powerful enough to persecute others. Once the empire got their hands on Jesus's movement, they enacted huge changes in its theology, narrative, organization, and relationship with political power. Gone was the simple, direct message of love from the homeless Jewish faith healer. In its place sprung up new hierarchies, ecclesiastical institutions, and endless dogma and doctrines.

More importantly, the merger of Christianity with imperial power led to it becoming a tool for political control, with countless spiritual teachings twisted for authoritarian purposes. Emperor Theodosius issued a series of decrees that enforced Christian rule—and suppressed pagan practices. As religion merged with empire, pagan temples were destroyed, pagans were executed for heresy, and marginalized pagans faced persecution for not conforming to the new normal. Jesus's movement was now officially being used to justify violence, oppression, and authoritarian control.

Paul may have ensured the survival and expansion of Christianity beyond Palestine. But we must always remember that his work with Jesus's movement, while building the religion, would eventually lead directly to the Crusades, the Spanish Inquisition, colonization, Manifest Destiny, modern Christian nationalism, and the official autographed Donald Trump Bible.

MASTER-RACE CHRISTIANS OF THE TWENTY-FIRST CENTURY, AND HOW TO DEBATE THEM

"Mark my word, if and when these preachers get control of the [Republican] party, and they're sure trying to do so, it's going to be a terrible damn problem. Frankly, these people frighten me. Politics and governing demand compromise. But these Christians believe they are acting in the name of God, so they can't and won't compromise. I know, I've tried to deal with them."

Barry Goldwater, 1994

"I distrust those people who know so well what God wants them to do because I notice it always coincides with their own desires."

Susan B. Anthony

I was raised to believe that the opposite of faith isn't doubt, as doubt is an essential part of any real faith journey.

The opposite of faith is *certainty*.

Religious extremists of all faiths are raised in, and live with, supreme and absolute certainty. They don't *think* they're better than you; they know for a fact that *God* thinks they're better than you.

Life's pretty simple for the authoritarian Christian. Since most of their opinions happen to also be God's opinions—and they believe that they're the folks who get to speak for God—they generally feel divinely obliged to control whatever part of society they see fit. Y'know, for God.

And if you're one of the anointed who speaks for the Almighty, eventually you're liable to believe that anyone who opposes you is, logically, on the side of Satan. And God's true people are never going to sit down and negotiate things like school curriculum, women's rights, or marriage equality with *Lucifer*. People who've been conditioned to think you're on the side of the devil aren't permitted to meet you halfway.

In contemporary America, the two most dominant forces within right-wing Christianity are fundamentalism and Christian nationalism. These two umbrella-term movements wield the Bible to gain control over society in different ways, and they both suffer life-threatening allergies to the actual teachings of Jesus.

FUNDAMENTALISM

Fundamentalists believe that all biblical events, in every chapter, both Old and New Testaments, are 100 percent literal historical records; all dialogue is the absolute, direct, and infallible word of God, with zero room for parable or metaphor.

And gosh-darn it, they think you should believe that, too.

High certainty, low empathy, science resistant. Fundamentalists are deeply into hierarchy, raised on patriarchy, and they always prop up oligarchy.

And they'll tell you they don't see themselves as better than anyone else—they're just "saved." Sound like anybody you might know?

The most important point I can make is this—fundamentalism is in *no* way restricted to Christianity. Within most of the world's religions, the far-right fundies are the angriest, most aggressive, most xenophobic members of every faith group, always telling others exactly who they should hate and why. The more right-wing the fundamentalism, the more any person *of any religion* will believe:

1. God decided women are second-class.
2. Sex is generally bad, especially when women or gay people enjoy it.
3. Violence is acceptable to God, if it's my side doing it.
4. Punishment is prioritized over healing.
5. Perpetual victimhood can justify anything.

These core beliefs are shared by extreme fundamentalist Christians, Muslims, and Jews, who have far more in common with each other than with the liberals and moderates of their own faiths.

Right now, some of you are thinking, "Wait, hang on, Mr. Fuselage—are you actually comparing our hardcore right-wing Christians to their hardcore right-wing Muslims?" Hell yes, if you believe in hell. And if you don't, the fundamentalists of all the great religions will do their best to create some hell, right here, for the rest of us.

CHRISTIAN NATIONALISM

Christian nationalism is like marching the Bill of Rights and the New Testament out into the woods, at gunpoint, together, and digging two holes.

It's become the current in-vogue term for a long-standing form of fundamentalism, a movement that manages to gloss over the well-documented wishes of both the founding fathers and Jesus in equal measure. It is, loosely, a belief system that America was created by God specifically to be a Christian nation.

In addition to not being especially catchy to pronounce, "Christian nationalism" is a term vaguely covering a wide spectrum of colorful devotees: the traditional religious right, MAGA folk, old-school hardcore God-and-country conservatives, all manner of white supremacists, assorted QAnon folk, Nazis, incels with unprocessed grief who spend too much time online, and guys who just read too many Tom Clancy books.

In the words of Dr. Anthea Butler, chair of the department of religious studies at the University of Pennsylvania, "It places love of country and political action over God, and assumes that God favors one nation over others."

Our nationalist and fundamentalist friends both see US governmental authority and their version of Christianity as destined to merge, like American supremacy and Christian supremacy having an evil Aryan baby.

And of course, history has shown that countries governed by religious nationalism tend to descend into authoritarian regimes where dissent and diversity are suppressed. Looking at you, Iran and Saudi Arabia. Or Spain under Franco. Or Russia, under Putin. Or the Puritan Massachusetts Bay Colony. Or the Buddhist nationalists persecuting Rohingya Muslims. We could do this all night.

Jesus taught love for all humanity, regardless of their nationality, ethnicity, or religious affiliation. But Christian nationalists are here to *fight* for Jesus—not *listen* to him.

IT'S ALWAYS BEEN ABOUT CONTROL

Kristin Kobes Du Mez is professor of history and gender studies at Calvin University and author of *Jesus and John Wayne: How White Evangelicals Corrupted a Faith and Fractured a Nation.* I asked her about this Christian obsession with power.

"Conservative evangelicals have tended to prioritize interpretations that justify exercising power over others—men's power over women, and Christians' power over society," Du Mez says. "Many theologians argue that Jesus rejected this approach to power. He emptied himself and refused to claim earthly power, which was very much within his reach. He said the first must be last, and that to follow him meant to take up one's cross, to sacrifice oneself for others. These are hard teachings, however. If you want to build a movement and claim power for yourself, these teachings will get in the way."

Christian nationalists want the US to be a Christian nation, but they don't want to follow the words of Christ. It's like irony and hypocrisy having violent hate-sex.

It's also the culmination of what Rome did to the Jesus movement—the triumph of Christian dominance over Christ teachings. And because Christian nationalists believe that God really does support anything they do, they're quite possibly the most dangerously entitled non-billionaires in America today.

THE BELIEF: THE SEVEN MOUNTAIN MANDATE

WHAT IT IS: A popular dominionist mission to gain control of the "seven mountains" of society: religion, government, business, education, media, entertainment, and the American family itself. It's like a vision board for theocrats.

This movement's very popular within some charismatic and Pentecostal Christian groups, especially the New Apostolic Reformation of US House Speaker Mike Johnson.

WHERE THE BIBLE SAYS ALL THIS: It seriously doesn't.

WHAT JESUS ACTUALLY SAYS: JC preached humility and gentleness, not coercion and power over other groups:

"Take my yoke upon you and learn from me, for I am gentle and humble in heart, and you will find rest for your souls" (Matthew 11:29).

"Whoever wishes to become great among you shall be your servant; and whoever wishes to be first among you shall be slave of all. For even the Son of Man did not come to be served, but to serve and to give His life as a ransom for many" (Mark 10:43–45).

Not the words of a control freak looking to run society and randomly cancel all foreign aid.

And remember the story they taught us in Matthew 4, where Jesus spends forty days in the wilderness before Satan comes to tempt him?

"The devil took him to a very high mountain and showed him all the kingdoms of the world and their splendor. 'All this I will give you,' he said, 'if you will bow down and worship me.' Jesus said to him, 'Away from me, Satan! For it is written: 'Worship the Lord your God, and serve Him only.'"

Christian nationalism is Jesus looking at the cross he has to carry, and then finally deciding, "Ya know what, Satan? I think I'll take that deal."

NO, THE FOUNDERS REALLY DIDN'T WANT AMERICA TO BE A CHRISTIAN NATION

In 2022, the Public Religion Research Institute (PRRI) released the American Values Survey, which reported that 31 percent of all Americans and 49 percent of Republicans believe "God intended America to be a new promised land where European Christians could create a society that would be an example for the rest of the world."

(Except European Christians didn't do the heaviest lifting to build that new promised land, if you know what I mean. I'd say more about who physically built America, but I don't want to get banned from teaching history in Florida.)

We're a nation raised on comic books, and we've given America a new origin story.

The Christian nationalists among us tend to get fussy when you point out that our Constitution doesn't contain a single mention of Christianity but does say "Congress shall make no law respecting an establishment of religion."

Even worse, Article VI forbids any religious test for holding public office, so it's a good thing the Heritage Foundation hasn't read the Constitution, either.

The founders kept religion separate from the state for a good reason. They knew from experience that mixing the two rarely—if ever—works well.

Many of the founders were Deists, emphasizing reason and natural law over religious doctrines. Deism generally dismissed beliefs like Jesus's divinity, instead believing in a distant, impersonal God who set up natural laws and principles to govern the universe but wasn't a fan of intervening in human affairs; like a boss who only works remotely and never pops in the Zoom meetings.

Thomas Jefferson, John Adams, and Benjamin Franklin all viewed Jesus as a great teacher and philosopher—but not as God. The first House of Representatives, while debating the First Amendment, specifically rejected the new US Senate's proposal calling for the establishment of Christianity as the country's official religion.

It should also be noted that enslaving people and slaughtering Indigenous people disqualifies America from ever pretending to have been founded on Jesus's movement, as we will see.

But the founders got this very simple and moral concept just right: the government never gets to dictate how you can or cannot pray, or that you must pray. They knew the dangers of merging government, which was designed to protect individual rights, with any religion, which was a matter of individual conscience.

The founders recognized that a government free from religious entanglements would be more inclusive and generally more drama-free. Mixing religion with government inevitably leads to factionalism and division, suppression of individual rights, and the mandatory imposition of one belief system—none of which would've helped establish stability for a new nation.

So they officially decided this country would be secular—to better protect all religions. And, best of all, they took the time to write it down. More than once.

This is the point where our right-wing friends will solemnly intone that the Constitution never actually uses the expression "separation of church and state."

And they're right.

But apart from a "Year of our Lord," the Constitution doesn't mention God, Jesus, or the Bible in any way. The First Amendment explicitly prohibits any national religion. The Establishment Clause stops the government from ever favoring one faith over another, and the Free Exercise Clause protects individuals' rights to practice their religion without undue government meddling. The two clauses are a full-time juggling act, keeping religious rights and government neutrality in the air at the same time.

Our official religion is All and/or None. Sorry, nationalists. You get to be Christian, and everyone else gets to be what they want to be. Sit down.

Christian Nationalism, by the Numbers

In 2024, the folks at PRRI released a survey titled "A Christian Nation? Understanding the Threat of Christian Nationalism to American Democracy and Culture." It measured American support for Christian nationalism based on responses to five statements:

- "The U.S. government should declare America a Christian nation."
- "U.S. laws should be based on Christian values [specific values not mentioned]."
- "If the U.S. moves away from our Christian foundations, we will not have a country anymore."
- "Being Christian is an important part of being truly American."
- "God has called Christians to exercise dominion over all areas of American society."

About 29 percent of us reject all five of those statements; about 40 percent *mostly* disagree. Approximately 10 percent of Americans are full-blown Christian nationalists, overwhelmingly agreeing with all five statements, and about 19 percent more are Christian nationalism sympathizers, who agree with the statements but not completely.

In other words, adherents and sympathizers of Christian nationalism comprise about 30 percent of the US population. But somehow, they manage to make up two-thirds of the Supreme Court.

WHEN DEBATING A CHRISTIAN NATIONALIST

Engaging in debates with nationalists and fundamentalists can be challenging, as these friends and neighbors are often resistant to alternative perspectives; as well as, on occasion, facts.

But I'll always believe that appealing to right-wing Christians with the words of Jesus is worth the effort—and far more effective than despising them.

Engage gently. Debate if need be. Stay relaxed, don't be intimidated, and try to frame your points around asking questions.

And do keep in mind:

1. Focus on Jesus's teachings—love, compassion, and social justice, which I understand for some are trigger words.
2. Try to know the Bible just a bit—be prepared to calmly reference specific verses while your opponent, who's probably never been thoughtfully challenged on scripture, calls you a globalist baby-killing snowflake.
3. Be ready to calmly challenge misinterpretations or selective readings of scripture by using crazy concepts like context, historical understanding, and what Jesus said versus what he didn't.
4. Remind them that parables are stories—which are open to interpretation. There are hundreds of different translations and word meanings that have changed over the millennia.
5. Focus on core principles we all agree on, like love, compassion, justice, and reconciliation. They're kinda required for Christianity. Get them to agree on that.
6. Model respectful dialogue, even if you're repelled by some opinions. Eye contact, smiling, and warmth are always good. Avoid, if you can, the personal attacks or dismissive language, even if they don't. You may get to model turning the other cheek.
7. Don't debate in a vacuum—try to have witnesses. You'll reach more people if you can show how an informed, civil person debates in public. You might not get all the onlookers on your side, but you won't give them reason to hate you.
8. Be open to listening, even if it's crazy-talk. They've been trained their entire lives by right-wing media to believe you don't care about them or their beliefs, so don't prove them right. Identify

those fleeting moments of agreement. They'll respect you, even if they don't like you very much.

9. Get them—gently—to acknowledge your points. They don't have to agree with you (and they won't), but ask them to confirm they at least *understand* the point you're making. It helps guarantee they won't instantly forget your point.
10. Remember to not give in to any hate they may throw at you. If you're going to debate something as personal as the Bible, your job is to remember to be the calm, patient person who doesn't hate back. If you're just there to antagonize, you'll only make your fundamentalist more cranky and wrathful. Some of these folks seriously enjoy being martyrs, and any hostility from you will give them license to act like one.

Ultimately, debating with nationalists and fundamentalists requires patience, empathy, and a commitment to *constructive* dialogue. With humility and respect, you really can achieve meaningful engagement.

If that's what you want.

But keep in mind: You may be prepared to debate a right-wing loved one or coworker. You might know all the arguments to refute their mean version of Christianity. You can probably ensure that you'll never again be steamrolled by that pious person.

But—you likely won't change their minds. And that's okay.

It's not your job to deprogram a zealot. This book is about taking Christianity back from the haters, not curing them.

You can do your part to beat the Christofascists at their own game. And you may even give strength to bystanders—their kids, their wives, and many other folks at the cookout.

THOU SHALT NOT TAKE ALL OF THIS TOO LITERALLY

"I do not feel obliged to believe that the same God who has endowed us with sense, reason, and intellect has intended us to forgo their use."

Galileo Galilei

"Jesus told the crowds all things in parables; without a parable he told them nothing. This was to fulfill what had been spoken through the prophet: 'I will open my mouth to speak in parables; I will proclaim what has been hidden from the foundation of the world.'"

Matthew 13:34–35 (NRSA)

Ever notice how some folks take the Bible very literally when they want to put down LGBTQ people or restrict the power of women, but not so much when Jesus tells them to give away all their stuff to the poor?

A 2019 Pew Research Center study reported that 61 percent of Southern Baptists accepted the Bible as the literal word of God, higher than the 31 percent among all US adults and 53 percent among other evangelical Protestants.

You may have had the pleasure of knowing and loving people who claim to take the entire Bible as absolute literal fact, those who maintain every single line of scripture is 100 percent accurate and inerrant, the 100-proof word of God. Especially the Creation account in the Book of Genesis. Packed with facts, I tell you.

The Bible is a source of guidance for millions, but not every passage is meant to be applied literally. Many passages reflect the societal norms of their day or address specific cultural dynamics that *might not directly apply to your century.*

And please understand that I sympathize deeply with the literalists. As a child, I was raised to believe in both the Bible and science. I remember desperately arguing with my second-grade teacher that snakes used to have the ability to talk, because that's in the Bible, but they gradually lost the ability to talk, because that's evolution. The other kids just stared. It made enormous sense to me at the time.

Many still insist that following the teachings of Jesus requires belief that the earth was made in six days, only about six thousand years ago, and that all species were created, in their exact current form, on Day 1. Or, if we're being literal about it, on Day 6.

And while seemingly harmless, a literal reading leaves no room for competing beliefs, scientific facts, or metaphorical understandings of the Bible. And it doesn't exactly set a kid up to succeed in the twenty-first century, either. Let's also not forget that taken literally, many of the rules in this book would swiftly land you in jail.

Literalist readings of scripture have historically been used to justify slavery, segregation, and restrictions on rights, particularly for women, LGBTQ people, and religious minorities.

But please understand—*nobody* believes *everything* that is in the Bible. A sizable chunk of this historic, wonderful, brutal book are in fact myths that *nobody takes literally.* Again, anybody who tells you they believe "all of it" either hasn't read all of it, or they're counting on *you* not having read all of it.

The Bible has a lot of truth, which is not the same as a lot of facts. And those who claim the loudest allegiance to the book's inerrancy tend to be the ones who know it the least.

- The Bible clearly commands us to kill anyone who works more than six days of the week.
- It bluntly forbids ever eating ham, or wearing clothing made of mixed materials.
- It forbids divorce, but not polygamy.
- It forbids playing football, but doesn't forbid slavery.
- It forbids gathering sticks on a Saturday, but doesn't forbid genocide.
- It forbids eating shrimp, but doesn't forbid trading your ten-year-old child for a goat.

Now there are many very nice believers who claim to be biblical literalists; this book is about the other kind. The wrathful literalists who never talk about the love of JC in the NT of the KJV; they're mad about BLM or DEI or CRT. Or whatever abbreviations we've been groomed to despise this year.

Embracing rigid literalism is lethal to reason, critical thinking, and the basic intellectual curiosity that's necessary for interpreting scripture—which is why religious authoritarians have always liked it. Real faith is not afraid of reason, and it can be enriched by engaging with the scripture thoughtfully and critically.

Author and theologian Dillon Naber Cruz frames it this way: "I don't think many Christians realize that the Bible is literally an anthology of texts that reflects what the various authors and editors of those texts believed about God rather than a single book. Those beliefs do not stay consistent throughout the texts, and sometimes not even within the same book.

"For instance, early in Genesis we see God described in very human terms taking a stroll in the garden of Eden, while in other places, God cannot appear in any sort of human form but instead is seen as a burning bush to Moses or heard speaking out of a whirlwind in Job."

You don't always need a clerical collar to spot what's possible, what's metaphor, and what's, respectfully, silly to argue as literal fact. Por ejemplo:

- In the Tower of Babel story of Genesis 11:1–9, our all-knowing God was afraid that humans would be able to build a tower to heaven—without any lighting, space heaters, pressurized suits, or oxygen tanks.
- In Jonah 1–2, Jonah is swallowed by a large fish (it's never called a whale) and survives with enough air in its belly for three days.
- Balaam's donkey talks to him in Numbers 22. Never understood what believing this had to do with Jesus.
- In Joshua 10:12–13, with the military command "Sun, stand still over Gibeon," the sun stops moving so the Israelites can have better lighting for their battle. Along with Psalm 19:4–6 and Ecclesiastes 1:5, we realize that these inspired Bible writers understandably believed the sun moved around the earth.

The New Testament, too, has laws or rules that virtually all Christians routinely ignore. Jesus commands followers to not have any witnesses when they pray. His teachings prohibiting divorce were taken quite literally, while his command in Matthew 5:33–37 to never swear any oaths was pretty much ignored by everybody but the Quakers.

Literalists can spend so much time trying to prove the facts that they miss the truths. If Jesus only spoke in parables, using story to tell a deeper truth, why is it so hard to imagine that parts of the Bible might be parable, metaphor, and poetry? These stories are designed to provoke reflection, not to serve as simplistic dictates.

The belief that every word of the Bible should be interpreted to the letter and applied directly to contemporary life is *not the point of faith.* Imagine Jesus ending a parable by saying "And the moral is that the Good Samaritan was one hundred percent a totally real guy, and I command you to believe that every part of that story really did happen. Amen."

Literal Bible Verses You Literally Don't Believe

Let's begin with something light:

Someday, God will force parents to eat their own children.

- "You will eat the flesh of your sons and the flesh of your daughters." (Leviticus 26:29).
- " . . . you will eat the fruit of the womb, the flesh of the sons and daughters the Lord your God has given you" (Deuteronomy 28:53).
- "I will make them eat the flesh of their sons and daughters, and they will eat one another's flesh" (Jeremiah 19:9).
- "And the king said unto her, What aileth thee? And she answered, This woman said unto me, Give thy son, that we may eat him to day, and we will eat my son to morrow. So we boiled my son, and did eat him: and I said unto her on the next day, Give thy son, that we may eat him: and she hath hid her son" (2 Kings 6:28–29 KJV).

I should warn you: If you quote these too early during the Thanksgiving Christianity debate, the bad guy at the reunion will be you, not the fundamentalist.

Sex slavery is condoned early on.

- In Exodus 21:7–8, "When a man sells his daughter as a slave, she will not be freed at the end of six years as the men are. If she does not satisfy her owner, he must allow her to be bought back again" (NLT).

Did you know rape can be a form of biblical courtship to win over a girl's dad?

- "If a man happens to meet a virgin who is not pledged to be married and rapes her and they are discovered, he shall pay her father fifty shekels of silver. He must marry the young woman, for he has violated her. He can never divorce her as long as he lives" (Deuteronomy 22:28–29).

In just two simple lines, women are confirmed to be property, and sexual violence is normalized.

God Himself will kill tens of thousands if it pleases Him.

- 1 Samuel 6:19: "And he smote the men of Beth-shemesh, because they had looked into the ark of the Lord, even he smote of the people fifty thousand and threescore and ten men: and the people lamented, because the Lord had smitten many of the people with a great slaughter" (KJV).

Kill 50,070 men for *looking* at something?

Yes, God smites women, children, and animals with equal enthusiasm.

- "Behold, with a great plague will the Lord smite thy people, and thy children, and thy wives, and all thy goods: And thou shalt have great sickness by disease of thy bowels, until thy bowels fall out by reason of the sickness day by day" (2 Chronicles 21:14–15, KJV).
- Did you know you can chop off a woman's hand if she seizes a man's private parts during a fight without his permission? I learned that in Deuteronomy 25:11–12: "If two men are fighting

and the wife of one of them comes to rescue her husband from his assailant, and she reaches out and seizes him by his private parts, you shall cut off her hand. Show her no pity."

I mean, they thought of *everything.*

LITERALISM, FAITH'S TRICKY PAL

I will confess that a very young me found the story in 2 Kings 2:23–25 to be one of the Bible's most disturbing passages. And while it was a bit of a challenge to accept literally, I tried my best.

The verses describe an incident involving the prophet Elisha: From there Elisha went up to Bethel. As he was walking along the road, some boys came out of the town and jeered at him. 'Get out of here, baldy!' they said. 'Get out of here, baldy!' He turned around, looked at them and called down a curse on them in the name of the Lord. Then two bears came out of the woods and mauled forty-two of the boys."

Now, it was very important to me as a kid to believe all of the Bible. And I will confess I spent years as a child, and well into adulthood, wondering: How the hell do two bears kill forty-two kids?

I mean, think about it. If you're a group of forty-two kids and you're suddenly attacked by two bears, you'd all most likely collectively panic and disperse in every direction, right? And if all of the kids ran off in multiple directions, how could two bears possibly catch all forty-two?

Also, forty-two kids are mauled, and there's not one sword-wielding adult around? Sounds a bit extreme, even for biblical free-range parenting.

Maybe if the bears were somehow in a deep pit with the forty-two kids? It would probably take days, but without any ladders they'd eventually eviscerate every last one of those bald-mocking brats.

Or maybe these were *divinely magical bears* with special God-given powers, so they could rapidly savage forty-two kids before any could escape.

And did Elisha think God was maybe being just a bit disproportionate in punishment, with violent mass child slaughter over being called bald?

Not to belabor this, but I used to hypothesize what the mechanics of this might involve:

- Could two mauling she-bears lead to trampling, or other life-ending injuries?
- Maybe some of the wounded kids actually took days to die?
- What if the number of mauled kids was exaggerated, emphasizing more the seriousness of the event rather than a literal body count of clawed-up and eaten kids?
- Couldn't the term "mauled" also mean various degrees of harm, not necessarily fatal injuries for all forty-two?

I spent a whole summer when I was nine obsessed with the science of this—because I knew I *had* to believe it to be a good person. The notion that the story might be symbolic, conveying the serious consequences of disrespecting God's appointed leaders, was not something I'd considered.

Nor was the possibility that the actual author might have been bald and thin-skinned, and projecting his own revenge fantasies all over the holy parchment.

Years later I saw the film *Cocaine Bear* and instantly remembered 2 Kings. "Hey, do you think two cocaine bears could get so high they could massacre forty-two kids all at once?" I asked my wife, who quietly inched just a little bit farther away from me on the couch.

THE WORLD'S LONGEST GAME OF TELEPHONE

When we read "the Bible," we're reading translations of translations of re-writes of copies of copies of stories, written by Greek-speaking believers, that had originally been passed down word of mouth, through the centuries.

Assembling the many books and letters that make up the modern Bible, and deciding which texts to include or exclude, was an incredibly complex endeavor that spanned centuries. And in many places we don't even know what the original authors of the Bible actually wrote.

This means if you believe the Bible is the absolute word of God, you've also got to believe that God doesn't want anyone to ever read the original text.

These stories existed in oral tradition, told around campfires for hundreds—even thousands—of years. Eventually the Old Testament stories were written down in Hebrew and Aramaic, from the twelfth to the second centuries BC.

The New Testament was written in Greek, mostly in the first century CE, and later translated to Latin. The Synod of Hippo (393 CE) and the Councils of Carthage in 397 and 419 CE (which both sound like legitimate hip-hop crews) decided on the official versions of the New Testament books.

Copies were all made by hand, mistakes were made in the copies, and those mistakes later got copied. If you needed a copy, you relied on aging scribes, writing on parchment, often by candlelight.

Martin Luther eventually translated everything to German (even though he and the Vatican couldn't agree on exactly which books belonged in the Bible). After many, many centuries, the books were finally translated into English—where they've continued to undergo endless revisions with each passing year.

And this, claim the fundamentalists, is the absolute, inerrant, 100-proof word of God.

Did you ever play telephone tag in school?

Thirty kids queue up in a row and whisper a phrase all the way down the line. The first kid whispers "My dog has fleas." Then each child whispers "My dog has fleas" to the next kid in the line, and by the time the information reaches the last kid, the message has become "My testicles are full of angry blue hamsters."

That's how the Bible was written, friends. Jesus said, "Welcome the stranger."

Our neighbors heard "Build a wall."

THE LITERAL PROBLEM

> "The most common misconception in my opinion is that the Bible is The Word of God. This is false. The Bible is a compilation of the words of men about God. The second most common misconception is that the Bible is inerrant. Nothing man does or touches is absent from error. Therefore, it is full of errors, contradictions, misrepresentations, and mistranslations. The Bible is many things, but the inerrant Word of God is not among them."
>
> Pastor Desimber Rose

The Bible often uses figurative language to express truth. Jesus described himself as the "bread of life" in John 6:35, but it's not interpreted literally. The man was a poet; he wasn't actually made of flour and yeast.

Biblical literalism feeds authoritarian tendencies by emphasizing obedience to rulers over critical thinking and individual freedoms. Leaders invoking "God's will" to justify their decisions discourage dissent and scare away accountability.

Literal interpretations usually lead to exclusivism, where those who do not share the same beliefs are deemed sinful, heretical, or condemned. Some interpret John 14:6 ("No one comes to the Father except through me") to exclude all non-Christians from salvation. This spiritual elitism has always led to intolerance, division, and hostility, even among Christians with differing interpretations.

Literalism rejects any scientific theories, such as evolution and climate change, that might conflict with a rigid interpretation of the Bible. This can seriously impede evidence-based policymaking and the collective IQ of a society. Efforts to introduce creationism or intelligent design in public school curricula don't advance the teachings of Jesus, and violate the line between religion and government.

Sadly, people who don't like science have no problem with US students falling behind the rest of the world in science.

But remember, *nobody* believes all of it. Really.

Yes, There Are Inconsistencies

While the Bible is unified in many overarching themes, it does contain contradictions that suggest different theological perspectives among the many, many, many guys who wrote it. You can study entire books and websites devoted to these inconsistencies, but here are a few points you might respectfully ask your fundamentalist about:

- Matthew 16 and Mark 8 agree that Peter makes the Good Confession in Caesarea Philippi, but Luke 9 indicates it was near Bethsaida. How am I supposed to function without knowing which is true?
- Matthew's version has Peter claiming Jesus is "the Messiah, the Son of the Living God." But Mark and Luke agree Peter says Jesus is "the Messiah of God." Who's lying?
- Is the Sermon on the Mount in Matthew 5–7 (where Jesus says the Beatitudes) the same as Luke 6:17–49's "Sermon on a Level Plain," where Jesus also says the Beatitudes? Which altitude is God's sacred preference?
- Do they believe the "days" in Genesis were twenty-four-hour periods? If so, how do they account for the existence of "evening and morning" before God created the sun on Day 4?
- Do they believe in a literal Garden of Eden? Where is it, and why hasn't it been discovered?
- If Genesis were proven to be figurative or allegorical, would this affect their faith? Why?
- Do they believe that Noah's ark contained every species of animal? How specifically would they have been fed, housed, and kept alive for the duration of the flood? Was all land on earth connected at the time, or did animals have to cross oceans to get to Noah's boat?

Want more? Here's a few more innocent contradictions one could mention:

- Did Noah bring two of each kind of animal onto the ark, or more?

  Genesis 6:19 says "You are to bring into the ark two of all living creatures, male and female."

  But Genesis 7:2–3 says "Take with you seven pairs of every kind of clean animal, a male and its mate, and one pair of every kind of unclean animal, a male and its mate, and also seven pairs of every kind of bird, male and female, to keep their various kinds alive throughout the earth."

  Who cares if it was two of each or seven of each? Noah's kids, who had to clean the damn boat, probably cared a great deal.
- Does God Change His Mind?

  Yes: "The Lord relented and did not bring on his people the disaster he had threatened" (Exodus 32:14).

  No: "God is not human, that he should lie, not a human being, that he should change his mind" (Numbers 23:19).
- How does Judas die?

  Matthew 27:5: Judas hangs himself.

  Acts 1:18: Judas falls headlong, his body bursts open, and all his intestines spill out.

  Most of us would be okay with either of these endings for Judas, but which of the two do you believe and which do you reject?
- How many women visited Jesus's tomb?

  One woman: Mary Magdalene (John 20:1).

  Two women: Mary Magdalene and "the other Mary" (Matthew 28:1).

  Three women: Mary Magdalene, Mary (mother of James), and Salome (Mark 16:1).

  More than three women: Joanna and others (Luke 24:10).

So, which Gospel is correct, and which are factually wrong? The central message remains: the tomb was empty, Jesus had risen, and the first people he appeared to were women.

What about Matthew 27:51–53? This passage deals with events *immediately* following Jesus's death on the cross.

"At that moment the curtain of the temple was torn in two from top to bottom. The earth shook, the rocks split, and the tombs broke open. The bodies of many holy people who had died were raised to life. They came out of the tombs after Jesus' resurrection and went into the holy city and appeared to many people."

Um, why is this only in Matthew? Wouldn't a number of dead people coming back to life and busting out of their tombs be headline news for the other Gospel writers? The passage doesn't provide details about who witnessed the resurrected saints or their subsequent actions. Did they eat? Go back to their homes? Get jobs?

And doesn't it diminish the uniqueness of Jesus's resurrection if several dozen other guys got resurrected two days before he did? Heck, Jesus coming back must've seemed pretty normal by Sunday.

And I know the question you're too polite to ask—were these people, in fact, zombies or were they not?

Arguing with Literalists for Fun and Relaxation

> "The people who most stridently contend they believe in a literal application of the Bible have simply not read the majority of it. They have been selectively armed with the verses that seem to reflect their prejudices, confirm their theology, ratify their politics, and echo the story they believe about God. The moment you give them a verse or a section that confronts their worldview, you take the pressure off of yourself by having them argue with God and not you."
>
> Pastor John Pavlovitz

You're probably not going to be debating with a person who shares your passion for logic and empirical proof, but that's no reason to be rude or dismissive. Respect fosters open dialogue rather than defensiveness. Also, some of them HATE it when you're nice.

Ask Questions. Encourage thoughtful reflection by asking:

- "What does belief in this have to do with what Jesus commands?"
- "How do you reconcile this belief with [scientific evidence, internal contradictions, or historical context]?"
- "If you believe [this part of a certain Bible chapter], don't you also have to believe [other, more unpleasant parts of same chapter, that they emphatically do not follow]?"

THE CLAIM: "God's Word must take precedence over fallible human science."

Science and biblical literalism don't mix, but science and faith can and do coexist. Both can answer different questions: Science explores how the universe works, while the Bible addresses why it exists. Millions of faithful Christians accept overwhelming scientific evidence of evolution and an old earth, and it doesn't threaten or compromise their kindness or their belief in a loving God.

THE CLAIM: "The Bible is the Word of God, divinely inspired and without error, so everything in it must be literally true."

THE SCRIPTURE: Most literalists rely on Paul's letter in 2 Timothy 3:16, which asserts that "all Scripture is God-breathed and is useful for teaching, rebuking, correcting, and training in righteousness." That means that nothing in the Bible ever goes out of date. None of it ever applies "only in certain situations" or to "particular people or centuries."

As we've already covered in the chapter on Paul, when he referenced scripture in his letter to Timothy, he was talking about actual scripture, not his letter he was writing to Timothy. More than two hundred years after Paul's death, the Council of Nicaea declared his letter also "scripture." This is called "citing Paul to argue that Paul is true."

THE CLAIM: "Rejecting literalism undermines moral and theological authority."

Faith does not require literalism; many Christians find profound meaning in the Bible without taking every word as fact. As author and theologian Keith Giles reminds us, "Many things are 'Biblical,' like genocide, patriarchy, slavery, polygamy. When I say these things are 'Biblical,' I mean that people have in the past—and even today—used the Bible to justify all of those things. So, yes, those things are Biblical. But none of those things are Christlike.

"And that's the point. We're called to follow Christ, *not the Bible*. In fact, please understand this: *the Bible does not tell us to follow the Bible*. The Bible tells us to follow Christ. But Biblical Christians follow the Bible. They do not, in fact, attempt to follow Christ."

THE CLAIM: "The early church fathers believed the Bible was literal."

Not altogether true. Several early Christian theologians, such as Origen and Augustine, read Genesis allegorically. In Augustine's work *The Literal Meaning of Genesis*, written in the early fifth century, he argued that the six days of creation were not twenty-four-hour days, but rather a symbolic framework for understanding the creation process, and that the true meaning lies in the theological truths they convey. Today, he'd be labeled a "globalist cuck."

Origen of Alexandria was a prominent scholar (184–253 CE) who taught that some parts of the Bible *must* be interpreted non-literally. Regarding Creation, he wrote: "Who is so silly as to believe that God . . . planted a paradise eastward in Eden, and set in it a visible and palpable tree of life . . . [and] anyone who tasted its fruit with his bodily teeth would gain life?"

But in the year 400, Theophilus, the patriarch of Alexandria, summoned a council that condemned Origen and all his followers as heretics for having taught that God was a spirit, not material form. This, they decreed, contradicted the only true position, which was that God had a literal, physical body resembling that of a human male.

Got that? God officially has a penis. Men said so.

Although it should also be mentioned that we've still never been told the specific context in which He might use it.

WHEN TALKING WITH ADULTS ABOUT A TALKING SNAKE

> "Genesis is a very important book as it provides the foundation for the rest of the Bible, for our Christian worldview, for all doctrine, and, in fact, for everything."
>
> Ken Ham, CEO behind the Creation Museum, "Genesis—It Explains the Origin of Everything!"

Creationism is the belief that God could create the heavens and earth in six days but couldn't find two naked people hiding in the woods. Many Jewish scholars view Genesis allegorically, focusing on the moral and ethical teachings of the text rather than its historical accuracy. But overwhelming scientific evidence and the common sense God hath given us doesn't tend to sway people who believe in talking snakes.

Now, you could get all huffy and try to convince your loved ones that science is a thing. Fossil records and thousands of ancient human remains have documented our evolutionary transition from earlier primates to modern humans, and DNA sequencing has shown many genetic similarities between humans and other primates.

And you'll even say "evolutionary theory" and not "evolutionary proof" because you understand that's not how science works.

But do remember that for whatever data, facts, or evidence you bring up, your literalists already have an invincible comeback line:

"Were you there?"

So, you explain up and down about *Homo habilis, Homo erectus,* Neanderthals, and various *Australopithecus* species. Be sure to mention how comparative genomics has identified specific genetic markers and mutations that distinguish humans from other primates, and traced our evolutionary history.

And they will swiftly cut down your pitiful research with:

"Were you there?"

Maybe you've been in this situation and you've behaved unwisely, as was often my youthful custom. Young Catholic Me would seethe over the absurdity. Who cares about the Book of Genesis? A talking snake has nothing to do with Jesus! What does that have to do with the moral heavy lifting the Bible requires?

And without needing any counterargument, they'd shut me down: "Were you there?"

And it's okay. You'll probably never convince them.

The order of creation in Genesis—light created before the sun, plants created before the sun, creation of humans before animals in one account, after animals in another—contradicts all established scientific understanding of the origin of the universe and development of life on earth. Snakes lack vocal cords and the cognitive ability necessary for speech, and always have. This presents a significant conflict with the natural history and biology of reptiles.

"Yeah, well, God could've made the snake talk just that one time."

Okay, that's possible, I guess. Maybe God was behind it all, and Eve really was framed.

But if you're Eve, nakedly sauntering through paradise, and a serpent pops up to persuade you to disobey God and eat of the Tree of Knowledge, it's reasonable to assume your first response might be "Holy crap, a talking snake."

Science has never made me doubt the existence of a loving God, but some Christians have.

Loch Ness Creationism

In 2012, it was reported that some private schools in Louisiana participating in the state's voucher program were using a curriculum from Accelerated Christian Education (ACE). ACE is a Christian curriculum provider that pushes a literal interpretation of the Bible and teaches creationism alongside—or in place of—actual scientific theories.

These curriculum materials, which promoted Young Earth creationism as science, cited references to the Loch Ness monster as evidence that dinosaurs coexisted with humans and have survived into modern times. Since Noah's flood was only four thousand years ago, it's logical that sea monsters survived. And because the Loch Ness monster is a totally real and living dinosaur, this proves evolution is false.

It's twenty-first-century American fundamentalism: taxpayer dollars for textbooks that disprove science by saying humans coexisted with dinosaurs and still do. Which is why I have no problem with creationism being taught in science class, as long as evolutionary theory is taught during Bible study.

Fun Activities with Hardcore Creationists

You may find yourself at a family gathering. And you may find yourself at a table with your most extreme right-wing religious relatives. The ones still mad about Pride Month at Thanksgiving.

Now, maybe you're a sensible person, and, not seeking unnecessary conflict, you politely steer away from politics or religion. I recommend sports.

But if you do decide to engage with a biblical literalist in a public setting, especially featuring loved ones, try to ask questions.

Do our creationist friends believe the passage of Genesis 6:1–4 that describes fallen angels mating with human females and creating a race of Nephilim, or giants? That's really there.

In Genesis 4:14–15, Cain is scared that "others" will kill him after he is exiled for murdering Abel. Who are these "others" if Adam, Eve, and Cain were the only humans at the time?

Where exactly did Cain's wife come from, please?

Where'd all the water go after the flood?

See? No fighting necessary. So, with that in mind, let me share my favorite question to ask your right-wing relatives at the next reunion:

Did God create man and woman at the same time, or did God put man here first?

You see, the Book of Genesis contains two different creation narratives in chapters 1–2, with different sequencing and events in each.

First, point out that in Genesis chapter 1, God creates man and woman at the same time:

"Then God said, 'Let us make mankind in our image, in our likeness, so that they may rule over the fish in the sea and the birds in the sky, over the livestock and all the wild animals, and over all the creatures that move along the ground.' So God created mankind in his own image, in the image of God he created them; male and female he created them" (Genesis 1:26–27).

Got that? God creates humanity—both male and female—in his image, simultaneously. Both genders share in the divine likeness, but we'll get to that in the scary chapter on feminism.

But in Genesis chapter 2, it's a different story.

Literally.

God creates Adam first, in Genesis 2:7, from the dust of the ground. Yes, folks who won't believe humans came from primitive primates believe that humans came from dirt.

God then places Adam in the Garden of Eden and gives him a big manly job: come up with names for all the animals (Genesis 2:8–20). Despite all the company, by Genesis 2:20 he's come to realize that none of these critters are a "suitable companion" for him.

And this part horrified me as a teen. None of the animals were *a suitable companion* for man? How many did he try out? And what were those auditions like, exactly? Was Adam attempting to get it on with goats? Birds? Ferrets? Who gets the rose in this ceremony?

Never fear, the Almighty's got this—in a way that would allow centuries of men to believe that while women's bodies can create life, men did it first.

"So, the Lord God cast a deep sleep on the man, and while he was asleep, he took out one of his ribs and closed up its place with flesh and that was Eve."

See? Two completely different accounts. So ask your literalist loved ones, respectfully—which is it? Did God create man and woman at the same time, or did God put man here first? You *can't* believe both, so which is the literal truth?

Nine times out of ten, your right-wing loved one will tell you that they believe God made Adam first, then used his rib to create Eve.

And then you can let the whole table know that these very nice folks here believe that the first-ever woman, in all of history, transitioned from a man.

You'll never be invited back, but they'll never forget you.

THOU SHALT NOT HATE FEMINISTS

"But I suffer not a woman to teach, nor to usurp authority over the man, but to be in silence."

St. Paul, 1 Timothy 2:12

"A wife is to submit graciously to the servant leadership of her husband even as the church willingly submits to the headship of Christ."

Official statement of Southern Baptist Convention, summer 1998

If God loves men and women equally, then God's a feminist.

Feminism is, quite simply, the controversial belief that women deserve the same rights and access as men. Conservative men in power have historically tried to control women's sexuality, education, participation in society, and bodily autonomy. And they've spent centuries trying to control how women feel about *themselves.*

It's consistent across all faiths—the more fundamentalist the sect, the more women are oppressed—and the more men will claim that's just how a male God wants it.

Christianity has not, generally, been an exception.

For centuries, the Old Church positioned itself as the arbiter of moral behavior while programming generations with sexual and bodily shame, on top of all that original sin. This allowed religious leaders to maintain control of people's fears and behaviors, while promoting themselves as the only guides for achieving purity and salvation.

Today, their ideological heirs strive to limit women's freedoms and their participation in the workplace, while scheming endless taxpayer dollars to fund private Christian schools that might just have to remind girls of their proper biblical gender roles.

Christian nationalists generally oppose feminist movements and any policies that promote gender equality. Feminism is a threat to their version of Christian morality, because a certain kind of male will never stop believing that God prefers him to a woman. They no longer attempt to own women as outright property, which is sanctioned by the parts of the Bible they prefer. But in their efforts to criminalize abortion—which the Bible *never* bans—they've finally found a way to control women's bodies in this century.

The question is simple: Does Jesus ever say anywhere that women don't deserve equal rights to men?

Women have it rough throughout the Bible. They're cursed; they're not allowed to speak in the temple. They're considered "unclean" after childbirth, and if their baby is female, they're "unclean" for twice as long. They're also systemically programmed to accept that they're inferior in the eyes of God. It's like the Gospel According to Ike Turner.

But then Jesus has to show up and ruin it all for the misogynists of ancient and modern times. Yeshua violates all kinds of anti-woman law: he includes women in his ministry, has public conversations with them (forbidden at the time), teaches women (*strictly* forbidden at the time), and has women disciples who play important roles in his movement.

These women include Mary and Martha, the sisters of Lazarus, as well as Mary Magdalene, who is not, at any point in the Bible, described as a prostitute.

In a first century where women were submissive, unclean, and disposable property, Jesus breaks all the social codes to treat them as equals. As with so many other bigotries, sexism requires rejecting his ways.

By treating women with equality and dignity, involving them in his ministry, and challenging the gender roles he'd grown up with, Jesus and his New Covenant align with the very modern feminist values of equality, inclusion, and justice.

And the controlling, overcompensating, spiritually weak beta males of modern right-wing Christianity don't want women—or girls—to ever find this out.

KEEPING WOMEN SUBMISSIVE: TOTALLY NORMAL AND NOT AT ALL INSECURE

THE CLAIM: "God Almighty Himself says women are naturally subordinate to men, and male dominance is a divine mandate."

THE SCRIPTURE: In Genesis 3, after Adam and Eve have eaten of the forbidden Tree of Knowledge, God tells Eve—and all women to come—exactly where they stand:

"I will make your pains in childbearing very severe; with painful labor you will give birth to children. Your desire will be for your husband, and he will rule over you."

THE APPROPRIATE FIRST RESPONSE: "So you're saying that painful childbirth, which all mothers experience, is literal punishment because Eve was tricked by a talking snake? This is your spiritual belief, Cousin Neckbeard?"

But seriously, ask them—nicely—to confirm if they feel this way.

This has been used to justify subordination of women for centuries. But men will remind you: these are the rules. Conveniently written, in full, by one gender.

BIBLICAL MISOGYNY: PROPERTY, AND/OR ICKY

It's important to know how women were expected to be treated in the world of the Bible, across multiple regions and faiths. Society was completely dominated by men, in both public and private. Women's status and security were tied to their relationships with men, be they fathers, husbands, or sons.

Girls were under the authority of their fathers before marriage, and then their husbands afterward. Women's roles were primarily domestic, their legal rights were few. They were expected to bear children, maintain the household, and support and "delight" their husbands.

Marriages were typically arranged, and girls—usually married off before age fourteen—had little say in the choice of their husbands. The primary purpose of marriage was to produce offspring, and maybe form a useful alliance between families.

Women didn't have anything resembling independent property rights. Laws regarding inheritance and marriage like Numbers 27:1–11 and Deuteronomy 21:10–14 consistently affirmed women as subordinate to men. Inheritance traditionally passed through male lineage.

And if a man decided to drop his wife, in many cases her only option was to attempt to move in with relatives somewhere. Otherwise, she could find herself homeless, or at best reduced to prostitution or begging to survive. Divorce could be a death sentence, and it could come at any time.

And of course, women's participation in religious rituals and roles was severely limited; they were excluded from the priesthood and many religious ceremonies.

Society saw women as commodities, inherently impure and the source of all sin, because the scriptures were written by men who saw it that way. Then, as now, biblical misogyny fell into two basic categories: (1) men who think women are property, and (2) men who think women are icky.

Women Are Men's Property

In many biblical accounts, marriage involved the payment of a bride price, a form of compensation paid by the groom's family to the bride's family. Similarly, dowries were sometimes provided by the bride's family as part of the marriage arrangement, reflecting the transfer of the woman's dependency from her father to her husband.

Either way, scripture made sure that everyone understood women were part of a man's collection of properties: "You shall not covet your neighbor's house. You shall not covet your neighbor's wife, or his male or female servant, his ox or donkey, or anything that belongs to your neighbor" (Exodus 20:17).

Daughters could be bought and sold, since they were also the property of men. Exodus 21:7 laid out the tasteful, thoughtful conditions for selling one's child into servitude: "If a man sells his daughter as a servant, she is not to go free as male servants do."

As we saw earlier, Deuteronomy 22:28–29 teaches us that a raped daughter—otherwise considered damaged goods—can, fortunately, be sold to her rapist.

1 Kings 11:3 shows that collecting wives and sex slaves was a terrific status symbol. If you could control them, that is: "He [Solomon] had seven hundred wives of royal birth and three hundred concubines, and his wives led him astray."

And of course, a girl's or woman's entire worth was defined by her sexual purity at the time of marriage. As Deuteronomy 22:20–21 makes clear, if a bride was found to not be a virgin, the whole town was encouraged to murder her. Well, not the whole town—just the guys. "If, however, the charge is true and no proof of the girl's virginity can be found, she shall be brought to the door of her father's house and there the men of her town shall stone her to death."

This "used brides deserve a horrible death" law has been used to terrify women and control their sexuality for literally centuries, by many fundamentalists of multiple religions.

God commands in Numbers 31:17–18 that women's bodies should be taken as spoils of war—but only the virgins:

"Now kill all the boys. And kill every woman who has slept with a man but save for yourselves every girl who has never slept with a man."

Deuteronomy 21:10–14 breaks down how attractive female spoils of war can be abducted, imprisoned, raped, and married. And if a guy decides he doesn't enjoy her after all that, he can just cut her loose.

"When you go to war against your enemies and the Lord your God delivers them into your hands and you take captives; if you notice among the captives a beautiful woman and are attracted to her, you may take her as your wife. Bring her into your home and have her shave her head, trim her nails, and put aside the clothes she was wearing when captured. After she has lived in your house and mourned her father and mother for a full month, then you may go to her and be her husband and she shall be your wife. If you are not pleased with her, let her go wherever she wishes. You must not sell her or treat her as a slave, since you have dishonored her."

Got that, women? It's nice how they let you mourn your slain parents.

"Biblical Marriage"

I asked author and theologian Keith Giles about "biblical marriage":

"According to the Scriptures, biblical marriage was always a contract between two men: the father of the woman and the father of the man. It was a business deal, not a romantic affair. In other words, the woman had little say in the matter and the arrangement was essentially another word for slavery. The man owned the woman. She was his property. She existed to serve him and to enlarge his legacy.

"Biblical Marriage isn't what many Christian leaders want you to think it was. It wasn't beautiful. It wasn't sacred or holy. It wasn't defined by religious texts. It was a secular business deal. On the Christian side, marriage wasn't made a sacrament until the 1500s. Meaning, prior to that time, Christians didn't think about marriage as something the Church had to bless or regulate or define. It was merely an arrangement between two families that took place in someone's home without involving the pastor, the priest, the bishop or any Christian leader."

Women Are Icky

The men who wrote the Bible had but a first-century understanding of the reproductive system. Women were merely the vessels for male seed, and their bodies played no role in developing the children they bore.

You may not be shocked to learn that the male authors of the Bible generally found menstruation to be totally scary and gross. They generally regarded the biological process that helps create life as a source of impurity and uncleanness, and they make damn sure the reader understands this.

Menstruating women are spiritually unclean in Leviticus 15: 19–31.

"When a woman has her regular flow of blood, the impurity of her monthly period will last seven days, and anyone who touches her will be unclean till evening. Anything she lies on during her period will be unclean, and anything she sits on will be unclean. Anyone who touches her bed will be unclean. . . . Anyone who touches anything she sits on will be unclean."

And in Leviticus 20:18:

"If a man has sexual relations with a woman during her monthly period, he has exposed the source of her flow, and she has also uncovered it. Both of them are to be cut off from their people."

More of this in Ezekiel, where menstruation is stigmatized by associating it with moral impurity—for men:

"He does not eat at the mountain shrines or look to the idols of Israel. He does not defile his neighbor's wife or have sexual relations with a woman during her period" (Ezekiel 18:6).

"In you are those who dishonor their father's bed; in you are those who violate women during their period, when they are ceremonially unclean" (Ezekiel 22:10).

Now, some historians argue that these menstrual laws had practical benefits for health and hygiene in ancient times, that these were purity rituals, not condemnation. And that may be true. But what's undeniable is that these verses of women as ritually impure led to centuries of stigmatization and body shame by turning women's biology against them.

And it must be mentioned that in the twenty-first century, Jews are often *way* ahead of Christians on women's equality. Jewish feminist movements have advocated for gender equality throughout communities and institutions; both Reform and Conservative Judaism have allowed women to serve as rabbis, cantors, and religious scholars.

And of course, Israel had its first female prime minister, Golda Meir, in 1969. But we've got high hopes the United States will be ready for a female president sometime in our second 250 years.

Modern Judaism no longer views women as property like the ancients, but the heirs of this belief include many Christians, still using government to exert control over women's bodies.

THE BIGGEST DAMN FEMINIST IN THE ENTIRE BIBLE

> "As we meet Jesus in the Gospels, we'll encounter a man who welcomes sexually notorious women while standing up to sexually self-righteous men. We find a man born into sexual scandal, who further scandalized his fellow Jews by loving women known for sexual sin. We find a man who never had a sexual relationship, but who loved women so well that they'd leave everything to follow him. We find a man who turned his back on the religiously powerful men of his day and had his longest recorded private conversation with a religiously despised woman."
>
> Rebecca McLaughlin, *Jesus Through the Eyes of Women*

Then this Jesus shows up, stubbornly refuses to treat women as inferior, and almost ruins the whole rigged game.

All four Gospel writers specifically cite Jesus rejecting the accepted cultural norms and treating women with respect. Not only did he break rabbinic laws of his day by teaching and talking to women, but he allowed women to touch him—including those considered "unclean" by the culture at large.

He begins in the Sermon on the Mount, Matthew 5:28, by essentially telling men, "Stop looking at her like that."

"You have heard that it was said, 'You shall not commit adultery.' But I tell you that anyone who looks at a woman lustfully has already committed adultery with her in his heart."

This could be the first recorded biblical utterance of "Eyes up here, buddy." Jesus's admonition to not look on women lustfully is not anti-sex—it's anti–sexual harassment.

The Samaritan Woman

John chapter 4 tells of a meeting between Jesus and a Samaritan woman that seems innocuous on the surface, especially for churchgoers who haven't been taught the backstory about how women were treated at the time.

Jesus's community generally despised the Samaritans and avoided their territory, a region between Judea and Galilee. But in this story, Jesus leads his followers on a detour through Samaria. Tired and thirsty, he stops at the well for a drink while the apostles do their own thing.

A woman shows up at the well, in the heat of the day, and Jesus engages her. Now, in the culture of the times, this violated two major codes of behavior. A man would never speak to a woman he did not know, and no respectable Jew would *ever* talk to a *Samaritan.*

But Jesus, fan of breaking down barriers and reaching out to outcasts, asks her for a drink and strikes up a conversation.

She's a bit shocked at first. "You are a Jew and I am a Samaritan woman. How can you ask me for a drink?" (For Jews do not associate with Samaritans.)

What follows is Jesus's longest recorded private conversation with anyone in the Bible—with a woman he was forbidden to have been speaking to.

As they converse, Jesus reveals details about her personal life. He knows she's had five previous husbands, and was currently living with another guy, out of wedlock. By the standards of the time, these were grounds for righteous, full-throated slut-shaming.

It's very possible that this woman was shunned by her own community. Women would generally go together to get water from the well in the morning or evening, but this woman was fetching water in the brutal heat of midday, all alone.

Jesus doesn't care about the rules. He doesn't care that she's a despised foreigner, and he does not shame or condemn her—at all—for her personal life. Instead, he promises to give her "living water," which would quench her spiritual thirst. He even tells her "salvation is from the Jews," which is why right-wing Christians never quote this one.

The woman immediately sees Jesus as a prophet and mentions the coming Messiah; Jesus then reveals to her that, yeah, I'm the guy.

This admission marks the first time in John's Gospel that Jesus ever tells anyone that he's the Messiah—and he says it to a deeply despised woman no rabbi would be permitted to talk to.

John 4:27 tells us how the apostles were not cool with this, but kept their mouths shut. "Just then his disciples returned and were surprised to find him talking with a woman. But no one asked, "What do you want?" or "Why are you talking with her?"

The story ends with the woman telling everybody about the encounter. "Many of the Samaritans of that town began to believe in him because of the word of the woman who testified" on his behalf (John 4:39).

Jesus broke down ethnic, gender, and religious barriers just by having a conversation. It's worth pointing out that Jesus keeps picking Samaritans, a very particular type of unpopular foreigner, whom his people were allowed and *encouraged* to hate, to be these examples of humanity.

(Sam Cooke & The Soul Stirrers' "Jesus Gave Me Water" is the best-ever up-tempo a cappella gospel pop song about this very encounter)

Martha and Mary in Luke 10:41–42

The familiar story of Martha and Mary, the sisters of Lazarus, in Luke 10:38–42 is another one that's often read at church but becomes more powerful (and logical) with context.

At the time, studying the Torah was traditionally reserved for men, but

Mary wanted to learn and Jesus wasn't going to say no. She's described here as one who "sat beside the Lord at his feet listening to him speak," which is usually the position of the top male disciple. Sitting at the feet of a rabbi meant that a person was one of his best students.

Meanwhile, Martha takes on the traditional woman's role of providing hospitality and doing what society expects of her—preparing food, doing housework, and always keeping busy. She's understandably not thrilled that she has to play hostess to Jesus and twelve other guys while her sister's sitting around, committing the sin of becoming educated.

But Jesus makes it clear to Martha that he doesn't expect her to take care of his men, or to constantly put their needs ahead of her own. He tells her that he's the one serving the real food, that Mary is right to sit and learn, and that Martha's stress and anxiety aren't helping.

"'Martha, Martha,' the Lord answered, 'you are worried and upset about many things, but few things are needed—or indeed only one. Mary has chosen what is better, and it will not be taken away from her.'"

Growing up, I heard this story often in church, but never in context. I felt sorry for Martha, who seemed overwhelmed, and I wasn't taught how subversive Jesus was being. He not only asserts that women can and should receive an education; he even says it's better to learn than to do housework. It's a classic example of a Bible story that's taught to kids before they can understand why it matters.

The Bleeding Woman

Not only did Jesus violate the rules of his day by teaching and talking with women, but he also allowed them to touch him—including women who'd been deemed "unclean" by the religious authorities. The very dramatic story of the woman who'd had a nonstop flow of blood for twelve years appears in Mark 5, Luke 8, and Matthew 9.

Like women of her time with any flow of blood, she was understood by the community to be unclean in the eyes of God. The fact that she'd been bleeding for a dozen years made her an absolute outcast, unable to participate in any part of society, or any religious rituals.

She'd spent her money on treatments, but nothing had worked. Anything she touched, or any person, was ritually unclean. Any person who *touched anything she had touched* was de facto unclean.

This desperate woman of this story believed if she could just touch Jesus's robes, she'd be healed. (Sam Cooke & the Soul Stirrers also immortalized this one in "Touch the Hem of His Garment.")

Hearing Jesus is in town, she ventures out in public, works through the crowd, and approaches secretly from behind, to touch the edge of said garment. Keep in mind, she was already breaking the law by approaching *anyone,* and under the law she never should've been allowed into a *crowd* where an innocent person might brush against her unclean state.

In the story, as soon as she touches his robe, she can tell that her bleeding has stopped, and she knows she's been healed. Jesus feels that the power has gone out from him; he stops and asks who touched him.

Again, for any woman to *ever* touch a man was forbidden. But in her defiled state, she had legally rendered Jesus unclean in the eyes of God.

Trembling, the woman comes forward and admits it was her. And Jesus responds to this woman, who has just violated so many rules made by men, saying, "Daughter, your faith has healed you. Go in peace and be freed from your suffering."

This is the only time in the Bible Jesus ever calls anyone "daughter." He refuses to view her as unclean, or worthy of punishment. An impure woman inappropriately touches him and he responds with intimacy, letting his "daughter" know she has every right to touch him.

She violates the taboo, and then Jesus breaks the taboo, for good.

It's amazing how misogynists pretend to follow this guy.

The Adulteress and the "Fallen Woman"

In the story of the adulteress in John 8:7, a few Pharisees lay a trap by presenting the guilty woman before Jesus to see if he'll reject Moses's law, which demanded that she be stoned to death. This story figures prominently in chapter 11, on the death penalty.

If Jesus took the woman's side, he was negating the law. If he took her accusers' side, he was negating all he'd taught about forgiveness. Either way, they figured, they had him this time.

But Jesus avoids the entire legal debate and calls them out with the fundamental truth that no one is without sin. He not only forgives the woman, but he also demolishes the law that commands her death.

Countless times, Jesus fulfills the law by ignoring its specifics and reorienting the law around love.

In Luke 7:37 and 38, a shamed woman anoints Jesus while he's dining with a Pharisee friend:

"A woman in that town who lived a sinful life learned that Jesus was eating at the Pharisee's house, so she came there with an alabaster jar of perfume. As she stood behind him at his feet weeping, she began to wet his feet with her tears. Then she wiped them with her hair, kissed them and poured perfume on them."

Again, by allowing the woman to touch him and in showing her compassion, Jesus was breaking social and religious rules of his time. "Sinful" women were seen then as inferior, as they are today. His Pharisee host—named Simon—is disgusted, warning Jesus of her ways. "If this man were a prophet, he would know who is touching him and what kind of woman she is—that she is a sinner" (Luke 7:39).

But Jesus forgives her for whatever she's done—he doesn't much care about humiliating her with specifics—and does not reduce himself to judging her. Not only does Jesus tell the woman that her sins are forgiven, but he also uses her actions to straighten out his offended host. Jesus's question to Simon is pointed: "Do you see this woman?" (Luke 7:44).

It's a powerful response, when you think about it. He doesn't judge the guy, but the question urges his host to look beyond the rules, to see this guilt-ridden woman as a human soul of great repentance, sincerity—and potential for goodness.

Jesus reminds that the one who's enforcing all the rules is not necessarily the better person. "I tell you, her many sins have been forgiven—as her great love has shown. But whoever has been forgiven little loves little" (Luke 7:47.)

If you're *ever* looking for permission to slut-shame, Jesus ain't your guy.

WHEN ANTI-DIVORCE WAS PROTO-FEMINIST

Over in the LGBTQ chapter we cover how this story has been twisted in recent years to claim Jesus opposes gay marriage, when in reality it was Jesus opposing straight divorce. The Nazarene challenges or overturns many religious laws, but divorce is one of his most direct.

Matthew 19:3–9: "Some Pharisees came to him to test him. They asked, 'Is it lawful for a man to divorce his wife for any and every reason?' . . . Jesus replied, 'Moses permitted you to divorce your wives because your hearts were hard. But it was not this way from the beginning. I tell you that anyone who divorces his wife, except for sexual immorality, and marries another woman commits adultery.'"

Now, it should come as no surprise that in the first-century Holy Land, divorce laws weren't written by the editorial staff of *Jezebel.* Deuteronomy 24:1 asserts that men could divorce their wives for trivial reasons, leaving women vulnerable and without support. Tired of her? Kick her to the curb. There was no such thing as alimony, and women couldn't get jobs or even an education. Divorce really could be fatal, but only for women.

So, while Jesus's rule may appear harsh, at the time he was being extremely progressive. He calls out Moses's divorce laws as "hard-hearted" and announces that men shouldn't be able to casually dump their wives anymore. He was standing up for women's rights and safety, and trying to keep them from being thrown away and left to starve.

Considering that Jesus changed Moses's divorce laws in the interest of protecting women, it's reasonable to believe that in the very different world of two thousand years later—when divorce is often a lifeline for women in abusive situations—the Nazarene wouldn't judge women for getting out of bad marriages.

MORE IRKSOME JESUS STORIES FOR MISOGYNIST BELIEVERS

- Luke 11:27–28 is another story told often in church, but free of context:

  "As Jesus was saying these things, a woman in the crowd called out, 'Blessed is the mother who gave you birth and nursed you.' He replied, 'Blessed rather are those who hear the word of God and obey it.'"

  Now, why would a nice Jewish boy like Yeshua negate a blessing on his mother? Can't you just say thank you, Jesus?

  But consider this—women of Jesus's time were expected to have children. That's it. Many societies consider women to be baby-making machines, and raising those babies is typically the extent of their value. Am I right, JD Vance?

  So when this woman praises Jesus's mother for her baby-making and baby-feeding abilities, Jesus corrects her. He doesn't want his mother blessed for birthing and nursing; he wants her blessed *for the choices she herself makes.* In front of everyone, Jesus affirms that women are not to be reduced to being only mothers, but should also be praised for having agency and doing the right thing.
- In Luke 15:8–10's parable of the lost coin, Jesus gives a metaphor that actually presents God as a woman.

  "Suppose a woman has ten silver coins and loses one. Doesn't she light a lamp, sweep the house and search carefully until she finds it? And when she finds it, she calls her friends and neighbors together and says, 'Rejoice with me; I have found my lost coin.' In the same way, I tell you, there is rejoicing in the presence of the angels of God over one sinner who repents."
- In Luke 8:1–3, Jesus is journeying from village to village, preaching and proclaiming. The twelve apostles are with him and several women are mentioned, too: "Mary (called Magdalene), from whom seven demons had gone out, and Joanna the wife of Cuza (Herod's household

manager), Susanna, and many others who provided for them out of their own resources." (NET)

That's right. In case you ever wondered who funded this whole operation, it was women investors who financially supported Jesus and his twelve disciples as he traveled, teaching and healing.

The fact that these women are called by name in the Bible is significant. In a culture and time where women couldn't own property or even testify in court, a woman's presence at an event wasn't even considered worth counting. Jesus included them as active participants in his ministry, brought them along in his travels, and had them help spread the Gospel.

Did your church ever teach you that women kept Jesus's ministry afloat financially?

MAKE BIBLE MISOGYNIST AGAIN

Guess Who's Back?

> "Christianity is inherently sexist because 'Christianity' did not originate with Christ. Christianity is an institution of systems created by men for men. Because of this, women can only fit into roles and ranks that accommodate the mind and motives of the men who created the system."
>
> Pastor Desimber Rose

Once Jesus is gone and Paul takes over, "women are property" and "women are icky" are both back on the menu.

Paul lets women know that God has totally signed off on their husbands' complete authority over them. "Wives, submit yourselves to your husbands, as is fitting in the Lord" (Colossians 3:18).

Millions of men who prefer He-Man Paul to Feminist Jesus have used this line to justify patriarchal views of marriage and gender roles. Oh, and in case you missed that submission thing? It applies to whatever a man wants: "Wives, submit yourselves to your own husbands as you do to the Lord. . . . Now as the church submits to Christ, so also wives should submit to their husbands in everything" (Ephesians 5:22–24).

Here's more submission—plus childbirth as a form of atonement:

"A woman should learn in quietness and full submission. I do not permit a woman to teach or to assume authority over a man; she must be quiet. For Adam was formed first, then Eve. And Adam was not the one deceived; it was the woman who was deceived and became a sinner. But women will be saved through childbearing—if they continue in faith, love, and holiness with propriety" (1 Timothy 2:11–15).

Oh, and by the way—women were created for men, and God *really* doesn't like the tops of their heads:

"For if a woman does not cover her head, she might as well have her hair cut off; but if it is a disgrace for a woman to have her hair cut off or her head shaved, then she should cover her head. A man ought not to cover his head, since he is the image and glory of God; but woman is the glory of man. For man did not come from woman, but woman from man; neither was man created for woman, but woman for man" (1 Corinthians 11:6–10).

Women should be seen, not heard:

"Women should remain silent in the churches. They are not allowed to speak, but must be in submission, as the law says" (1 Corinthians 14:34).

This last passage has been used to exclude women from leadership roles and public speaking in religious settings for centuries.

Now remember, Paul also ordered slaves to be obedient to their masters. Most of us would disregard that admonition as coming from a flawed man from an archaic era, right? Take note of anyone who thinks Paul's order for women to submit shouldn't be weighed in a similar context. Paul is not, in fact, Jesus.

But here's the strange part. Not three chapters earlier (1 Corinthians 11:5), Paul instructed the women who were *prophesying and praying in the church* to do so while wearing culturally appropriate head coverings.

So Paul just told women *how* to speak in church, and now he's telling them *not* to speak? How is that consistent?

Also, remember—all throughout his letters, Paul reminds the church that they are no longer subject to the old law's condemnation because of their faith in Jesus:

"Now before faith came, we were imprisoned and guarded under the law until faith would be revealed. Therefore, the law was our disciplinarian until Christ came, so that we might be justified by faith. But now that faith has come, we are no longer subject to a disciplinarian, for in Christ Jesus you are all children of God through faith" (Galatians 3:23–25, NRSVA).

So how does that fit with his declarations that women sin against the law by speaking in church? It doesn't make sense—and reveals an inconsistency in Paul's teachings that has confused people much smarter than me for many years.

As mentioned earlier, there's evidence that Paul, despite his most infamous words, wasn't a complete misogynist. Paul acknowledges the work of many women in the early church. In Romans 16:1 he praises a woman called Phoebe, who's described as a deacon, telling the Christians in Rome, "I ask you to receive her in the Lord in a way worthy of his people and to give her any help she may need from you, for she has been the benefactor of many people, including me." Phoebe was a wealthy businesswoman and a supporter of Paul's work. Once again.

Other women mentioned by Paul include Priscilla, described with her husband, Aquila, as "my co-workers" who "risked their lives for me"; Prisca, Mary, Persis, Julia, Nereus's sister, Tryphena, Tryphosa, Rufus's mother, Chloe, Euodia, Syntyche, and Junia, who in Romans 16:7 is praised as "outstanding among the apostles."

It's unfortunate that Phoebe, who helped fund Paul, came to be overshadowed by the misogyny sprinkled through his work.

Of course, that's nothing compared to what happened to Mary Magdalene.

What Mary Magdalene Wasn't

THE SCRIPTURE: Luke 7:36–50; Luke 8:1–3

Mary Magdalene was a pivotal figure in Jesus's ministry and the early Christian movement. She was part of that group of women who traveled with him and supported his ministry financially (Luke 8:3). She's first introduced in the Gospels as a woman healed by Jesus, from whom he cast out "seven demons" (Luke 8:2). This phrasing could symbolize spiritual or emotional healing rather than literal possession. (Having said that, I'd totally watch a movie exclusively about Jesus's side gig as an exorcist).

Magdalene is with Jesus until the end, a witness at the Crucifixion—after most of Jesus's male disciples had fled (Mark 15:40–41, John 19:25). She was also the first to witness and announce the resurrection, earning her the title "Apostle to the Apostles" in early Christian tradition (John 20:1–18, Matthew 28:1–10).

But you might know her as a prostitute.

Christian lore has long associated Mary Magdalene with sex work, or some vague sexual sin. In films like *King of Kings* (1961) and *The Greatest Story Ever Told* (1965), she's portrayed as a woman with an undefined but troubled past. Barbara Hershey's stunning performance in Martin Scorsese's *The Last Temptation of Christ* goes deep on its depiction of her prostitution, reflecting the novel that inspired the film.

Of course, Mary Magdalene is never once referred to as a prostitute in the Bible. But that didn't stop early Christian leaders from conflating her with other women in the Gospels, feeding this misconception. Instead of being recognized as a faithful follower and benefactor of Jesus, she's been—well, you know.

In the sixth century, Pope Gregory I delivered a homily where he identified Mary Magdalene as the unnamed sinful woman who anointed Jesus's feet in Luke 7:36–50. He suggested that Magdalene was a prostitute who repented of her sins, leading to her association with penitent sinners.

Many scholars argue that identifying Magdalene as the sinful woman of

Luke 7 is dead wrong, and there's no biblical basis for labeling her a prostitute. We don't even know if the nameless woman in Luke 7 *was* a prostitute. Pope Gregory just made it up, his contribution to the ongoing game of biblical telephone tag.

This willfully erroneous portrayal was likely influenced by efforts to undermine the authority of women in the early church. Magdalene's prominent role clearly posed a challenge to patriarchal structures. Nevertheless, the smear has stuck for fifteen hundred years.

THE HE-MAN WOMAN-HATER'S CULT

> "Every woman should be filled with shame by the thought that she is a woman."
>
> St. Clement of Alexandria (c. 150–c. 215)

Things didn't get much better for women after Paul put them back in their place.

Listen to early church father Tertullian (c. 155–c. 240), "the father of Latin Christianity." He's known for his influential writings on theology, like "Woman is a temple built over a sewer."

If that seems a bit ambiguous, he also said, "You [woman] are the devil's gateway: you are the unsealer of that [forbidden] tree: you are the first deserter of the divine law: you are she who persuaded him whom the devil was not valiant enough to attack. You destroyed so easily God's image, man. On account of your desert—that is, death—even the Son of God had to die."

Pretty sure the Son of God's horrible death was his dad's overall plan all along, but you go ahead and blame the ladies, Tert.

Jesus's respect for women was not as appealing to the guys who inherited his operation. St. Augustine of Hippo (354–430) was one of the most significant figures in early Christian theology, and a beautiful writer and theologian. But a hero to women, he was not:

"What is the difference whether it is in a wife or a mother, it is still Eve the temptress that we must beware of in any woman. . . . I fail to see what use woman can be to man, if one excludes the function of bearing children."

"Woman was merely man's helpmate, a function which pertains to her alone. She is not the image of God but as far as man is concerned, he is by himself the image of God."

In at least eight US states today, a guy could run for office on that message and win.

Martin Luther's legendary passion for reform didn't extend to gender roles within the church; he deeply opposed the education of women beyond basic literacy:

"The word and works of God are quite clear, that women were made either to be wives or prostitutes."

"If they become tired or even die, that does not matter. Let them die in childbirth; that's why they are there."

That's nothing. Wait till we get to how he felt about the Jews.

Or take it from enlightened reformer John Calvin: "Woman is more guilty than man, because she was seduced by Satan, and so diverted her husband from obedience to God that she was an instrument of death leading to all perdition. . . . This is reason enough why today she is placed below and that she bears within her ignominy and shame."

My God. Imagine how bad these men must've been at basic foreplay.

From Franklin Graham to Jerry Falwell Jr. to Roy Moore, Christian misogyny has come a short way. After two thousand years, Christian nationalists' opposition to women in power is still rooted in the cultural attitudes they were raised in, and an unmanly fear of women in power.

Pat Robertson famously warned that feminism encourages women to "leave their husbands, kill their children, practice witchcraft, destroy capitalism and become lesbians."

During former Vice President Mike Pence's time in Congress, he boasted that his Christian virtue was so great, he had never—and would never—eat a meal alone with a woman other than his wife. Fundamentalists swooned at the depths of Pence's piety. Some pointed out that this is exactly how gender discrimination works in professional settings, because only male colleagues could be lucky enough for one-on-one time with such a noble statesman.

Stephen Wolfe, author of *The Case for Christian Nationalism,* openly says that under Christian nationalist rule, women can't be in charge, because they are too empathetic and inclusive. Only a male-dominated church can guarantee "blasphemy is punished" and "atheism is crushed."

Right-wing pastor and desperate cry for help Joel Webbon coedited "The Statement on Christian Nationalism" manifesto (co-drafted by James Silberman and Oklahoma state senator Dusty Deevers), which states that the US must officially "acknowledge the Lordship of Christ" in all its laws. In a 2024 viral podcast appearance, Webbon proudly asserted that if he could wave a Christian nationalist "wand," the Nineteenth Amendment would be abolished, and US women would lose the vote.

Speaking of his wand, Pastor Webbon justifies his misogyny because politics is war, and "the sword has been given to men."

"The sword is—without being crude, I think this is a fact—it is a phallus. It is assigned by God to men."

Got that, ladies? Joel's penis was assigned by God Himself. And it's like a sword. This means he's special, and you're not.

These deep spiritual thinkers promote an obnoxious Christian misogyny that cuts across politics and media platforms to poison the minds of very weak men.

NO KNOB, NO JOB

Of course, many Christian sects have come a long way, and today women enjoy leadership roles in churches throughout the world. And then there are the Catholics, who have, at times, permitted women to "participate."

If the Virgin Mary came back, would the Vatican let her say mass? Despite no convincing biblical, scientific, or moral evidence, the church's policy on female priests has remained the same for centuries: God made humans in His own image, but 51 percent just happen to be unworthy of a clerical collar.

THE CLAIM: "The twelve apostles were all men, so clearly Jesus only wanted men as priests and popes. Who are we to question?"

THE REALITY: As we've seen, in addition to the twelve male apostles—whom Jesus repeatedly calls out for getting things wrong, by the way—women accompanied his journeys as part of his ministry. When Jesus was arrested and the apostles all scattered, it was the women who never abandoned him, who never hid, who never denied knowing him. In the Resurrection story, Jesus reveals himself to the women before any of his male disciples.

We know that Mary Magdalene, along with Martha and Mary, the sisters of Lazarus, were fellow travelers. To a sane person in the twenty-first century it might seem obvious that there were actually fifteen apostles, at least.

Wrong, says the church. Those women might have always been with JC and the twelve, but they didn't have full apostle passes. They just followed Jesus from gig to gig, working the merch tables like it was a boy band tour. The church continues to treat these women as secondary figures rather than leaders.

In 2010 the Vatican issued new clerical rules that reinforced its ban on female clergy. The statement said that any priest who ordains a woman is guilty of a "grave crime"—which is the exact language the church had used to describe the abuse of children, by its priests.

The gender that's caused over 99 percent of the sex abuse problems also makes the rules about which gender is worthy, and which isn't. The Vatican will one day realize that they need women more than women need the Vatican.

THE BIBLICAL SLUT-SHAMING HALL OF FAME

Okay, since this is a book about the Bible and all, let's talk about sluts.

The word dates back to the 1400s and has come to mean any woman who's promiscuous. And in America, "promiscuous" means "anybody getting more than you."

It's long been used as an ugly slur, usually out of fear, envy, or rage when a far sluttier male gets turned down.

In the twenty-first century, we've ushered in a new Golden Age of Slut-Shaming—a time where the culture, the media, and the men demand women sexualize themselves to prove their societal value, and then punish the ones who dare to enjoy it.

Slut-shaming is social control of female sexuality—admonishing or attacking women over how they dress, how they love, what they believe. It's typically perpetrated by low-frequency males who crave female sexuality, as long as they can control it.

It's also used to shame women who've been victimized by sexual assault—in the Middle East, Africa, Asia, Europe, and right here in the USA. We saw it in the Ariel Castro trial, if you recall the Ohio monster who'd abducted three women and kept them as sex slaves for ten years. At his sentencing hearings, he tried to shame his victims by pleading to the court that they'd all had multiple partners before he kidnapped them, so it's not like he did anything bad.

The granddaddy of modern slut shaming, of course, is still the late Rush Limbaugh, racist and Presidential Medal of Freedom recipient. When college student Sandra Fluke testified before Congress that access to birth control was a legitimate women's healthcare issue, Limbaugh went on the air and famously dismissed Ms. Fluke as a "slut."

I think mediocre men hate sexually independent women because they can't handle the truth. And the truth is that "slut" is secretly an acronym for "Sexually Liberated, Unapologetic, and Truthful."

1. Tamar

The story of Tamar, found in Genesis 38, is an amazing narrative of a powerless and shamed woman with the agency and resourcefulness to challenge the patriarchal structures that oppress her.

We first meet Tamar in Genesis (see the upcoming chapter about sex hang-ups). She's the unfortunate woman married to Er, smited by God for reasons unknown. She was then obliged to reproduce with her dead husband's brother, Onan, to fulfill the custom of levirate marriage, where a brother must produce an heir for his deceased sibling. But then God killed Onan when he couldn't go through with it.

After these deaths, Tamar was a childless widow with no prospects for survival. Old Judah, father of Onan and Er, promised that she could marry his youngest son, Shelah, once he was older. She lived in Judah's home, expecting her levirate-marriage right.

But Judah, afraid that his last son might also die, withheld him from Tamar rather than allow the required marriage (Genesis 38:11).

To protect herself from being cast out, and to produce heirs, Tamar devised a rather intense plan. She disguised herself as a prostitute and waited for Judah on the road. Not recognizing his own daughter-in-law, old Judah solicited her services, as one does. In the story, Judah promised to compensate her with a young goat. But Tamar demanded he give her some collateral, so Judah gave her his signet ring, cord, and staff.

After no luck conceiving with two of Judah's sons, Tamar became pregnant from this encounter. But when her pregnancy was discovered, Judah immediately condemned his sons' widow to be burned alive:

About three months later Judah was told, "Your daughter-in-law Tamar is guilty of prostitution, and as a result she is now pregnant."

Judah said, "Bring her out and have her burned to death!" (Genesis 38:24).

But before the righteous men can burn a pregnant woman to death—*because fetuses are not considered people in the Bible*—Tamar reveals Judah's signet ring, cord, and staff as proof of his role in the conception. In other words, "Judah, you are the father."

Judah acknowledges his wrongdoing and recognizes Tamar's righteousness in seeking to fulfill her legal marriage obligation.

Now, you could spend half a testament unpacking this one. The narrative highlights the vulnerability of women in patriarchal societies and brutally reveals the unequal treatment they face. Judah solicits sex from a prostitute—then condemns his daughter-in-law for being a prostitute and demands her death.

And Tamar fiercely challenges the power dynamics that deny women agency and autonomy. She's forced, by religious law and marriage customs, to secure her rights and safety any way she can after Judah's broken promise. And she's held to a drastically different standard than Judah, whose actions are never condemned.

Tamar's deception is a brave response to injustice, exposing Judah's hypocrisy and securing her future. The Bible portrays this deeply wronged woman as an intrepid figure who acts with brilliance and self-respect.

In fact, it's such an inspiring biblical story of justice and female ingenuity that none of these conservative Christian broadcast groups have *ever* tried to make a movie out of it.

2. Bathsheba

The story of Bathsheba and King David, in 2 Samuel 11–12, is one of the most morally complex in the Bible. It reveals how innocent women can be preyed on by men—and then blamed for causing the very violence they suffer.

It has inspired many, many paintings, as well as Leonard Cohen's "Hallelujah." And even though the scriptures themselves never blame or slut-shame Bathsheba, she's been scandalized through the centuries by men who've held *her* responsible for the violence of a powerful man.

The story begins when King David, walking the roof of his palace, spies a beautiful woman bathing. Consumed by lust, he's told that she's Bathsheba, wife of Uriah the Hittite, one of his generals.

It never says she was bathing "on a roof" as has long been commonly believed; just that *David* was on the roof, and spied a woman bathing . . . somewhere.

David sends messengers to bring her to his palace, where he sleeps with her. The matter of consent is not mentioned; it was not hers to give.

Soon, Bathsheba sends word to the king that she's pregnant. To cover it up, David summons Uriah back from the war in hopes that he'll sleep with his wife and then believe the baby to be his own. But when Uriah refuses to leave the battlefield, David arranges to have him moved to the front lines, where he's quickly killed.

David then marries Bathsheba, but the child born from the "affair" falls ill and dies. Their next child is Solomon, and Bathsheba persuades David to make him first in line to the throne. Upon David's death, this child famously becomes King Solomon the Wise.

Over the years, the story's been reinterpreted to suggest that Bathsheba was provocatively bathing on an open roof to be seen, implying she was trying to seduce poor David. But the text never describes her as being on a roof—just the king, and that's how he first spots her.

By the seventeenth century, painters highlighted Bathsheba's allure, always bathing out in broad daylight. She came to be depicted as a bold temptress, rather than the victim of sexual violence.

St. Augustine of Hippo and John Calvin both framed Bathsheba as complicit in David's violence—but the Bible itself never accuses or maligns her. And her later actions, ensuring her son Solomon's succession to the throne (1 Kings 1–2), highlight her resilience. Like Tamar, Bathsheba rises above the situation her world puts her in.

3 Rahab "the Prostitute," aka Rahab "the Harlot"

The story of Rahab, found primarily in the Book of Joshua, chapters 2 and 6, offers another example of a biblical heroine who's faced significant sexual shaming throughout history.

Rahab is a Canaanite and prostitute living in the city of Jericho, which the Israelites are preparing to invade and conquer. When Joshua sends two spies to scout out Jericho, they lodge at Rahab's house inside the city walls, where she hides the spies and gives them crucial information about the city's defenses. In exchange, she asks for protection for herself and her family when the Israelites invade.

The spies promise Rahab that her family will be spared if she ties a scarlet cord in her window to identify her house. She does so, and when Jericho is conquered, Rahab's family is indeed protected.

It's a good story, and Rahab is presented as a brave and resourceful woman of faith. Yet over the years, her profession has been emphasized to distinguish her from other characters in the Bible. In medieval and Renaissance art, Rahab was often depicted with an emphasis on her physical appearance and sensuality rather than her role as a civilian hero of the battle of Jericho.

She's not Rahab, brave hero of Jericho; not Rahab, loyal servant of Israel who protected her family. She's forever Rahab the prostitute, redeemed in the Bible, but not in her earthly rep.

4. The Levite's Concubine

Judges 19 describes a period of political corruption and moral anarchy, and features one of the most harrowing and disturbing passages in the entire Bible. It involves a Levite who stays in the town of Gibeah with his concubine, where they're offered shelter by an old man. In the same vein as Sodom and Gomorrah, a mob of local men gather outside the house and start demanding to gang-rape the visiting Levite.

To protect himself, the Levite throws his helpless concubine out to the mob. We're never told her name, and her lack of agency—and options—underscore the horrific objectification and violence she experiences.

The concubine is brutally abused throughout the night, and by morning she has died from the assault just outside the old man's door. In response, the Levite—who threw her to the mob—dismembers her body into twelve pieces, and sends the body parts to the Twelve Tribes of Israel, stirring outrage and leading to civil conflict.

Even though this story is framed as a condemnation of the evil men of Gibeah, the heinous treatment of this unnamed, powerless woman—and her depiction as a disposable sexual object a man uses to avoid his own assault—has further served to normalize violence against women.

5. Oholah and Oholibah

Ezekiel 23:1–49, often referred to as "The Allegory of the Two Sisters," uses poetic sexual imagery to describe unfaithfulness. This passage is a vivid and graphic allegory meant to criticize the idolatry and infidelity of the Kingdoms of Israel and Judah. The names "Oholah" and "Oholibah" are symbolic rather than personal names, representing Samaria and Jerusalem, respectively.

It's a mighty fun read. Oholibah is punished for "harlotry," and despite being banished "she became more and more promiscuous as she recalled the days of her youth, when she was a prostitute in Egypt. There she lusted after her lovers, whose genitals were like those of donkeys and whose emission was like that of horses."

Now you try to find a better Bible passage for a Sunday morning than that. Where I grew up, they'd stay for a second Mass just to hear that again.

GENEALOGY OF JESUS

Remember back in the Jesus chapter, we subjected you to Matthew 1:1–17's very long recitation of all the ancestors of Jesus? Well, that lineage includes Tamar, Rahab, and Bathsheba.

Each of these women has a story that involves elements of sexuality or scandal. Each has been slut-shamed throughout history. But according to the Gospel of Matthew itself, they're all direct ancestors of Jesus's family.

Kristin Kobes Du Mez says, "That his own genealogy includes women who wouldn't pass an evangelical purity test is worth pondering. Jesus came into a fallen world to save and to restore."

The Bible's letting you know—without these "sluts," there'd be no Jesus.

6

THOU SHALT NOT HATE THE GAYS

"Homosexuals are brute beasts . . . part of a vile and satanic system that will be utterly annihilated, and there will be a celebration in heaven."

Rev. Jerry Falwell

"God has shown me that I should not call anyone impure or unclean."

Acts 10:28

While the Hebrews of Jesus's day forbade male-male sexual conduct, it was very much the norm over in Rome and Greece. Jesus was, of course, aware of all this, but somehow never got around to condemning same-sex relations.

What Jesus does is demand a radical love that transcends social boundaries and embraces all people, including those marginalized or rejected by society. Which is why antigay Christians have traditionally relied on their favorite Bible verse, "Anything but Jesus."

You'd think that teachings like "Judge not, lest you also be judged," or "Do unto others as you'd have them do unto you," or even "Love your neighbor as yourself" would pretty much cover "don't be a total dick to gay people." But not to Christian homophobes.

See, gay people are kind of like cannabis plants or foreskins—if an almighty God really hated them, He'd stop creating so many.

There are less than ten references to homosexuality in the Bible, and most of them have been twisted to serve a prejudice that's directly at odds with the teachings of Jesus. And yet, Christianity has allowed the homophobes to set terms that Jesus himself clearly *rejected*.

If anyone's trying to use the Bible to justify any meanness to LGBTQ people, they've *always* got to go around Jesus. Being gay is natural; hating gay is a lifestyle choice. And unlike being gay, homophobia is highly curable.

But some Christian guys are powerfully attracted to antigay hate. At some point when they were young, they may have experimented with hate a little, and now it always gets them turned on.

As recently as the early twenty-first century, many states had sodomy laws criminalizing homosexual acts, supposedly justified by Christian moral teachings. These "Christian moral teachings," however, have never been based on any words of Christ.

GAY MARRIAGE WILL DESTROY US, AT SOME POINT, SOMEDAY

THE CLAIM: "Gay marriage will lead to bestiality."

THE SCRIPTURE: There is none.

And yet this is a mainstream right-wing Christian talking point. In a 2004 op-ed for *The Times* (Shreveport, LA), future Speaker of the House Mike Johnson wrote: "Society cannot give its stamp of approval to such a dangerous lifestyle. If we change marriage for this tiny, modern minority, we will have to do it for every deviant group. . . . There will be no legal basis to deny . . . a person [the right] to marry his pet."

Here's a tip—if you think letting consenting taxpaying adults marry who they love will lead to bestiality, you are *not* a champion of Jesus—you're a guy who thinks too much about bestiality.

Ralph Reed, TV fixture and founder of the Faith and Freedom

Coalition, said, "No one should have special rights or privileges or minority status because of their sexual behavior."

This was, post-AIDS crisis, the most widespread and acceptable bias against gay people—that letting them marry who they love was somehow giving them "special rights."

But marriage equality was never about special rights, just *equal* rights. "Special rights" are for political churches that don't have to pay taxes.

Former Vice President Mike Pence believes in a God who really, really doesn't like all those gay people He's created. As a member of Congress, Pence tried to get HIV funds diverted to conversion therapy—that charming form of child torture that was already banned in multiple states. As governor of Indiana, Pence had championed a "religious freedom" law that legalized discrimination of LGBTQ Americans, delighting homophobic Christians everywhere. It was more than a little ironic, as Pence's general look and demeanor resemble that of what some might call a dominant daddy power-top.

Not for nothing, but it's Genesis 2:18 where God says, "It is not good for man to be alone." God didn't intend for the queer people He created to be isolated, shamed, and lonely—we all deserve a chance at love and companionship.

Oh, and any guy who tells you same-sex attraction is a "choice" to be resisted probably has some experience resisting it.

Now, it's one thing to knock down traditional homophobic taunts, and quite another to fully debunk Bible-based bigotry.

"You know what's gonna happen if you let a man marry a man?"

"Yes. It means two more women for you to strike out with."

Or

"God made Adam and Eve, not Adam and Steve!"

"Actually, Reverend, God made Adam and Steve, too. And they can adopt some of them there 'accidents' that Adam and Eve don't want."

Debunking biblical homophobia is trickier than just pushing back on ignorant jabs. You should know that the Christian homophobe is forever seeking a Jesus loophole, something in the book they can point to as being more meaningful and authoritative to Christians than, y'know, Christ. To accomplish this, they can go one of two directions—backward or forward. The Old Testament or Paul.

PART I: THE OLD TESTAMENT, FOR HOMOPHOBES

The first half of the Christian Bible, the Hebrew scriptures commonly referred to as the OT, has the most frequently cited passages used to condemn gay people—despite the fact that the words "homosexual" and "homosexuality" never appeared in the original Bible, and didn't *exist* in Hebrew, Greek, or Aramaic.

Those words came into use near the end of the nineteenth century, when psychologists began to discover and understand sexuality as an essential part of the human personality. The word "homosexual" was first added to an English translation of the Bible in the Revised Standard Version, 1946. Prior to that, nobody could agree on what certain biblical translations meant.

Problems, as they say, ensued.

The Bible condemns idolatry, exploitation, cruelty to immigrants, and violence, but with a few exceptions never even mentions same-sex relations.

Helping the poor, by contrast, is commanded *over three hundred times.* Which is why that's all conservative Christians talk about, isn't it?

Sodom and Gomorrah, Genesis 19:1–11

If you never learned the details of this tale of two cities, don't feel bad—it doesn't make it into too many Bible coloring books. This is the earliest Bible story historically used to claim gay people are evil and deserve punishment; it's also where we get the term "sodomy."

THE CLAIM: "God destroyed the ancient cities of Sodom and Gomorrah over homosexual behavior, and that's proof God didn't want Elton John to marry his boyfriend."

THE SCRIPTURE: Look, I'm not going to lie—from everything we know, Sodom and Gomorrah were horrible places filled with evil, nasty people. Their citizens murder, they lie, they abuse visitors and poor people, they worship false gods, they forward chain emails, they don't leash their dogs, they use speakerphone in public, just awful humans. And these two cities are right next to each other, like an even more depraved Minneapolis and St. Paul.

Abraham elegantly bargains with God to spare the evil cities if there are still but ten righteous people there, which strongly indicates that God's not big on judging entire groups of people just because some of them do wrong.

God sends two angels—called "messengers"—to check out the city and see how bad things have gotten. Lot, Abraham's nephew, greets the angel-men, welcomes them into his family's house, feeds them, and offers to put 'em up for the night. So far, it's a lovely story, right?

The messengers warn Lot that he needs to bounce; God's about to drop the hammer and shit's about to jump off. I paraphrase from the Hebrew.

But then a large mob gathers outside the house, shouting at Lot and the others, demanding to know who the two strangers are. "Where are the men which came in to thee this night? Bring them out unto us, that we may *know* them." And if you've seen *Oz* season 2 on HBO, you know exactly what they're talking about.

Now, in the modern age of blocking and muting trolls, you might not see much sense in trying to reason with a gang of sweaty guys in the desert who've made up their minds to gang-rape two angels. But Lot goes outside and makes them an offer—if they promise to leave the two messengers alone, they can have his two virgin daughters, to do with as they will.

Yes, Lot offers his two virgin daughters up for gang rape. Remember, this is the heterosexual hero of a story used to teach us that gay people are bad.

But this mob doesn't want the two virgins; they insist on angel-rape. These men wanted to dominate and humiliate the "messengers" because that's what rape's all about.

The angels blind the crowd; Lot, his wife, and daughters escape; and God rains down burning fire on Sodom and Gomorrah. Lot's wife turns back to view the devastation, and for this transgression is turned into a pillar of salt. Which soon becomes eerily convenient.

Lot goes on to settle in the mountains with his two childless daughters, who then decide to get Lot drunk and take advantage of him. Both daughters sleep with their drunken father and later give birth to their own child-siblings. The End.

And the moral of that story—we are told—is that God really doesn't want us to ever bake a cake for a gay wedding.

THE DEBUNKING: Sodom and Gomorrah is a story of God's anger at a people who reject and abuse strangers, instead of welcoming them. Throughout the Bible, Sodom and Gomorrah keeps coming up not as an example of the dangers of same-sex relations, but rather as an example of *how really bad people treat strangers and the less fortunate.*

In fact, God specifically tells the ancient Jewish prophet Ezekiel why He nuked them:

"Now this was the sin of your sister Sodom: She and her daughters were arrogant, overfed and unconcerned; they did not help the poor and needy. They were haughty and did detestable things before me. Therefore I did away with them as you have seen" (Ezekiel 16:49–50).

When Jesus talks about Sodom in Matthew 10:14–15 and Luke 10:10–12, he never mentions same-sex relations. Rather, he says that cities that reject his disciples—thereby committing the terrible sin of inhospitality—will receive judgment harsher than Sodom received.

If you're going to believe that God destroyed Sodom and Gomorrah because of gay people, you've got to believe that God's okay with offering up virgin girls for gang rape and having incestual relations with your dad, as those behaviors don't seem to merit any punishment.

Finally, there's nothing in this story about sexual orientation, same-sex relationships, or same-sex attraction. God does not condemn a city of gay men given to brunch, racquetball, and antiquing. He punishes a gang of men looking to rape. And rape is not about love, pleasure, or sexual preference. It's about power.

So remind your homophobe—if he thinks consensual same-sex relationships and gang rape are the same thing, he's seriously dating the wrong guys.

Leviticus, Which Absolutely No One Truly Follows

We covered this a bit in chapter 1, but let's briefly recap:

Imagine you're going to marry a very powerful man, and he gives you a simple prenup—that's the Ten Commandments. Then, after a few years, he delivers twenty-six chapters of extensive fine print—that's Leviticus.

Your wife's on her period? Well, she's unclean and you're not allowed to touch her. Mildew? As bad as leprosy. Did you plant two seeds in the same hole? Okay, that's bad, too. If you don't like big government poking around your private life, Leviticus is a funny chapter to hang your hate on.

THE BIG CLAIM: God said, "Man shall not lie with man, that is an abomination."

THE SCRIPTURE: Of all the Bible passages used to condemn LGBTQ people, Leviticus appears to be the easiest slam dunk. It features two of the only Bible verses that seem to divinely criticize same-sex relations:

First, Leviticus 18:22: "Thou shalt not lie with mankind, as with womankind: it is abomination."

Then, Leviticus 20:13 reminds you "If a man also lie with mankind, as he lieth with a woman, both of them have committed an abomination: they shall surely be put to death; their blood shall be upon them" (both KJV).

Leviticus has twenty-seven chapters and 859 verses, and these are the two that Americans have most likely heard of. For centuries, Christians have used these verses to justify all manner of condemnation, and to let a divinely sanctioned hate run wild and free.

The problem is there's no way any Christian on earth can ever cite Leviticus, because no Christian on earth actually follows thirty-five-hundred-year-old Jewish rule books—and they're technically *forbidden* by Jesus from doing so. Context is a wooden stake to Christian homophobia.

Let's break these verses down, one at a time.

Leviticus 18:22—The "Abomination" Verse

If one is going to judge others by the standards of Leviticus, one should prepare to *also be judged* by the standards of Leviticus, no? The Holiness Code outlaws quite a few things the average twenty-first-century homophobe probably isn't ready to part with.

In Leviticus 11, God also declares shellfish and pork to be "abominations." Which means that shrimp cocktail with bacon bits JD Vance just scarfed down at the Focus on the Family fundraiser makes him every bit as biblically abominable as George Michael Night at the Ramrod Bathhouse.

Next time your homophobic Christian uncle is over, classing up the holiday by calling rainbow flags "abominations," be sure to ask how many of these other Leviticus teachings he actually lives by. And votes by, too:

- Leviticus 11:7–8 bans people from touching pigskin, but we never hear "Hate the sin, not the NFL."
- Leviticus 23:3 forbids ever working on the Sabbath. Tough break, NASCAR.
- Leviticus 18:19 forbids men from having sex with a woman on their period. Actually, most homophobes I've known might obey this one.
- Leviticus 19:19 forbids the wearing of mixed-fiber clothing, thereby damning any gay-hater who's ever worn polyester.

But there's good news—if you've committed this heresy, there's a process you can undertake for repentance (that's "teshuvah" in Hebrew, by the way). This may involve animal sacrifice, but what are you gonna do? Leviticus is what good Christian homophobes believe in, right?

- Yes, Leviticus 19:28 really does ban tattoos. "'Do not cut your bodies for the dead or put tattoo marks on yourselves. I am the Lord." Homophobes must now condemn the US Marine Corps and most decent bands.
- Leviticus 19:27 forbids males from trimming their beards. Which is bad news for clean-shaven politicians, good news for Brooklyn hipster atheists. Although most of those guys have tattoos, so the beards can't save 'em. It's almost like these rules you homophobes celebrate were designed by very orthodox ancient Hebrews.

Today many scholars argue that Leviticus 18:22 should be understood within the broader context of Leviticus 18. Why? Most of the sexual condemnations in Leviticus 18 are for different forms of incest.

God forbids sexual congress with one's mother, stepmother, sister, half sister, mother's brother, father's brother, daughter in-law, sister-in-law, and stepdaughter. God's clearly taken the time to think through every possible family incest dynamic He can forbid.

Since most of Leviticus 18's prohibitions are for incest, scholars believe 18:22 refers to the same-sex kind. Others point out that the actual text refers to a man who lies with men as he usually does with women. Which could simply mean a married guy who's on the down-low, aka adultery.

Now that second verse is even rougher:

Leviticus 20:13: "If a man also lie with mankind, as he lieth with a woman, both of them have committed an abomination: they shall surely be put to death; their blood shall be upon them" (KJV).

The traditional punishment for transgression back then was simple: When somebody was guilty of violating a particular law, everybody else got to throw rocks at them until they were dead. No trial, no hearing, no three strikes. Every sinner must get stoned.

Which means that if you're claiming that you oppose gay relationships on religious grounds because this *one* part of the Bible that you dutifully follow calls it "an abomination," you probably need to start gathering rocks. Which is bad.

But as a true Leviticus adherent, you're also obliged to slay a slew of nongay people, including:

- **Blasphemers**—Leviticus 24:10–23 commands the faithful to kill, via stoning, anyone who insults the name of God. Again, the overlap of our fundamentalist Christians and fundamentalist Muslims becomes clearer.
- **Psychics**—Leviticus 20:27 states that any man or woman who consults the spirits of the dead shall be stoned to death, which covers all mediums, fortune-tellers, and every high school student to use a Ouija board.
- **Bestiality**—Leviticus 20:15–16 states that if a man or a woman has sex with an animal, they must be put to death, and the animal, too. How awful is that for the sheep? As soon as one guy finishes doing something extremely nasty to you, another guy shows up to kill you for it.
- **Certain Women**—If a priest's daughter becomes a temple prostitute, she must be burned alive as per Leviticus 21:9. I realize this sort of thing isn't all that common, but they certainly found some creative ways to kill women.
- **Adulterers**—Leviticus 20:10. Looking at you, MAGA Christians.

Remember that the goal of prohibiting all these behaviors was to help keep a nomadic Jewish nation alive in the desert for forty years. Healthy procreation was essential, which is why they'd strongly discourage incest, sex between guys, bestiality, and sex during menstruation.

Also, allow me to point out that one should definitely never kill any of these people, or any other people, in perpetuity. (Thanks, legal department.)

If They Still Claim to Follow Leviticus . . .

Finally, if you have a homophobe in your family or at the office who still clings to the one truly antigay passage in the Bible, remind them that they need to believe this part of Leviticus, too . . .

"The foreigner residing among you must be treated as your native-born. Love them as yourself" (Leviticus 19:34).

Or even better—Leviticus 25:35: "If any of your fellow Israelites become poor and are unable to support themselves among you, help them as you would a foreigner and stranger, so they can continue to live among you."

If they wanna hate the gays, they've gotta love the immigrants.

Tellingly, there are no records in the Bible of anyone ever actually being executed for same-sex relations. Because killing off your members is also not ideal for keeping the tribe's numbers high.

And remember, Gentiles, Jesus brought a New Covenant. You don't get to hide behind a book you don't truly follow just to hurt a people Jesus commands you to love. Paul goes deep on this. Remember, Christianity's first big selling point was that traditional Jewish laws don't apply to this new operation. Paul, the former Pharisee, teaches that people get right with God *not* by following Levitical law, but by faith in Jesus's teachings and sacrifice.

Remember Galatians 3:24–25: "So the law was our guardian until Christ came that we might be justified by faith. Now that this faith has come, we are no longer under a guardian."

That's it. Your devotion to Old Testament laws about gay dudes being an abomination has *nothing to do* with Christianity.

Deuteronomy and Kings

THE CLAIM: "Yeah, but there are still other parts of the Bible that condemn homosexuality!"

THE SCRIPTURE: Deuteronomy 23:17 states, "There shall be no whore of the daughters of Israel, nor a sodomite of the sons of Israel" (KJV). There are similar verses in 1 Kings 14:24, 15:12, and 22:46, and 2 Kings 23:7.

THE DEBUNKING: For many years, scholars have debated what certain translations of these words—which could refer to temple shrine prostitutes—actually mean. Just like today's scholars, authors of the Bible couldn't agree on the right term for "male whore."

And while the passages from Kings aren't usually invoked by homophobes, Deuteronomy is occasionally cited because of the word "Sodomite." In the original Hebrew, the word used was "Qadesh," which historically referred to male temple prostitutes, associated with pagan religious practices.

Believe it or not, pagan rent boys were not terribly popular among the orthodox Jews who wrote the Torah.

After the centuries of Bible telephone tag that led to the King James Version, English translators finally decided Qadesh meant "Sodomite." As previously shown, the sin of Sodom was never described as consensual same-sex action, but that didn't stop twentieth-century translators from morphing the term for male concubine into "homosexual"—despite the fact that there was no such word when the Torah was written.

If your antigay Christian should persist on Deuteronomy, I recommend repeating what we learned in Leviticus and calling them out on their selective obedience to a book's many rules. If you're going to claim your homophobia's sanctioned by God because you follow Deuteronomy, you've also got to support:

- Killing people who don't listen to priests (Deuteronomy 17:12)
- Killing women who aren't virgins on their wedding night (Deuteronomy 22:20–21)

- Killing any fellow Israelites who serve other gods (Deuteronomy 13:6–11)

I asked Rabbi Danya Ruttenberg about Christians who pick and choose parts of ancient Jewish law they don't otherwise follow to justify antigay prejudice. She said:

"Focusing on a couple of clobber verses here and there but ignoring the fact that the Torah commands us no less than 36 times to love and care for the stranger in our midst is an absolute desecration of the sacred, in my opinion. Or ignoring the demands from Deuteronomy through the prophets to protect those most marginalized by our society. Talk about missing the point of 'everyone is created in the divine image'?"

And we should acknowledge once again that the Jews have often made greater progress on this issue than many Christians. Israeli LGBTQ couples have the same pension, inheritance rights, and medical coverage as heterosexuals. Employment discrimination on the grounds of sexual orientation was first made illegal in 1992. LGBTQ people have been formally accepted in the Israeli military since 1993, and LGBTQ couples have been able to adopt each other's kids and enjoy full rights as parents since 2005.

They've moved beyond the ancient rules, but some Gentiles can't let go . . .

The Story of David and Jonathan

David and Jonathan's relationship in the Book of Samuel is portrayed as incredibly committed and deep. Most readers see a friendship characterized by loyalty, mutual respect, and transformative love. But strictly as friends, bro.

What about some less platonic interpretations? Well, you tell me. These are two emotionally intense gentlemen.

1 Samuel 18:1–4—They meet:

- **18:1:** "After David had finished talking with Saul, Jonathan became one in spirit with David, and he loved him as himself."
- **18:3–4:** "And Jonathan made a covenant with David because he loved him as himself. Jonathan took off the robe he was wearing and gave it to David, along with his tunic, and even his sword, his bow and his belt."

So it's their first meeting, and David goes home in Jonathan's tunic. Not much to read into there.

1 Samuel 20:16–17—This passage highlights the depth of Jonathan's love for David: "Jonathan made a covenant with the House of David, saying, 'May the Lord call David's enemies to account.' And Jonathan had David reaffirm his oath out of love for him, because he loved him as he loved himself."

That's a passage about two men sharing oaths of love to each other in the Bible, in case you're wondering.

1 Samuel 20:41 describes an emotional farewell between David and Jonathan: "David got up from the south side of the stone and bowed down before Jonathan three times, with his face to the ground. Then they kissed each other and wept together."

2 Samuel 1:26—This is David's lament for Jonathan after his death: "I grieve for you, Jonathan my brother; you were very dear to

me. Your love for me was wonderful, more wonderful than that of women."

Now, I don't know about you, but I've had several gay male friends assure me that they're more wonderful at many things than women. But the best part of this story is that it's been incredibly meaningful and inspirational to many gay Christians, whether David and Jonathan were a thing or not.

PART II: THE NEW TESTAMENT, FOR HOMOPHOBES

The only sexual sins Jesus ever specifically calls out are adultery and abandoning your wife. When it comes to people's sexuality, he's clear enough with "Love one another."

He didn't suffer from sexual hang-ups, which might seem surprising, as sexual hang-ups are the rock upon which many churches are built. He asks that we give love to despised and marginalized peoples, and stand up for those on the lowest rungs of life. None of which can get you elected in the current Bible Belt.

Now, ten years into marriage equality in America, Christian homophobes who've given up on using Leviticus have a favorite passage they've weaponized against those marrying gays.

THE CLAIM: "Jesus clearly opposed gay marriage because he affirmed marriage as being one man and one woman; therefore, Christians must oppose marriage equality for same-sex couples."

THE SCRIPTURE: Matthew 19:4–6—Jesus says: "Haven't you read . . . that at the beginning the Creator 'made them male and female,' and said, 'For this reason a man will leave his father and mother and be united to his wife, and the two will become one flesh? So they are no longer two, but one flesh. Therefore what God has joined together, let no one separate."

Now, some of our friends who believe that God creates gay people just to watch them be hated are very fond of this one. Like most passages used by antigay folks, it's taken deeply out of context.

THE DEBUNKING: As covered in the feminism chapter for quite different reasons, this is where some of the Pharisees approach Jesus in Judea and try to trip him up by asking, "Is it lawful for a man to divorce his wife for any and every reason?"

Jesus answers in a revolutionary way that has nothing to do with gay people, and everything to do with respecting women. He reminds them when a righteous man marries a woman, it's supposed to be for life—and unless she's cheated on him, he cannot abandon her. God made them male and female, and the twain shall be one flesh.

That's it. Absolutely nothing about loving consensual same-sex relationships not being recognized by the state in this entire exchange.

Which means if you're a Christian who truly cares about "protecting marriage" because of Matthew 19, then it's time to stop fighting gay weddings and start fighting straight divorce.

But wait, Jesus says *what*?

Jesus challenging a law from Leviticus or Deuteronomy was nothing new. He famously challenged or overturned Moses-era rules on food purity, Sabbath observance, and the death penalty.

But this new rule that a man who gets married has to keep his wife for life is a bit shocking to the apostles. In Matthew 19:10, they remark," If this is the situation between a husband and wife, it is better not to marry."

Now this next part is lots of fun to debate, and is essential to any argument using Matthew 19 against gay people. Jesus's reply should end the homophobia argument for good.

No, he doesn't endorse gay marriage; that concept is a twenty-first-century phenomenon. But he does assert that while his marriage laws apply to most men—*there are exceptions.* Who are the exceptions? The three kinds of men who will *not* be marrying. Here's where it gets interesting.

For these three different types of men who will not be marrying women, Jesus uses the umbrella term "eunuch."

"Not everyone can accept this word, but only those to whom it has been given. For there are eunuchs who were born that way, and there are eunuchs who have been made eunuchs by others—and there are those who choose to live like eunuchs for the sake of the kingdom of heaven. The one who can accept this should accept it" (Matthew 19:11).

"Eunuch" in the ancient world referred to any kind of man who wasn't going to be getting together with a lady. The third type, "those who choose to live like eunuchs for the sake of the kingdom of heaven," refers to devoutly religious men who've made themselves celibate.

The second type, "eunuchs who have been made eunuchs by others," clearly refers to males who have been castrated.

But when Jesus starts with "eunuchs who were born that way," he's not talking about those astronomically rare boys born without genitals. He's talking about the men who, since birth, are clearly *never going to be marrying women.*

That's right. The one chapter used to argue that Jesus opposed gay marriage is the same chapter where Jesus says, calmly and matter-of-factly, that gay men are born that way.

Jesus asserts some boys are born who will never be interested in girls, that they are the minority, and that God made them that way. And nobody bats an eye at this.

"The one who can accept this should accept it."

Jesus then leaves it at that and moves on to pray with some kids. Because Jesus knows that, hey, some guys aren't into women, and it's not that big a deal. Because Jesus, time and again, refuses to be a dick.

The Roman Centurion

The story of Jesus healing the Roman soldier's servant is found in both Matthew 8:5–13 and Luke 7:1–10. It's one of the most fascinating and moving stories in the Gospels.

Jesus and crew arrive in Capernaum and are sought out by a centurion. It's easy to miss the significance of this exchange even happening.

Centurions were the professional officers of the Roman Empire. They commanded military units and were essential to maintaining discipline and order throughout Roman territories, which included Judea. They enforced Roman law, which frequently conflicted with local Jewish beliefs and customs.

Centurions were armed, oppressive symbols that the Jewish people had lost their independence; they're the men who would eventually execute Jesus.

But despite being a leader of the foreign occupying forces, this particular officer approaches humbly, seeking help. He pleads with Jesus to heal his dying servant—or slave, depending on what translation and what Bible you're reading.

Jesus offers to come see the dying young man, but the officer declares himself unworthy; and assures Jesus that he understands there's no need for him to come in person—he knows the miracles can work remotely.

Jesus is so impressed with the Roman's faith that he pronounces the servant healed, on the spot. And so ends another lovely miraculous story about Yeshua accepting everybody at his table, even pagan colonizers.

Episcopal Bishop John Shelby Spong of the diocese of Newark first taught me that this story goes much, much deeper. The original Greek word used to describe the servant in Matthew's account was *pais,* a term that had several meanings: boy, son, and "*beloved* boy." It carries cultural connotations of a younger male beloved by an older male in certain contexts, potentially implying a much deeper relationship.

(I'm choosing to believe, by the way, that someone has given this book to their angry right-wing stepdad, and this is the point he finally, disgustedly throws it across the room. But read on, it gets good.)

What do we know about the Roman Empire at the time of Jesus? History tells us that Roman men would regularly engage in sex with other men and avoid any stigma, as long as they assumed the dominant penetrative role. It was quite normal for men of higher status—like, say, *centurions*—to have young male companions who could be servants or slaves. These relationships varied widely, from the purely work-oriented to something more personal or intimate.

In fact, it was not uncommon for a soldier to leave his wife at home and bring a special boy along for extended tours of duty. In the Luke passage, the soldier doesn't shy from referring to the young man as his *entimos doulos* or "honored slave." And while such a relationship may be repugnant to us, and was likely repugnant to Jesus's traditional Jewish apostles, these relationships were not uncommon in the Rome of Jesus's day.

Finally, ask yourself—would an officer in the occupying army seek out a homeless Jewish mystic faith healer and publicly beg him to heal some servant if the young man were nothing more than a common slave?

When viewed from this perspective, the story becomes even more powerful and revolutionary. At no point does Jesus judge the man for having a young male lover or being a pagan or being a part of the occupying military that crucifies Jews for Rome. I'm sure some of apostles were *thrilled* about this one.

After the centurion leaves, Jesus tells the presumably shocked onlookers in Matthew 8:11–12, "Many, I tell you, will come from the east and the west to sit with Abraham and Isaac and Jacob at the banquet in the kingdom of heaven. But the heirs of the kingdom will be thrown into the outer darkness" (NCB).

Again, the Nazarene challenges the spiritually smug expectations about who gets into heaven, asserting that many unlikely people will get there, but the "heirs"—those who think salvation is their birthright—may be out of luck.

And even if the centurion's relationship was totally platonic, bro, it's a story of Jesus healing an unknown pagan's servant without hesitation, again showing a radical inclusivity for people outside his own national, religious, and ethnic boundaries.

If you'd like to see a cinematic adaptation of this story, check out Ernest Borgnine's very fine portrayal of the centurion in Franco Zeffirelli's *Jesus of Nazareth*. I'm guessing Mr. Borgnine had no idea about the Greek translation.

Have at It, Paul

THE CLAIM: "The New Testament does too condemn homosexuality! "

THE SCRIPTURE: Romans, Timothy, and Corinthians are the last stand for the biblical homophobe. Which is ironic, because when you list them it sounds like a gay Italian leather bar.

This may seem a bit in the weeds, but let's stretch this chapter out a little bit longer, okay? Your Christian homophobe will definitely be citing Paul, and way out of context.

As we've covered, Paul's a fascinating, complex, and often contradictory figure. Most of the sexual hang-ups in the New Testament come from Paul, who believed the world would soon end and so everyone should be celibate like him. Zero judgments, Paul.

Romans 1:26–27: Here, Paul discusses two of his favorite subjects—humanity's sinfulness and the righteous anger of God—in a letter to the fledgling Christian church in Rome, around 57 AD.

Romans 1:26–27 says, "For this cause God gave them up unto vile affections: for even their women did change the natural use into that which is against nature: And likewise, also the men, leaving the natural use of the woman, burned in their lust one toward another" (KJV).

So finally, good news for Christians who want to hate some gays, right? How is this *not* late-inning, airtight proof that God can't stand Neil Patrick Harris?

THE DEBUNKING: This is the one line of Romans that most antigay Christians will ever know. But if you read what comes before, it's clear that Paul's talking in the past tense about God punishing otherwise *heterosexual* Romans for worshiping Roman animal gods. How? By giving them up unto "vile affections."

"[They] changed the glory of the uncorruptible God into an image made like to corruptible man, and to birds, and fourfooted beasts, and creeping things. Wherefore God also gave them up to uncleanness through the lusts of their own hearts, to dishonor their own bodies between themselves: Who changed the truth of God into a lie, and worshipped and served the creature more than the Creator, who is blessed for ever. Amen" (Romans 1:23–25, KJV).

That will bring us back to "For this cause God gave them up unto vile affections."

This is a very important point to convey to your homophobic loved one—if these men are changing their "natural use of the woman" to "burn in their lust" for each other, where exactly does the *gay* part come in?

They're clearly not gay guys: They're *straight* guys hooking up with *other straight guys.* That's exactly how Paul describes them.

And they're not hooking up with each other to spite God—God's "giving them up unto" it, to punish them. In the fetish community, this is sometimes called "forced bi." Or so I've read.

In the Bible, idolatry is equated with adultery, because the Bible depicts God's covenant with people as a marriage. Using graphic sexual imagery to metaphorically rebuke the worship of other gods appears in Ezekiel 22:23–23:27, as well. The only "gay men" Paul's talking about are straight men who worshiped ancient Roman animal-gods two thousand years ago.

What this passage teaches is that certain Roman dudes were committing idolatry and partying with each other, and Paul was totally grossed out. That's it. Paul thought these were nasty people. And Paul wrote that in a letter and sent it to the early Roman church.

It's not God telling your school board to ban books.

BUT WAIT, THERE'S MORE

But if your homophobe still believes that one line of Romans chapter 1 gives them the right to condemn gay people, ask if they've ever read the *first line* of Romans chapter 2?

"You, therefore, have no excuse, you who pass judgment on someone else. For at whatever point you judge another, you are condemning yourself, because you who pass judgment do the same things."

That's Paul, foreshadowing all those Gen Z libs saying "projection is reflection."

Also:

- Do the homophobes who live by Paul's letter to the Romans bless their persecutors, as Paul commands in Romans 12:14?
- Do they eagerly pay their taxes? Paul orders that in Romans 13:6–7: "This is also why you pay taxes, for the authorities are God's servants, who give their full time to governing. Give to everyone what you owe them: If you owe taxes, pay taxes; if revenue, then revenue; if respect, then respect; if honor, then honor."
- Best of all, when these devoutly spiritual guys meet their fellow gay-haters, do they kiss each other? Because they must, according to Romans 16:16. That's where Paul instructs all *real* Christians to greet one another with a custom reflecting the familial nature of early Christian communities: "Greet one another with a holy kiss. All the churches of Christ send greetings."

  The holy kiss was a greeting in many cultures of the ancient Mediterranean world, signifying peace, respect, and community. For Paul, this must have been a very important custom of his time, because he writes about it much more than he writes about gay people.

  So every Christian man who uses Romans to justify homophobia is biblically obliged to start kissing every Christian dude he knows, every time they meet.

  Sorry, guys, but you're the ones who chose Romans over Jesus. Pucker up.

THE SCRIPTURE: 1 Timothy 1:8–11: "We also know that the law is made not for the righteous but for lawbreakers and rebels, the ungodly and sinful, the unholy and irreligious, for those who kill their fathers or mothers, for murderers, for the sexually immoral, for those practicing homosexuality, for slave traders and liars and perjurers—and for whatever else is contrary to the sound doctrine that conforms to the gospel concerning the glory of the blessed God, which he entrusted to me."

THE DEBUNKING: This is a favorite verse of the gay-haters, so let's remember that Paul wrote all of his letters in Greek. The two-thousand-year-old Greek word Paul used, that was later translated to "homosexuals," is *arsenokoitai*. Its exact meaning is debated among scholars, who believe it may just be something Paul made up. It's a compound word from *arsen* (meaning male) and *koitai* (meaning bed).

Many historians assert that this term refers more broadly to sexual exploitation, or abuse, rather than consensual same-sex relationships (we're back to those ancient Roman pastimes here). The word was originally thought to mean "male concubines," later came to mean "pederasts," and in much later translations came to be construed as "sodomy for gay and straight guys." Some scholars suggest Paul, like in Romans, was addressing pagan rituals where same-sex acts were part of idolatrous worship.

Most of what's now referred to as "homosexual" in the Bible probably referred to heterosexual married guys fooling around with other guys, or boys, and often paying for the pleasure.

This ancient world had no concept of sexual orientation as we do today—"homosexual" is a twentieth-century word, and they're still trying to attach it to a two-thousand-year-old term.

And by "they" I could be referring to secretly gay gay-basher Pastor Tom Brock. Or secretly gay gay-basher Pastor Ted Haggard. Or gay-bashing, rent-boy-hiring Family Research Council founder George Rekers. Or gay-bashing, restroom-cruising GOP Senator Larry Craig. Or gay-bashing and dude-groping CPAC chair Matt Schlapp. You get the idea.

Citing Timothy to be antigay asserts that being gay is on the same level as killing one's parents and enslaving people. And if the right-wingers are going to use Timothy to condemn the gays, remember that Paul goes out of his way here to also condemn slave traders. Which means these true believers need to drop any defense of anything related to the Confederacy. Break it to them gently.

Finally, when Christians who can't separate Jesus from Paul *really* want to condemn LGBTQ people, they'll always wind up at Paul's letter to the Corinthians.

THE SCRIPTURE: 1 Corinthians 6:9–10: "Know ye not that the unrighteous shall not inherit the kingdom of God? Be not deceived: neither fornicators, nor idolaters, nor adulterers, nor effeminate, nor abusers of themselves with mankind" (KJV).

THE DEBUNKING: The short version: Jesus said anyone can be saved. Why should we listen to Paul instead of Jesus?

The more specific version: In Corinthians, Paul again rails against the *arsenokoitai,* but also throws in the term *malakoi,* a Greek word that's often translated as "soft" or "effeminate" in various Bible versions (though its actual meaning is also debated). Some interpretations view *malakoi* as referring to men who are simply seen as lacking masculinity. Again, it likely refers to exploitative or abusive practices common in Paul's time.

A few centuries later it was decided that *arsenokoitai* meant "abusers of themselves with mankind." Again, it's like a big game of gay-panic-euphemism bingo.

Martin Luther's later German translation of this word used the term *Knabenschänder,* which specifically means "boy molester" or "pederast," reflecting the cultural and historical context of Luther's time. And to be honest, *Knabenschänder* just sounds nastier.

Literalists cling to Corinthians to avoid the commands of Jesus—love, grace, justice, and the dignity and worth of all people, including LGBTQ individuals, even including Roman rent boys. But do your homophobic relations follow the rest of Corinthians?

- Do they believe it is better for a man to be celibate and never have sexual relations with a woman?
- Should women only speak in submission to men?
- Should men be banned from having long hair?
- Should Christians never file civil lawsuits?
- Finally, do they support economic equality for the poor? "Our desire is not that others might be relieved while you are hard pressed, but that there might be equality" (2 Corinthians 8:13).

If their answer to any of these is no, then they don't follow or obey Corinthians, so they don't get to weaponize it.

By the way, in the next chapter, Paul says it's better for men to marry than to burn with lust. Which, ironically, could be the top biblical argument for gay marriage.

And Don't Forget to Enrage Your Homophobe with This

Some academics and theologians suggest that Paul's strong condemnation of sexual immorality, particularly same-sex relations, might be influenced by his *own* repressed or unacknowledged sexuality. Paul never mentions having a wife, unusual for a Jewish man of his time. This absence—and his many hang-ups—have led to widespread speculations about his personal life, which could explain his struggles with his own unholy urges.

I first read about this theory in Bishop John Shelby Spong's excellent *Rescuing the Bible from Fundamentalism*. The bishop had posited that Paul's personal struggles with his own sexuality could have influenced his very anti-sex writings and positions.

I first got to meet Bishop Spong when we appeared together on Bill Maher's show. He was much taller and faster than me, and as we were both whisked down a hallway by producers to the greenroom, I was like a groupie to a rock star.

Trying to keep up, I asked the elderly bishop about that Paul theory (because for me, that's ice-breaking small talk). Without breaking stride, Bishop Spong replied, "Meh, it's not a theory. Of course Paul was a closeted homosexual; it's the only explanation that makes any sense."

Remember that in Romans, Paul describes those same-sex relations he despises so much as a consequence of humanity's rejection of God. Paul and Freud could've spent *months* together.

But it's worth pointing out that Paul didn't just hate same-sex couplings; he disdained heterosexual sensuality as well. Paul felt that anyone who put their own pleasure first was putting God second—which means he condemned straight lust and gay lust equally.

And Then There's Jude

Jude 1:5–8: This epistle isn't brought up very often, but you'll occasionally see it grouped with the traditional clobber passages.

The author here identifies himself as "Jude, a servant of Jesus Christ and a brother of James" (Jude 1:1). This James is traditionally understood to be James the Just, a leader of the Jerusalem church and the brother of Jesus, which would make Jude *another brother* of Jesus (Mark 6:3; Matthew 13:55).

Here, Jude references well-known examples from Jewish history to warn against false teachers and immoral behavior.

"I want to remind you that the Lord at one time delivered his people out of Egypt, but later destroyed those who did not believe. . . . In a similar way, Sodom and Gomorrah and the surrounding towns gave themselves up to sexual immorality and perversion. They serve as an example of those who suffer the punishment of eternal fire."

As previously noted, the primary sin of Sodom was pride, inhospitality and violence, as backed up by Ezekiel 16:49–50.

Jude: Also not Jesus; also not antigay.

PART III: TWO OTHER LETTERS IN LGBTQ

In 2013, America witnessed the story of Carla Hale. Ms. Hale is a phys ed teacher—or was, until she lost her job at Bishop Watterson Catholic High School in Columbus, Ohio.

When her mother died, the newspaper obituary listed all the survivors—including the name of Ms. Hale's longtime partner. A student's parent read the obituary and sent an outraged anonymous letter to the school, calling the diocese "disgraceful" for employing a lesbian as a gym teacher. And all she'd done was bury her mom.

Ms. Hale had taught at Bishop Watterson for over a decade, but as soon as she returned to her job after a few days of bereavement leave, she was called into a meeting with administrators. They showed her the anonymous letter—and immediately fired her.

But here's the worst part: Ms. Hale's termination letter actually said, "Your written spousal relationship violates the moral laws of the Catholic Church."

Well, here's the good news—those "moral laws of the Catholic Church" are based on literally nothing in the Bible. And no Christian sect can ever use the Bible to justify cruelty to gay women, because the Bible never condemns gay women.

God never mentions them; neither does Jesus. In fact there's only one passage of the entire Bible that homophobic Christians use to condemn lesbians—we return yet again to Paul's letter to the Romans.

THE CLAIM: "Lesbians are condemned in Romans 1:26–27!"

THE SCRIPTURE: We've covered how Paul's letter to the Romans mentions normally straight men hooking up with each other. But then we get to the go-to line for every Christian who's ever condemned queer women:

"For this cause God gave them up unto vile affections: for even their women did change the natural use into that which is against nature" (KJV).

And there you have it. Centuries of shame and persecution, and that's the only alleged reference to lesbians in the entire Bible. And, just like Hilary Swank and Chloë Sevigny in *Boys Don't Cry,* they're not even technically lesbians.

THE DEBUNKING: Once you get past the fact that referring to women's "natural use" is one of the nastiest bits of misogyny in the book, all this verse says is that one time, some Roman women did something that Paul thought was "against nature."

That's it. We now live in a world where you can inject botulism into your forehead, but Melissa Etheridge is "against nature."

Dearly beloved, the most common form of sexuality that's "against nature" is pretending to be straight when you're not.

Which brings us back to Ms. Carla Hale, the Ohio gym teacher. She filed a complaint with the city of Columbus, which prohibits firing employees based on sexual orientation—and her local union chose not to support her.

Of course, the school could have just given her the job back, but that would've been the Christian thing to do.

I always wonder how anti-lesbian Christians handle Ruth 1:16–17. You've probably heard this one read at a ton of weddings; it's notable for its themes of loyalty, commitment, and love.

"Where you go, I will go, and where you stay I will stay. Your people will be my people, and your God my God. Where you die, I will die, and there will I be buried."

Many in the pews who hear this beautiful passage never even know it's actually about two women—Ruth and Naomi.

The Bible never specifically states they're romantically close, but it celebrates their love and uses the same Hebrew word ("dabaq") used to describe how Adam felt about Eve.

And this vow—a vow between two women—has come to represent what a marriage covenant is all about.

No, the Bible Isn't Anti-Transgender Either

At the 2024 Southern Baptist Convention, five thousand people voted to deny that transgender people even exist. And they say bisexuals are confused.

Every generation of American Christians seems to find a new marginalized group that feels righteous to persecute. When I was a kid, it was feminists and gay people. As I grew up, the acceptable feel-good targets for Christian prejudice shifted to Muslims or "illegals." As of this writing, transgender Americans—especially children—are having their moment in the crosshairs.

The diagnosis of gender dysphoria (which not all trans people experience) is used to describe the clinically significant distress some people feel at the difference between their gender and the sex they were assigned at birth.

It's not a mental illness; but many trans people grow up in communities and churches that fear and despise them, which can and does lead to mental health and self-esteem issues.

Some Christian groups have advocated for state-level Religious Freedom Restoration Acts (RFRAs) that allow businesses to deny services to transgender taxpaying citizens based on religious beliefs. Other Christian groups and leaders endorse pseudoscience conversion therapy for transgender individuals.

You can't groom a kid to be transgender—but you can groom a douchebag to think he's Christian. And Christian transphobia is yet another stark rejection of the words of Jesus.

"Love your neighbor as yourself" is a commandment, not an option. It's an order that transcends social boundaries, identities, and comfort levels. Jesus goes out of his way to preach compassion for any outsiders a society has decided it's allowed to hate.

Jesus lived in a time when people were often confused by biological phenomena they couldn't understand. People with leprosy or disabilities were often believed to have been punished with their afflictions for some sin. For many, the belief that these folks "deserved" their conditions made it *a lot* easier to not care for them.

But in John 9:1–3, Jesus removes this smear of "sin" from those born differently than you:

"And as Jesus passed by, he saw a man which was blind from his birth. And his disciples asked him, saying, Master, who did sin, this man, or his parents, that he was born blind? Jesus answered, Neither hath this man sinned, nor his parents: but that the works of God should be made manifest in him" (KJV).

So who are these right-wing Christians to say that being born intersex, or gay, or trans, or bi are sins, rather than being the work of God, that you might witness God's works through them as well? Sorry to get all *Conclave* and churchy, but these people make me want to flip a table.

If anything, Paul (of all people) gives Christians the best reason to drop their transphobia in Galatians 3:28, when he makes it clear that Jesus doesn't discriminate against any type of person:

"There is neither Jew nor Gentile, neither slave nor free, nor is there male and female, for you are all one in Christ Jesus."

Trans people are a tiny, vulnerable group of Americans. Their lives are challenging enough without small *c* christians believing they're biblically justified to bully them.

Helpful Facts About Trans Folks for Nervous Christians

The reality is that you're statistically far more likely to be groomed and/or sexually assaulted by a priest than a trans person. Like, it's not even close. America actually has arrest records to prove it.

- Childhood gender dysphoria is a medical diagnosis—not a surgical one—that does not require treatment, other than maybe individual or family therapy, until a kid reaches puberty.
- The World Health Organization no longer classifies being transgender as a mental disorder.

- The American Academy of Pediatrics recommends a gender-affirming, nonjudgmental approach to help kids feel safe in a society that stigmatizes those seen as different.
- Trans people are *four times* more likely to be victims of violent crimes (sexual assault, murder, assault) than cisgender people (Williams Institute at UCLA School of Law).
- Trans people are nearly nine times more likely to attempt suicide.
- They are four times more likely to experience depression.
- They are three times more likely to have an anxiety disorder.

Sounds like a group of people who could use the support of a religion based on inclusion and love.

A loving God welcomes people of all genders and sexual identities. And if you believe in the Trinity, then God identifies as "they."

An Ethiopian Eunuch in Gaza

And by the way—this empathetic Jesus talk applies to even those *without* a sexual identity. In Acts 8:26–40, an angel tells Philip, one of the five deacons, to travel the desert road that leads from Jerusalem to Gaza. Along the way, he meets an Ethiopian eunuch, an important official in charge of the treasury of the Ethiopian queen.

Now, eunuchs were excluded from many religious rituals, on account of a commandment in Deuteronomy 23:1, which informs men that if your genitals have tragically been damaged, you're not welcome in church: "He that is wounded in the stones, or hath his privy member cut off, shall not enter into the congregation of the Lord" (KJV).

But the Holy Spirit tells Philip to approach this Ethiopian eunuch in Gaza, a sentence that would horrify most TV evangelists. They share the Gospel, and then the eunuch asks Philip if even someone like him could be baptized. And before Philip can finish saying "Lemme find some water," he baptizes the man.

The eunuch rejoices, and it is understood that long ago, Christianity began as a nondiscriminatory movement that ostracized *no one*. This Ethiopian eunuch, despite his status and his fear that he'd be excluded due to his condition, is fully accepted and baptized.

Because the early church was established in *diversity, equity, and inclusion.*

A Few Troublesome Questions for Gay Panic Christians

What chapter of the Bible that *you yourself* follow and live by says that being gay is a sin?

Please show the chapter and verse where Jesus, himself, condemns homosexuality.

Sodom and Gomorrah is about attempted gang rape of angels. Do you understand the difference between gang rape and consensual same-sex relations?

Matthew 19 (marriage is between one man and woman) is Jesus coming out against heterosexual divorce, not gay marriage. Do you oppose heterosexual divorce?

How is being supportive of gender identity against the word of Jesus?

How is making life harder for transgender people Christlike?

Same-sex relations are not forbidden in the Ten Commandments and Jesus never condemns them. Why should Christ followers oppose LGBTQ equality?

THOU SHALT NOT HATE PEOPLE WHO HAVE ABORTIONS

"I have always felt that it was only after a child was born and had a life separate from his mother that it became an individual person."

Wallie Amos Criswell, president of the Southern Baptist Church, 1973

We've now reached the operating principle of modern right-wing Christianity. The issue that re-empowered white supremacists like Falwell after civil rights and Dr. King took away their mojo. The issue that reenergized a political party after the scandal and shock of Nixon's resignation. The political football that's driven conservative politics and come to define Christianity in the US media for most of our lifetimes.

The issue is safe and legal access to abortion. As you probably know, God, Jesus, and the Bible condemn abortion, repeatedly, in both the Old and New Testaments—oh wait, no, that's adultery. Never mind.

Christian denominations vary widely in their teachings on abortion. Some, like the Roman Catholic Church, strictly oppose it; others allow for more nuanced positions—usually in cases of rape, incest, or danger to the mother's life.

America doesn't actually have an abortion problem. We have an unwanted pregnancy problem, and an abortion symptom. And it will continue to divide us.

As a male, my opinion on the matter of abortion is that male opinions on abortion don't matter. I'll try to stick to the facts. This is a well-intentioned chapter about how the most important issue in US Christianity has nothing to do with, well, Christ.

Number of times the Bible demands punishment for ending a pregnancy: 0

Abortion—which was practiced in Jesus's time—is not directly referenced once in the entire Bible, nor is it specifically prohibited. I'm not saying the Bible is proabortion, or that Jesus would volunteer as a clinic escort on his free weekends.

But these are two facts that politicians, media, and fundamentalists always overlook: the Bible never forbids it, and Jesus never mentions it.

He opposes the death penalty, directs us to love and forgive each other, commands individuals and nations to care for the poor and welcome the stranger. He instructs his followers to pay their taxes and put away their swords. But Jesus never once gets around to condemning women who terminate pregnancies, or the individuals who help them.

- Never preaches that government should force citizens to be pregnant against their will.
- Never says government should force low-income women to have children they can't afford, or to punish the poor with greater poverty.
- Never calls for incarceration or execution for abortions.
- Never commands governments to force twelve-year-old rape victims to remain pregnant by their rapist.

And there's a good reason for this. Jesus was a first-century Jew, and Judaism does not forbid abortion. Generations of very nice conservative Christians have been groomed to prioritize something Jesus never mentions far above all of his actual commandments.

The Authorized King James Bible contains over 783,000 words. God, Moses, Jesus, the prophets, and Paul never use any of them to condemn abortion, and they all had plenty of chances.

I realize some of you may be starting to get upset, so let me do what my court-appointed therapist calls "de-escalation."

Again, nobody's saying Jesus is proabortion. But there's zero reason to believe that if Jesus met a woman who'd made that choice he would've shamed her, or tried to have her jailed. And that's another difference between Jesus and some of his unauthorized fan clubs.

If our right-wing friends would actually focus their efforts on preventing unwanted pregnancies, they'd stop far more abortions than their politically coercive methods have accomplished. But that wouldn't help politicians get elected, so the issue is never going away, and will continue to bitterly divide America.

WHEN BANNING ABORTION TOOK OVER CHRISTIANITY

I grew up on Long Island in the eighties, where "abortion" is actually pronounced "uh-baw-uh-shun."

See, throughout large swaths of the Isle of Long, many words—especially proper names—tend to adopt the schwa sound as a regional improvement, like Jennif-uh, Meliss-uh, or Tony Danz-uh.

Somehow, we managed to add a fourth syllable to abortion—"uh-baw-uh-shun." If you say that out loud enough times, you will sound convincingly Lawn Guylandish.

Growing up in America from the eighties onward, if your TV featured an interview with an antiabortion person, they were exclusively Christian, and most Christians on TV were exclusively antiabortion.

And while my parents would never call themselves pro-choice, they always—like the majority of Catholics—voted for abortion rights politicians. As a Catholic kid, I understood that having big families had once been essential to increase the number of Catholics in the world. That's why the church still officially opposes birth control.

But I also understood we no longer lived in an age—like my grandparents did—where half of all children could die in childbirth or before the age of twelve.

THE CLAIM: "Christians have always opposed abortion rights."

THE REALITY: It's become controversial to talk about how *not* controversial *Roe v. Wade* was when the US Supreme Court made the federal right to abortion the law of the land in January 1973.

Don't get me wrong—some Christians were always against the practice. Catholic leaders had long opposed abortion, especially in the 1930s when Depression-era poverty led to more women seeking the procedure. Of course, the Catholic Church is also against birth control and sex ed in the schools, which is great if your goal is more unwanted pregnancies.

Evangelicals had never collectively opposed abortion rights prior to *Roe v. Wade*. In 1968, Billy Graham's newspaper *Christianity Today* held a symposium which affirmed that there were instances in which abortion was appropriate. They even noted that Christians need to be sensitive to the conditions many impoverished children might be brought up in.

In 1971, the National Association of Evangelicals passed a resolution recognizing the need for therapeutic abortions, suggesting that it could be acceptable in cases where the health of the mother was at risk or in cases of rape or incest.

The Southern Baptist Convention, Rev. Jerry Falwell's denomination, was officially pro-choice throughout the 1970s; antiabortionism was considered a Catholic thing. At their 1971 meeting in St. Louis, SBC delegates passed a resolution calling for the legalization of abortion, which they reaffirmed in 1974 (one year after *Roe*) and again in 1976.

The views were not so drastic then; the general consensus was if abortion was such a big deal in Jesus's day, he would've mentioned it.

Many prominent Republicans supported abortion rights, such as former Governor Ronald Reagan of California, who had signed the most liberal abortion bill in California history. *Roe .v Wade* was generally seen as part of the trend toward expanding personal freedoms.

The GOP tried out abortion as a campaign issue in the 1978 midterms, but when Rev. Jerry Falwell started the Moral Majority in 1979, it was still not a priority. Instead, the hot issue for evangelical leaders in the 1970s was the loss of tax-exempt status for racially segregated schools, like the one Falwell founded in 1966. "Jimmy Carter's IRS" was the rallying cry of the former segregationists, furious that a Christian president would challenge their on-campus racism. It took five years after *Roe v. Wade* for a Falwell sermon to even *mention* abortion.

By 1980, things had changed. Ronald Reagan had already flipped from pro-choice to staunch antiabortion Republican. But many conservatives still supported abortion rights in 1980, including former CIA director and Reagan's rival for the GOP presidential nomination George H. W. Bush.

During his tenure as a Texas congressman (1967–1971), Bush had been moderate on social issues, including abortion. He supported family planning initiatives and never called for criminalization. Only after Reagan invited him to be his running mate did Bush Sr. become rabidly opposed to women's reproductive freedoms—but he did, overnight.

Abortion has since served as a litmus test for every Republican politician and Supreme Court nominee. As author and professor Kristin Du Mez explains, "Abortion has proved to be effective not only in forming a coalition, but also in giving the entire conservative agenda a moral foundation—or moral veneer, depending on one's perspective. For many evangelicals who grew up in Christian communities from the 1980s on, promoting abortion rights is unthinkable. Thus, voting for Democrats is also unthinkable. This contributes to a sense where anything Republicans promote is seen as 'moral' and anything Democrats put forward is evil."

Only in America can you be pro death penalty, pro war, pro drone bombs, pro torture, pro cutting services for the poor, pro for-profit privatized healthcare, pro dismantling USAID, and still call yourself "pro-life."

THE BIBLICAL ARGUMENTS AGAINST ABORTION (NONE OF WHICH MENTION ABORTION)

THE CLAIM: "The Bible says that the unborn have the same rights and value as the born."

THE REALITY: Not really.

In the Book of Exodus, God states that if men who are fighting somehow injure a pregnant woman—and her fetus is lost—the offender must pay a fine to the woman's husband:

"When men strive together, and hurt a woman with child, so that there is a miscarriage, and yet no harm follows, the one who hurt her shall be fined, according as the woman's husband shall lay upon him; and he shall pay as the judges determine. If any harm follows, then you shall give life for life, eye for eye, tooth for tooth, hand for hand, foot for foot, burn for burn, wound for wound, stripe for stripe" (Exodus 21:22–25, RSV).

Got that? The fetus is not given equal status to the mother. God makes it clear that if a man injures a pregnant woman who miscarries, a monetary fine is imposed, to be determined by men, if she suffers no other harm beyond the miscarriage. However, if the pregnant woman herself dies, the punishment escalates to the law of retaliation ("life for life"). Then, and only then, does "eye for an eye" apply.

There are those who dispute the text being about miscarriage. Some editions use differing language, like "if her fruit should depart." Some conservative Christians point to this as an indication that the passage is talking about a healthy early childbirth. But if that were the case, why would there be a fine?

I asked Rabbi Danya Ruttenberg about Exodus 21. She said:

"That text is clear (if you read the Hebrew and not the KJV!) that if she dies, it's treated as manslaughter, and if she does not die but she does have a miscarriage, one is to pay monetary damages. A fetus is not treated with the status of personhood."

The loss of the fetus is treated as a financial matter, because fetuses were not yet considered to be another life or a fully independent human. God says a fetus is property—of the father. If this fact enrages your fundamentalist, please remind them that you didn't write it.

THE CLAIM: "Life begins at conception."

THE SCRIPTURE: In the Bible, life begins at birth—when a baby draws its first breath. The Bible defines life as "breath" in several significant passages, including the story of Adam's creation in Genesis 2:7.

The notion that the soul enters the body with a newborn's first breath, known as "neshamah," has always been a part of Jewish mystical and philosophical traditions. The breath of spirit is what creates actual life; that's what God defines as being alive, as per Ezekiel 37 9–10, Job 34:14–15, and Job 33:4, which reads, "The Spirit of God has made me, and the breath of the Almighty gives me life."

The Jewish law Jesus knew didn't consider fetuses to be a full persons, with protections equal to those accorded to human beings. Rabbinic teachings viewed the fetus as a *potential* life with value, but not equivalent to a fully born person.

Before 1869, Christian doctrine (as always, determined by men) was that ensoulment happened well after fertilization, perhaps at quickening, when a woman feels fetal movement. Pope Pius IX moved the soul clock back to the moment of fertilization. Evangelical men would adopt this position when they embraced the GOP and began their decades-long quest for governance of the womb.

THE CLAIM: "How do you explain Jeremiah 1:5, 'Before I formed you in the womb I knew you'?"

THE SCRIPTURE: God said, "Before I formed you in the womb I knew you, before you were born I set you apart; I appointed you as a prophet to the nations."

THE CONTEXT: The Book of Jeremiah is actually a sort of prequel to Jesus. In Jeremiah 31:31–34 he introduces the concept of a New Covenant, foreshadowing the dawn of Christianity.

If you read the entire Jeremiah 1:5 quote, you'll see that God is not making any kind of pronouncements about all fetuses. God is *specifically telling Jeremiah* that his soul is eternal, and that He knew Jeremiah before he was even conceived, because Jeremiah was always destined to be a prophet. That's the context. And it's very beautiful. It's not antiabortion.

Later in the same book comes Jeremiah's lament, where he expresses anguish and despair over his prophetic mission and the suffering he's endured because of it. If you ever think you've had a bad day, listen to this:

"Cursed be the day I was born! May the day my mother bore me not be blessed! Cursed be the man who brought my father the news, who made him very glad, saying,"A child is born to you—a son! . . . For he did not kill me in the womb, with my mother as my grave" (Jeremiah 20:14–18).

The poor guy was really going through it. And as you'll note, Jeremiah wishes his father had "killed him in the womb," indicating that this was a practice that people could and would engage in at the time, a practice neither testaments of the Bible ever get around to prohibiting.

THE CLAIM: "Yeah, but what about 'Thou shalt not kill'?"

Yes, "Thou shalt not kill"—that's why Jesus opposes the death penalty.

Again, Genesis states that life begins with first breath, and as we see in Exodus 21, God makes it clear that He does not assign a fetus the same value as a woman. By this biblical definition, abortion's not the same as killing a person.

At various times the Bible does require the death penalty for many specific crimes. You can stone people to death for adultery, being a "stubborn son" (Deuteronomy 21:18–21), or even for picking up sticks on the Sabbath (Numbers 15:32–35). But abortion is not among the many, many, many prohibited activities listed.

Neither, by the way, is miscarriage. Women don't get punished for that in the Bible. Only in certain parts of America.

THE CLAIM: "Okay, but what about Psalm 139:13–16?"

This argument usually comes next. The Book of Psalms is a collection of 150 songs, prayers, and poems that express a wide range of human emotions and theological insights. Many are comforting and beautiful, some are quite angry, and one verse has been adopted by the criminalize-abortion movement.

THE SCRIPTURE: "For you created my inmost being; you knit me together in my mother's womb. I praise you because I am fearfully and wonderfully made; your works are wonderful, I know that full well. My frame was not hidden from you when I was made in the secret place, when I was woven together in the depths of the earth. Your eyes saw my unformed body; all the days ordained for me were written in your book, before one of them came to be."

THE CONTEXT: While lovely, the passage itself does not address the legality or morality of abortion rights. It says that God knows your soul, and that God—not humans—controls exactly what's going to happen to it.

It doesn't really suggest screaming "baby killer" at people. So please, don't remind your loved ones about what comes two Psalms earlier, 137:8–9, where we're treated to this pro-life gem:

"O daughter of Babylon, who art to be destroyed; happy shall he be, that rewardeth thee as thou hast served us. Happy shall he be, that taketh and dasheth thy little ones against the stones" (KJV).

A wish for violence against children does somewhat undercut the argument that Psalms is all about protecting the little ones, no?

This should all be enough to make for an awkward church social. But if you really need to get into it, there's Numbers 5:11–31.

If you're by any chance snacking while perusing this humble tome, now might be the time to put down your food. In the passage known as "The Test for an Unfaithful Wife," God prescribes a disturbing ritual to determine whether a pregnant wife has been untrue.

If a man suspects his expectant wife of infidelity, but has no witnesses and zero evidence, he is to bring his wife to the priest, along with a grain offering. The priest then makes a concoction called "bitter water" by mixing holy water with dust from the tabernacle floor. The woman's hair is then unbound (a sign of submission), and she must hold the grain offering while the priest pronounces an oath, cursing the water. Then, she's *forced to drink the water* that the priest just cursed.

Oh, you never heard this one in church?

Here's the really scientific part. If innocent, she'll be unharmed by the potion and can still conceive children. But "if she has defiled herself and has broken faith with her husband, the water that brings the curse shall enter into her and cause bitter pain, and her womb shall swell, and her thigh shall fall away, and the woman shall become a curse among her people."

The physical symptoms (swelling womb and falling thigh) would affect her reproductive organs and eliminate the adulterous seed. It's an induced miscarriage, also known as abortion.

This is the only actual mention of what might be real abortion in the entire Bible, and it's instructions on how to get one. The fact that the woman might be mutilated by the experience is apparently no big deal.

Not everyone agrees that this process is about abortion as we understand it, but it's hard to read it and reckon how the adultery-fetus is expected to survive the process.

There's also the distinct possibility that the entire ritual was just a psychotic hazing, designed to terrorize wives into obedient fidelity. Either way, right-wing Christians should appreciate how familiar it all must feel. In this passage—just as in Texas—the woman has no choice.

WHAT DOES JESUS'S RELIGION HAVE TO SAY ABOUT ABORTION?

One of the unpleasant truths conservative religious movements tend to overlook is that they can't actually end abortion—they can only end the safe, legal, regulated kinds. That's because abortion has always been around, and whether people like it or not, abortion will always be around.

THE CLAIM: "The Bible never mentioned abortion because abortion wasn't a thing back then."

THE REALITY: Abortions were known and practiced throughout biblical times, although the methods differed quite a bit from today. In ancient Egypt, it appears to have been relatively accepted, particularly when necessary for the health or well-being of the woman. The Ebers Papyrus, dating back to around 1550 BCE, one of the oldest and most important medical documents from ancient Egypt, contains many references to contraception, fertility issues, and ending a pregnancy.

Abortion was also practiced in ancient Greece and Rome. Various methods were employed, including the use of herbal abortifacients and surgical procedures. Medical texts from the period, such as those by Hippocrates and Soranus, discuss these practices.

And for centuries, certain medicinal plants have been used to induce miscarriage, including pennyroyal, mugwort, Queen Anne's lace, tansy, and blue cohosh, which only sounds like a cannabis product; it's traditionally been used by Indigenous women to induce labor, or to induce miscarriage.

Other religions, including Islam and the Baha'i faith, allow abortions out of medical necessity.

The Jewish law Jesus knew was well established. If a woman felt threatened by a pregnancy, it was her decision to abort it. In the Talmud, Mishnah Oholot 7:6 states, "A person who is having trouble giving birth, they abort the fetus and take it out limb by limb, because existing life comes before potential life. If most of the child has come out already they do not touch it, for we do not push off one life for another."

Which is to say, the Bible, as we know it, was written in a world where terminating pregnancies was permitted. The Hebrew and Greek words for "abortion" don't appear in the Old or New Testament of the Bible.

Moreover, Judaism considers abortion up to fifteen weeks as a God-given right. A US abortion ban is, by definition, an infringement of religious freedom of Jews guaranteed by the Constitution. In Israel, abortions are legal—and free. The procedures must be approved by a health committee, which typically includes a gynecologist, a social worker, and another physician. While it seems a very formal approval process, the majority of requests are approved, making abortions safe and accessible in practice.

How many right-wing Christian friends have you heard demanding an end to US foreign aid to Israel? Zero, because most don't even know this. Right-wing media has not instructed them to be outraged when Israel does it.

And while Jesus loves and cares for children, he didn't express any special concern for the unborn during the anticipated end times: "How dreadful it will be in those days for pregnant women and nursing mothers!" (Matthew 24:19).

THE LEAST PRO-LIFE CHARACTER IN THE BIBLE

When it comes to biblical child killing, God ain't squeamish, and He doesn't hold back.

The God of the Bible frequently commits panoramically violent mass killings, or delegates the job to certain lucky humans. In Numbers 31, God commands the Israelites to wage war against the Midianites, killing 120,000, including male children and women who aren't virgins. And in Numbers 25:4–9, Jehovah sends a plague and casually orders Moses to help slaughter 24,000 idolatrous Israelites, saying, "Take all the heads of the people, and hang them up before the Lord against the sun" (KJV).

In numerous instances God permits—or even commands—the death of fetuses as part of broader judgments or punishments. Now, you probably don't need tons of Bible verses that command the murder of children—or unborn fetuses—so I won't list *too* many. But:

- In Deuteronomy 2:34, God has the Israelites kill everyone in Heshbon, including babies.
- In 1 Samuel 15:3, God tells the Israelites to kill all the Amalekites, including babies.
- In Hosea 13:16, God promises to kill the infants of Samaria and

says, "Their little ones will be dashed the ground, their pregnant women ripped open."

- And who could forget Numbers 31:17–18: "Now therefore kill every male among the little ones, and kill every woman that hath known man by lying with him. But all the women children, that have not known a man by lying with him, keep alive for yourselves" (KJV).

And please bear in mind—if they believe that the Noah's ark story is literal fact, then they believe that one time God drowned every pregnant woman and every unborn fetus on earth, on the same day, because He felt like it.

And if you still think the God of the Bible prioritizes the innocent lives of children, let me remind you Gentiles about Passover, when God killed all Egyptian firstborn children as punishment for the sins of grown-ups.

Oh, and don't forget the two magical cocaine bears God sent to maul forty-two kids for mocking Elisha's baldness. I certainly can't.

So Pro-Life, We'll Kill You

As the New Testament constantly reminds us, Jesus's teachings emphasize nonviolence, compassion, and love for others. But when it comes to violence against women's healthcare clinicians, Christian extremists are quite convinced they get a pass:

In 1993, a Christian antiabortion activist murdered Dr. David Gunn in Pensacola, Florida.

In 1994, a Christian antiabortion activist attacked two clinics in Brookline, Massachusetts, killing multiple receptionists.

In 2009, a Christian antiabortion activist murdered Dr. George Tiller, who'd been repeatedly harassed by right-wing media figures like Bill O'Reilly as "Tiller the Baby Killer," while the doctor was attending church in Wichita, Kansas.

In 2023, South Carolina Republicans filed a bill to make abortion a death penalty crime, because all life is sacred.

In 2024, the Texas Republican Party's official platform endorsed defining abortion (which Jesus never mentioned) as homicide—punishable by the death penalty (which Jesus actually opposed).

There's also the 1998 bombing of clinics by Eric Robert Rudolph, and the 2015 Planned Parenthood shooting in Colorado Springs.

If your devotion to the unborn justifies murdering the born, your concerns stopped being Christian a long time ago.

Pro-life murder. And irony hangs itself in a Motel 6.

AMERICA, POST-ROE

> "I do think criminalizing abortion has become a substitute Gospel for Christian nationalists. I'm sure you know the evangelicals who criticize their pastors for quoting the Sermon on the Mount as 'too liberal.' You can effectively demonize the poor, reject LGBTQI people, be racist and sexist; and as long as you are against abortion you are a 'good Christian.' It's alarming to several evangelical leaders as it is kind of a 'get out of hell free' card."
>
> Rev. Susan Brooks Thistlethwaite

In the first two years after the Supreme Court *Dobbs* decision ended the constitutional right to abortion, over a dozen Republican-led states banned all or most abortions, leaving women in nearly a quarter of US counties more than two hundred miles from an abortion provider. Amid many legal challenges, the US would soon witness some of the highest rates of maternal mortality among high-income countries—with the worst outcomes experienced by lower-income women in states where abortion was banned completely. Federal documents show that complaints of pregnant women turned away from US emergency rooms spiked in 2022. Praise Jesus, I guess.

Following the *Dobbs* decision, American news headlines began to feature a steady stream of newly familiar phrases.

"Woman Left to Bleed for 10 Days from Incomplete Miscarriage After Being Turned Away by Hospital Post-Roe" (*Independent,* July 17, 2022)

"'I Had to Carry My Baby to Bury My Baby': Woman Says She Was Denied Abortion for Fetus Without Skull" (ABC News, August 26, 2022)

"Affidavits: 2 More Pregnant Minors Who Were Raped Were Denied Ohio Abortions" (*Cincinnati Enquirer,* September 27, 2022)

"Texas Woman Nearly Loses Her Life After Doctors Can't Legally Perform an Abortion: 'Their Hands Were Tied'" (*People,* October 18, 2022)

"Ohio Abortion Law Meant Weeks of 'Anguish,' 'Agony' for Couple Whose Unborn Child Had Organs Outside Her Body" (CNN, February 8, 2023)

"3 Abortion Bans in Texas Leave Doctors 'Talking in Code' to Pregnant Patients" (NPR, March 1, 2023)

"Florida Woman Denied Abortion Miscarried in Hair Salon Bathroom, Lost Half Her Blood" (*Jezebel,* April 10, 2023)

"Texas Woman Almost Dies Because She Couldn't Get an Abortion" (CNN, June 20, 2023)

"Emergency Rooms Refused to Treat Pregnant Women, Leaving One to Miscarry in a Lobby Restroom" (Associated Press, April 19, 2024)

"Catholic Hospital Offered Bucket, Towels to Woman It Denied an Abortion, California AG Said" (*National Catholic Reporter,* October 10, 2024)

"A Woman Died After Being Told It Would Be a 'Crime' to Intervene in Her Miscarriage at a Texas Hospital" (*ProPublica,* October 30, 2024)

The continuing accounts of women left to suffer have proven the lethal shortsightedness of a movement that only cared about banning a procedure, and not about what would follow.

A study published in *JAMA Pediatrics* revealed an 8 percent increase in Texas's infant mortality rate following the state's near-total abortion ban. That's because abortion bans force people to give birth to babies they know won't survive.

Thanks to the zeal of right-wing Christians, a wave of preventable agony was unleashed on women, their families, and of course, the babies forced to suffer horribly during their very brief lives. But our anti-abortion-access friends sleep soundly, knowing they're the righteous champions of matters Jesus really did mean to mention, at some point.

According to another research estimate published in 2024 in *JAMA Internal Medicine* and headed up by the medical director at Planned Parenthood of Montana, more than sixty-four thousand women and girls were projected to have become pregnant by rape in fourteen states that banned abortion after Roe was overturned. Most of these states had no exceptions for ending pregnancies that occurred as a result of rape.

Christian men, forcing rape victims to be pregnant, against their will, over something the Bible does not forbid.

Republicans will often cite the statistic that only 1 percent of abortions are obtained because of rape. They generally don't mention the fact that three out of four sexual assaults go unreported—and out of every one thousand rapes, only five perpetrators ever get convicted.

Are you feeling any Jesus vibes around any of this yet?

WHEN DEBATING ABORTION AND THE BIBLE

You probably already know it's not a fun debate to have. I've been called a "baby killer" hundreds of times; the fact that my baby made it to middle school just proves I'm a failure at killing it, I guess.

You will, most likely, never get an antiabortion coworker, neighbor, or loved one to agree that such choices are between a woman, her doctor, and

God, and that it's none of the government's business. But that doesn't mean we shouldn't engage respectfully and honestly on this issue.

And after you've acknowledged their feelings, I recommend politely asking them to acknowledge some facts:

- According to data from the CDC, both pregnancy and childbirth are more dangerous to a woman's life and health than abortion.
- Over 90 percent of abortions happen in the first trimester (by thirteen weeks).
- More than 60 percent of abortion patients have a religious affiliation.
- The majority of women who seek abortions are already moms.
- 59 percent of women seeking abortions are moms facing a high risk of poverty.

You might point out that after all the elective abortions performed since 1973, the Christian right still refuses to support programs that are proven to reduce abortions, like sex education or family planning that stresses contraception.

You can even remind them that abstinence-only education doesn't work; please avoid any temptation to call it "ignorance-only."

Be ready to acknowledge that US Christians are allowed to fight to criminalize abortion and have the right to try to incarcerate Americans for performing or having abortions. Ask them if incarceration is one of the goals of criminalizing the procedure. They may not have considered it before.

They also have the freedom to fight for an America where the only abortions that happen are dangerous, illegal, and unsafe. Try to get them to acknowledge that people have always ended pregnancies, and always will, whether it's legal or not.

They even get to fight for a forced-birth society where a rapist can potentially pick out the unwilling mother of his next child. Maybe save that one for later in the evening.

But they *don't* get to pretend their crusade is in any way sanctioned by Jesus.

And who knows? You may be able to get them to agree that if men could get pregnant, all abortions would be safe, legal, and free. And locker room schmucks would be bragging over who's had more.

Finally, a Note to the Catholics

This issue has divided American Catholics, literally. Slightly more than half of US Catholics support safe and legal access to abortion. That doesn't mean they like it; they just don't want it criminalized. This divides families, parishes, and clergy, too.

In 2004, Catholic presidential candidate John Kerry faced significant controversy within the church due to his pro-abortion-rights stance. Some bishops publicly stated that Kerry should be denied holy Communion as a sort of punishment, because they think bishops actually own the love of Jesus and may hold it back when they so choose.

In 2021, the US Conference of Catholic Bishops debated whether Catholic politicians who support abortion rights—specifically, the second Catholic president, Joe Biden—should be denied Communion. San Diego Bishop Robert McElroy objected, saying, "I do not see how depriving the president or other political leaders of Eucharist based on their public policy stance can be interpreted in our society as anything other than the weaponization of Eucharist . . . to pummel them into submission."

The Vatican, under Pope Francis, advised caution on this one. The Congregation for the Doctrine of the Faith urged US bishops to avoid politicizing the Eucharist and to focus on dialogue and unity within the church.

But a year later, the archbishop of San Francisco, Salvatore Cordileone, proudly announced to the world that he would no longer allow House Speaker Nancy Pelosi to receive holy Communion in her home diocese. Of course, the archbishop gladly still offered holy Communion to pro-death-penalty politicians.

How many Catholics have US bishops barred from receiving holy Communion due to:

Turning away refugees? 0
Drone assassinations? 0
Denying care to the sick? 0
Exploiting the poor? 0
Supporting executions? 0
Calling refugees "illegals"? 0
Covering up child rape? 0

In case you thought this had anything to do with Jesus.

Polite Abortion Questions for Right-Wing Loved Ones

1. Where in the Bible is terminating a pregnancy defined as murder?
2. Where does Jesus specifically mention ending pregnancies?
3. Where does the Bible ban or condemn ending pregnancies?
4. Genesis, Job, and Ezekiel all state that life doesn't begin until a human draws their first breath. Where does the Bible say life begins at conception?
5. If God really opposes abortion, why didn't He authorize Moses, Jesus, or Paul to issue one definitive statement on the subject?
6. Why did God, who loves the unborn and hates abortion, kill so many unborn babies, children, and adults throughout biblical history?
7. When a woman's body spontaneously miscarries, it is considered medical waste. But if a woman consciously aborts, is that same fetus a murdered baby with a soul?
8. What's the more "pro-life" position: lowering abortion rates through sex education and birth control or outright banning safe access to abortion?
9. Why does God perform the most abortions—through miscarriages—if abortion is a biblical evil? Why does God murder untold millions of these "persons" every year?
10. The number-one killer of children in America is gun violence. What is the pro-life plan to save the born children?

11. Every day around the world more than forty thousand people, mostly children, die from starvation or malnutrition. Why is it more important to focus your energy on the unborn than to protect and cherish the right to life of the already born?
12. Do American citizens have a right to not be pregnant if they don't want to be or should the government have the power to force citizens to be pregnant against their will?
13. If God is omnipotent, omnipresent, and omniscient, does He know the future of all embryos?
14. Does God know which embryos will become actual babies and which won't?
15. Does God knowingly ensoul fetuses that He knows are going to be aborted?
16. If God won't give souls to fetuses He knows won't become babies, how is abortion killing a human?
17. At what point does someone else's pregnancy become your business?

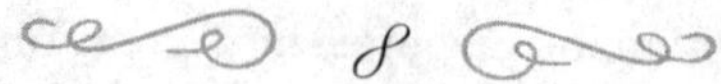

THOU SHALT NOT HATE "ILLEGALS"

> "It's hypocrisy to call yourself a Christian and chase away a refugee or someone seeking help, someone who is hungry or thirsty, toss out someone who is in need of my help."
>
> Pope Francis, 2016

> "Shall oppressed humanity find no asylum on this globe?"
>
> Thomas Jefferson, letter to Albert Gallatin, 1806

Immigration is one of the most controversial and morally complex subjects in both America and modern Christianity, one that demands both nuance and thoughtful, studious discourse. Historically, the Christian right hasn't been interested in that—but they're divine at reducing things to catchy xenophobic catchphrases:

"Build the wall!" "Send them home!" "Go back where you came from!" "Deport them all!" "Keep America American!" "Stop the invasion!" "Jobs for Americans, not illegals!" "No amnesty!" etc. I guess "no room at the inn" was taken.

But for our Christian nationalist pals who thought the Bible was on their side with abortion or homophobia, I'm afraid there's more bad news.

The God of the Bible consistently takes an unambiguously compassionate stance toward immigrants and strangers. Jesus commands individuals and nations to welcome the stranger and warns they'll be judged by how well they do it. Cruelty to immigrants, while deeply popular, violates those tedious woke themes of compassion, justice, and inclusivity in both Old and New Testaments.

And before our conservative friends get upset, I acknowledge that societies need to have restrictions on who can enter. I'm not calling for open borders or amnesty; that was Ronald Reagan. But people can support restrictions on immigration without weaponizing the Bible to smear refugees or asylum seekers as criminals.

The point of this chapter is that humans don't need to hate or scapegoat immigrants, and Christ followers aren't technically allowed to.

Let's begin with the Old Testament and test this out:

THE CLAIM: "They're 'illegals.'"

THE SCRIPTURE: The basic Christian belief that all humans are made in the image of God, in Genesis 1:27, inconveniently affirms the inherent dignity and worth of every person.

"God created mankind in his own image, in the image of God he created them; male and female he created them."

Recognizing the divine image in every human was the original plan to get Bible readers to treat everyone with respect and compassion, naïve though that may seem.

As we move forward, God consistently calls for the Israelites to treat foreigners with kindness and love, which would've made it very difficult for them to fully enjoy Fox News.

- "Let them live among you wherever they like and in whatever town they choose. Do not oppress them" (Deuteronomy 23:16).
- "You are to allot it as an inheritance for yourselves and for the foreigners residing among you and who have children. You are to consider them as native-born Israelites; along with you they are to be allotted an inheritance among the tribes of Israel" (Ezekiel 47:22).

God keeps commanding His people to have empathy and keeps giving them the same reason:

- "The foreigner residing among you must be treated as your native-born. Love them as yourself, for you were foreigners in Egypt" (Leviticus 19:34).
- "And you are to love those who are foreigners, for you yourselves were foreigners in Egypt" (Deuteronomy 10:19).
- "Do not mistreat or oppress a foreigner, for you were foreigners in Egypt" (Exodus 22:21).

Hey, that's God giving the *same exact commandment three different times.* Seems pretty specific.

Alas, dear xenophobes, the God of the Old Testament is unambiguously pro immigrant AND pro being nice to them. And as painful as that may be, Jesus isn't gonna make it any easier for you.

Open-Border Bible

So not only does God command us to welcome the strangers, no asterisks attached, He won't even let us push them around:

- "Cursed is anyone who withholds justice from the foreigner, the fatherless, or the widow" (Deuteronomy 27:19).
- "Do not take advantage of a hired worker who is poor and needy, whether that worker is a fellow Israelite or a foreigner residing in one of your towns" (Deuteronomy 24:14).
- "Administer true justice; show mercy and compassion to one another. Do not oppress the widow or the fatherless, the foreigner or the poor" (Zechariah 7:9–10).
- "So I will come to put you on trial. I will be quick to testify against sorcerers, adulterers and perjurers, against those who defraud

laborers of their wages, who oppress the widows and the fatherless, and deprive the foreigners among you of justice, but do not fear me" (Malachi 3:5).

CHRISTIANITY, A SANCTUARY CITY

From the Roman centurion to the woman at the well, Jesus frequently interacted with and helped outsiders from differing tribes. His teachings regularly command love and hospitality toward immigrants and strangers, and at no point in the Bible does anyone ever call him an open-borders globalist.

- "Love your neighbor as yourself" is quite inclusive and universal, extending beyond those who look and talk like us to include all of humanity.
- Jesus deliberately makes a despised foreign minority the hero of the Good Samaritan story.
- In Luke 4:24–27 a new-to-preaching Jesus enrages a hometown Nazareth crowd when he speaks of the Widow of Zarephath (1 Kings 17) and Naaman the Syrian (2 Kings 5) as outsiders who were blessed by God during periods when the Israelites were not. He challenges any nationalist or ethnocentric beliefs about who God loves and aligns himself with foreign outsiders. The crowd responds by trying to throw him off a cliff.
- And of course, the small matter of Jesus clearly stating that he'll judge us on that welcome-the-stranger business in Matthew 25:40, "Truly I tell you, whatever you did for one of the least of these brothers and sisters of mine, you did for me."

So what's an immigrant-hating Christian to do?

THE CHRISTIAN NATIONALIST CASE AGAINST WELCOMING STRANGERS

There aren't really any Bible verses devoted to "repelling the stranger." But Christians who hate the undocumented have found a way around this: by ignoring all of the Old Testament, all of Jesus, and talking about law and order.

THE CLAIM: "Illegals are lawbreakers, so Jesus's teachings don't apply."

In April 2018, Trump White House Attorney General Jeff Sessions announced a "zero tolerance" policy for undocumented entry into the US. Under this policy, all adults caught crossing the border illegally were to be criminally prosecuted, while their children were classified as "unaccompanied minors" and placed in the custody of the Department of Health and Human Services. This led to a policy that separated children from parents as a deterrent. America was stealing migrant kids.

Sessions, a Methodist, cited Romans 13 to justify the policy: "I would cite you to the Apostle Paul and his clear and wise command in Romans 13, to obey the laws of the government because God has ordained them for the purpose of order."

Romans 13? *Hello again, Paul.*

THE SCRIPTURE: Romans 13:1–2: "Let everyone be subject to the governing authorities, for there is no authority except that which God has established. The authorities that exist have been established by God. Consequently, whoever rebels against the authority is rebelling against what God has instituted, and those who do so will bring judgment on themselves."

White House Press Secretary Sarah Huckabee Sanders supported Sessions's use of Romans 13, emphasizing that it is "very biblical to enforce the law."

THE DEBUNKING: First, if one wishes to interpret Romans 13:1–2 as divine endorsement of governmental authority, one must ignore all those inconvenient biblical themes of compassion, hospitality, and justice for the stranger and the marginalized. Scholars call this "throwing out Jesus and the entire Old Testament to pathetically cling to one line of Paul."

Moreover, whenever a Democratic president has been in office, our Republican friends haven't been so keen on "respecting the governing authorities," as you may have noticed over the past few decades.

Finally, any foreigner standing on US soil has the right to claim asylum. So where does the "illegal" part come in?

Paul, however, is not the anti-immigrant hero Christian nationalists have waited for. Consider the chapter than comes just before:

"Contribute to the needs of the saints; extend hospitality to strangers" (Romans 12:13 NRSVA).

And be sure to get your immigrant-hating, Romans-citing friend's take on:

"Let no debt remain outstanding, except the continuing debt to love one another, for whoever loves others has fulfilled the law" (Romans 13:8).

"Love does no harm to a neighbor, therefore love is the fulfillment of the law" (Romans 13:10).

Paul even goes on to say:

"Do not forget to show hospitality to strangers, for by so doing some people have shown hospitality to angels without knowing it" (Hebrews 13:1–2).

THE CLAIM: "God's intention is for people to live in distinct and segregated nations."

THE SCRIPTURE: Some anti-immigration fundamentalists are fond of Genesis 11:1–9, aka the Tower of Babel. Humanity, united by one language, settles on a plain in Shinar and begins constructing a tower to reach the heavens and make a name for themselves. God, annoyed, confuses their languages and disperses them, ending the construction.

Many choose to interpret this story as God wanting firm borders. But the central issue in Genesis 11 is not the separation of people, but their collective pride and attempt to challenge God's authority. Yes, God confuses the language and scatters everyone, thereby creating linguistic and cultural diversity. But all that proves is that within the Bible, diversity is presented *as part of God's divine plan.*

God doesn't spend much time obsessing over the invisible lines in the ground we've created to separate our tribes.

THE CLAIM: "We must take care of our own first."

It's very human to justify prioritizing resources and attention for native-born citizens over immigrants or refugees, especially if the human is JD Vance. However, as you may have guessed, this take is fundamentally at odds with Messiahs who emphasize self-sacrificial love, inclusion, and care for the vulnerable regardless of nationality or identity.

THE SCRIPTURE: None.

The parable of the Good Samaritan is Jesus specifically rejecting the idea of limiting compassion to one's own group. A despised foreigner is the character who fulfills God's command to "love your neighbor as yourself." Jesus wraps this up with the command: *"Go and do likewise."* This directly refutes any charming argument that Christians should prioritize care for "their own."

Jesus called for his followers to sacrifice themselves at the expense of others:

- "Whoever wants to be my disciple must deny themselves and take up their cross and follow me" (Matthew 16:24).
- "Sell your possessions and give to the poor" (Luke 12:33).

How far individuals take this is, of course, up to them. But these teachings challenge any notion of hoarding resources for oneself—or one's precious group—at the expense of others in need. Take it up with Jesus, nationalists.

THE CLAIM: "God told Nehemiah to build a wall, so Trump's wall is totally biblical."

In 2016, Donald Trump's racist fantasia of a wall to keep out migrants and refugees offended Pope Francis, who'd said while visiting Mexico: "A person who thinks only about building walls, wherever they may be, and not building bridges, is not Christian. This is not in the Gospel." Pope Francis clarified that he was not telling Catholics how to vote, but it didn't matter.

After years of publicly suggesting that President Obama was secretly Muslim, an outraged Trump cried, "For a religious leader to question a person's faith is disgraceful."

And that's how he got into a fight with *the pope*.

The *nice pope*.

His Holiness versus His Assholiness.

Of course, Pope Francis calling Donald Trump "not Christian" is like James Brown calling Trump "not Black." But when it was pointed out that a wall spanning our southern border violated the Bible's commandments to welcome the stranger, the right found a brand-new way to go around Jesus.

THE SCRIPTURE: The book of Nehemiah.

Nehemiah was a Jewish official and cupbearer to the Persian king Artaxerxes I (likely Artaxerxes I of Persia, who ruled 465–424 BCE). Being the official "cupbearer" likely meant Nehemiah was a eunuch, a class of people who were, in Deuteronomy, forbidden access to temple worship.

But Nehemiah was ordered to rebuild the walls of Jerusalem, which had been destroyed during the Babylonian conquest. This was a symbol of restoration, renewal, and the fulfillment of God's promises to His people.

I can't tell you how many times I've heard this presented as proof that Christians are supposed to build walls to keep out the undesirables. Why listen to Jesus when you can disfigure Old Testament stories to demonize migrants?

THE DEBUNKING: The only problems with this thesis would be that:

1. God never actually speaks to Nehemiah.
2. Nehemiah didn't build a wall to keep out immigrants and asylum seekers.
3. Nehemiah lived five hundred years before Christ, aka it's not Christian.
4. Jesus, whom Christians are supposed to follow, commands us to *welcome* the stranger.
5. Nehemiah was a eunuch.
6. They're comparing Donald Trump to a eunuch.

Why "Illegals" Is Racist, Even If You Don't Mind It

Not to be preachy in a book about the Bible, but calling undocumented immigrants and refugees "illegals" dehumanizes people, many of whom are Christian; it reinforces negative stereotypes and perpetuates systemic biases. Which is the driest, most academic way of saying it's totally racist.

From a human rights standpoint, everyone has the right to seek asylum from persecution. Both the Universal Declaration of Human Rights and the 1951 Refugee Convention recognize the rights of individuals to seek protection, irrespective of their documentation status. Calling refugees "illegals" criminalizes people seeking safety and better lives, often in dire circumstances, which is why it's not Christian. And since seeking asylum or fleeing persecution are not criminal acts, it's not terribly American, either. Have you ever, on any US broadcast, heard the noun "illegal" used to refer to white lawbreakers?

Dehumanizing terms lead to greater hostility toward migrants and refugees, which is the point. If you humanize them, it's a lot harder to get otherwise decent Christians to sign on to the cruelty.

I recommend calling them "Christian refugees." It's accurate, and will enrage exactly the right people.

"TWO THOUSAND YEARS AGO, A YOUNG FAMILY BECAME REFUGEES"

In 2023, the *Houston Chronicle* published an editorial on Christmas Eve, titled "How Would Governor Greg Abbott Treat Mary and Joseph at the Border?"

Governor Abbott was by then known as one of the harshest and most inhumane Christian politicians when it came to border crossings. He wanted voters to see him being as cruel as possible to those undocumented brown folks who keep coming here for all those jobs white Texan employers keep handing out.

Abbott was not, it must be noted, interested in punishing the employers who hire undocumented labor, which is, again, the reason they come here. That's how we generally know this is all a scam.

Abbott launched Operation Lone Star in March 2021, which deployed the Texas National Guard and Department of Public Safety to the border, arresting asylum seekers who were legally entitled to seek protection. He began busing migrants from Texas to other states in very public media stunts that used vulnerable and confused humans as pawns.

But in 2022, Governor Abbott topped himself when he ordered the installation of razor wire along sections of the Rio Grande River. What better way to honor Christ's commandment to welcome the stranger than slicing up some of the more desperate ones?

A federal judge and the US Supreme Court all ordered Abbott to remove the razor wire. The governor, apparently not a fan of Paul's letter to the Romans about respecting authorities, ignored the orders and continued to let migrants be shredded in the river.

The *Houston Chronicle*'s Christmas Eve 2023 editorial was devastating: "Like Joseph and Mary and their child, more than 100 million people around the world are estimated to have been displaced this year, many of them on the move this very night. Refugees and migrants, they are fleeing persecution, grinding poverty, war, and unspeakable violence."

The editorial finished with: "The Christmas story we tell, the story the infant Jesus grew up to tell, counsels sympathy toward the less fortunate, compassion for those in need, kindness toward strangers."

Now, this shouldn't have been controversial. You don't have to like undocumented immigration to agree that these are humans who deserve to be treated like humans.

The day after Christmas, Abbott tweeted, "[The *Chronicle*] doesn't know the story of Mary & Joseph. They weren't 'refugees' (look up definition) Read Luke 2:1–10 They were ordered by the govt to go to Bethlehem to register for the census. Nice distortion. Doing Devil's work."

THE CLAIM: Calling Mary and Joseph "refugees" is "doing devil's work."

THE SCRIPTURE: Luke 2:1–10 tells the story of Mary and Joseph traveling to Bethlehem for the census: "In those days Caesar Augustus issued a decree that a census should be taken of the entire Roman world" (Luke 2:1).

Let's note that there's no historical evidence of any Roman census with those requirements ever being carried out. And if you'll take a moment to think about it, on what planet would any government order a nationwide census to return to your ancestral home?

What the governor really gets wrong is that the census story isn't even what the *Chronicle* was talking about. The editorial wasn't referencing Joseph and Mary's journey to Bethlehem, but their flight *to Egypt,* to flee persecution.

After Jesus's birth, they had to escape Herod's decree that all male children under two should be killed. "An angel of the Lord appeared to Joseph in a dream. 'Get up,' he said, take the child and his mother and escape to Egypt. Stay there until I tell you, for Herod is going to search for the child to kill him'" (Matthew 2:13).

Mary and Joseph were absolutely refugees according to both the dictionary and the Gospel of Matthew. They fled Herod's kingdom to escape violence, took their child to Egypt and stayed there for years, in hiding.

Our right-wing Christians are fighting to turn away the most desperate foreign refugees, all while worshiping Jesus, who was once a foreign refugee.

This means that Joseph and Mary most certainly did not "respect the governing authorities." It also means that Jesus of the Bible spent his formative years as an undocumented kid.

ON "SHITHOLE COUNTRIES"

Perhaps Donald Trump's most infamous xenophobic blurting occurred January 11, 2018, during an Oval Office meeting with lawmakers about immigration reform. This was part of the negotiations for a bipartisan proposal that sought to protect immigrants from Haiti, El Salvador, and certain African nations.

According to the *Washington Post,* Trump questioned why the US would want to accept immigrants from places with majority nonwhite populations instead of countries like Norway. He reportedly said, "Why are we having all these people from shithole countries come here?"

(Never mind the fact that Norway has universal healthcare, free college, strong social safety nets, higher environmental quality, and relatively low levels of income inequality. All that socialism the angry white people scream about *over here* is why those nice white people enjoy living *over there.*)

The *Post* quoted several sources, including a US senator, confirming the comment. International reaction was swift and negative. The UN called the remarks "shocking and shameful," and Trump's secretary of state, Rex Tillerson, was dispatched on an apology tour to all offended nations.

Right-wing pastor Robert Jeffress immediately defended the slur: "What a lot of people miss is, America is not a church where everyone should be welcomed regardless of race and background."

If only there was a term for not welcoming people because of their race or background.

But what a lot of xenophobic Christians miss, besides the brutally obvious racism, is this: Jesus himself came from an undesirable foreign place that could credibly be called a "shithole."

Nazareth was a remote enclave of a few hundred people, a typical agricultural community where people worked hard and lived simply.

Archaeological excavations in Nazareth have revealed small stone homes with no public buildings or infrastructure, indicating it was a modest, isolated rural settlement, smack in the middle of nowhere. It wasn't along any major trade routes and was not a place of any political or economic importance. I'm strongly resisting the urge to call Nazareth the Tatooine of the Bible.

Here's what a shithole Nazareth was considered to be: In John 1:45–46, when Philip tells Nathaniel about Jesus of Nazareth, Nathaniel replies, "Nazareth! Can anything good come from there?"

But according to the book our Christian nationalists claim to follow, God chose to have His only begotten son grow up a nonwhite refugee from a shithole place, and that son grew up to command us all to welcome . . . well, you know.

Awkward Questions for Migrant-Hating Loved Ones

- What does the Bible say about welcoming strangers?
- How do you reconcile your views with Jesus's teachings on loving your neighbor?
- How do you interpret the command to treat foreigners with justice?
- What's wrong about Jesus's example of ministering to despised outsiders?
- How do you address the biblical call to unity and equality among all people?
- How exactly does a Christian get from "welcome the stranger" to "no room at the inn"?

THOU SHALT NOT HATE ON POOR PEOPLE

"The modern conservative is . . . engaged . . . in one of man's oldest, best financed, most applauded, and, on the whole, least successful exercises in moral philosophy. That is the search for a superior moral justification for selfishness."

John Kenneth Galbraith, 1967

America leads the world in Christians who believe Jesus wants us to help the poor by cutting programs that actually help the poor.

But the Bible has a lot to say about poverty, and its teachings may be surprising to many. This book bluntly commands generosity, justice, compassion, and fairness toward the poor and marginalized. And it doesn't ask nicely.

- The Bible commands lending to the poor without expecting repayment or interest.
- The Law of Moses requires a "Year of Jubilee" every fifty years, when debts were to be forgiven, slaves freed, and land returned to its original owners, ensuring a reset of economic inequalities.
- Jesus commands individuals and nations to care for the poor and asserts that all will be judged by how well they did it.

- In the parable of the loaves and fishes, Jesus encourages everyone to give the food away instead of selling it, aka free guaranteed nutrition for everyone.
- In Mark 12:17, Jesus supports paying taxes the government will redistribute.
- The early church, in Acts of the Apostles, practiced a radical economic form of communal living where wealth and resources were shared.
- The Bible often depicts God directly identifying with the poor and oppressed, suggesting that how one treats the poor is indicative of their relationship with God: Proverbs 19:17 says, "Whoever is kind to the poor lends to the Lord, and he will reward them for what they have done."

Particularly since the early 1980s, the US has often pursued policies that favor the wealthy and increase economic inequality, which economists and theologians have come to label "the exact freaking opposite" of Jesus's teachings about caring for the poor—and the dangers of wealth—as stated in Matthew 19:24 and Luke 16:19–31.

Christian America has been caught up in the long con of trickle-down economics, a rigged system that gives massive tax cuts to the wealthiest, who need them the least, and all too often punishes struggling people with cuts to social services, fare hikes, and a degrading minimum wage. Years of leadership (and media) demonizing the poor as worthless, lazy welfare cheats has helped millions of Christians make peace with the suffering of the least of us.

But social programs exist because of the conclusive failure of the world's Christians to adequately provide for others the way God commands in the Book. Christianity *should* put the welfare state completely out of business due to lack of customers, but that hasn't happened. So if you want His will to be done, on earth as it is in heaven, it's going to require a lot of voting.

Biblical Priorities

Number of times the Bible forbids or demands penalties for abortion: 0

Number of times the Bible justifies keeping out immigrants: 0

Number of times Jesus condemned homosexuality: 0

Number of times the Bible addresses poverty, justice, and compassion for the poor: over 2,000

SMEARING THE POOR, FOR INSPIRATION AND PROFIT

Many a false prophet has dehumanized the poor, the sick, and the least of us with ugly stereotypes and cruel policy, but the Rev. Jerry Falwell was the Grand Master.

Falwell and his allies vilified poverty itself as a result of personal failings—and the intoxicating allure of welfare dependency.

Believing that economically struggling people are lazy enough to deserve their suffering permits us to internally justify policies that reduce support for those in need. Falwell's audience was conditioned to hate *the very idea* of a Christian nation that would help the least of us:

> "We are developing a socialistic state in these United States as surely as I am standing here right now. Our give-away programs, our welfarism at home and abroad, is developing a breed of bums and derelicts who wouldn't work in a pie shop eating the holes out of donuts. And they will stand in line at an unemployment office rather than go look for a job."
>
> "Conditions Corrupting America," 1976 Falwell sermon

By the time Franklin Roosevelt became president in Depression-era 1933, it was tragically obvious that churches were not able to adequately care for America's elderly poor. Social Security lifted millions of seniors out of poverty, while being called "socialist" by people like Falwell.

Yet the Falwell model has endured, as it's proven to be more convenient than the joyless drudgery of caring about poor people.

- Ronald Reagan often cited the "welfare queen" stereotype, so people would innately understand that safety nets encourage laziness and fraud.
- Former House Speaker Paul Ryan suggested that poor people suffer due to a "culture of poverty" where people are not instilled with a work ethic, a tastefully modern way of messaging "poor people are lazy."
- The first Trump administration proposed cuts to SNAP (food stamps), Medicaid, and other social programs in every one of its budgets, arguing these cuts were necessary to reduce dependency and promote self-sufficiency. In other words, the only way to help the poor is to punish them with greater poverty.
- Then there's the never-ending narrative that poor people—of all colors—are morally deficient. *The Bell Curve,* coauthored by Charles Murray in 1994, tried to link poverty to intelligence and behavior, suggesting moral and intellectual deficiencies among the poor.

The poor-haters never talk about generational poverty, systemic inequality, automation, deindustrialization, historic redlining, educational inequities, union busting, globalization, outsourcing, or inadequate access to resources as reasons why people are mired in poverty. Instead, these Christians push a "makers versus takers" binary to smear those ungodly government aid parasites.

Rev. Barry Lynn, former executive director of Americans United for Separation of Church and State, points out, "The Bible is thoroughly committed to the eradication of poverty. . . . There is a certain convenience to focusing on miracles . . . Raising people from the dead, bringing sight to the blind are powerful stories of inspiration. When one moves into the 'social justice' teachings, things start to get more difficult. In the Gospel of Luke Jesus says that if you have two coats give one away. There is no 'means test' and no question about why the person who gets one of your shirts didn't save enough to buy one at the market himself. This is fundamentally at odds with Religious Right views that people who are poor are somehow responsible for their poverty themselves."

If the USA was truly a "Christian nation," we'd vote to take care of the poor and sick, and let private charity bail out Wall Street.

HOW TO GET AROUND JESUS TO DEMONIZE THE POOR

Jesus warns us, rather constantly, against the dangers of wealth and the pursuit of material possessions (Luke 12:13–21, Matthew 6:19–24). His movement emphasizes community, mutual care, and sharing resources with those in need, also known as "takers." Jesus gave welfare to the poor constantly—free food and healthcare—and never asked for a co-pay. "You have received without payment; give without payment" (Matthew 10:8 ISV).

And you'd think it would be hard for Christians to twist words like these around.

THE CLAIM: "The Bible says if you don't work, you don't eat."

THE SCRIPTURE: 2 Thessalonians 3:10: "For even when we were with you, we gave you this rule: 'The one who is unwilling to work shall not eat.'"

Apparently, the Bible wants us to believe that Jesus sent poor people to bed without their dinner, and sternly told them all to think about what they did.

Ronald Reagan quoted 2 Thessalonians 3:10 during a 1982 radio address, saying, "The Bible teaches that if a man will not work, neither shall he eat" to support welfare cuts.

Former Speakers of the House Newt Gingrich and Paul Ryan have both quoted this one, as have right-wing pastors Robert Jeffress and Franklin Graham, along with deep spiritual leaders Sean Hannity and Rush Limbaugh.

THE DEBUNKING: Once again, our extremists are quoting our old pal Paul. That pattern should be clear by now, no?

In Paul's day, some members of the fledgling Thessalonian church believed that Christ's return was so imminent that they stopped working and became idle; maybe because Paul kept preaching that Jesus was gonna come back real soon, any day now.

Disorderly conduct among a fledgling first-century religious sect ensued. These early rapture-philes were hurting the church's bottom line and threatening a functioning society of Thessalonica. Paul had to straighten out those nutjobs by telling them if they didn't do their jobs to build the church, the church was gonna stop feeding them.

This was not a general command for all Christians, forever. Paul wasn't talking about poor people, and he was not laying down rules for twenty-first-century demagogues to deny care to the suffering. He was telling a story, past tense, about how he handled this end-of-the-world panic in a first-century Roman Empire Christian community.

And again, Paul had no idea his letters would one day be cited by guys who wanted a meaner Jesus.

THE CLAIM: "Yeah, Jesus said we should help the poor—but taxation is theft."

WHAT JESUS SAID: Jesus said to pay your damn taxes.

In Matthew 22:15–22, a small group of Pharisees approach Jesus to ask him about the imperial tax, hoping to trick him into treason. "Tell us then, what is your opinion? Is it right to pay the imperial tax to Caesar or not?"

This question was a political trap. If Jesus said yes, he risked alienating his Jewish followers who resented Roman taxation. If he said no, he risked being accused of sedition against Rome. His response avoids taking sides, while making a profound point about obligations to both earthly authorities and God.

"'You hypocrites, why are you trying to trap me? Show me the coin used for paying the tax.' They brought him a denarius, and he asked them, 'Whose image is this? And whose inscription?' 'Caesar's,' they replied. Then he said to them, 'So give back to Caesar what is Caesar's, and to God what is God's.' When they heard this, they were amazed. So they left him and went away."

By stating, "Give back to Caesar what is Caesar's," Jesus acknowledges earthly governments and their authority to collect taxes. Which confirms that participating in civic duties, such as taxation, is theoretically compatible with Jesus.

Later, in Matthew 25, Mr. Pay Your Taxes also commands individuals and nations to care for the poor and sick.

So if you don't want your tax dollars to help the poor and less fortunate, then maybe stop saying you want a country based on "Christian values."

THE CLAIM: "Yeah, but Jesus said the poor will always be with you."

THE SCRIPTURE: Matthew 26:11: "The poor you will always have with you" (also echoed in Mark 14:7 and John 12:8).

THE VERY IMPORTANT CONTEXT: This line—it's actually only half of a line—is frequently misused to suggest that efforts to address poverty are ultimately futile, so why try so hard?

In this scene, known as the Anointing at Bethany, Jesus is anticipating his arrest and execution when a woman anoints him with expensive perfume. The apostles, particularly Judas, criticize her, arguing that the money could have been used to help the poor.

Jesus responds: "Why are you bothering this woman? She has done a beautiful thing to me. The poor you will always have with you, but you will not always have me."

Jesus acknowledges the kindness as preparation for his imminent death, emphasizing the fleeting moment of his presence with them. This exchange is set to music, quite awesomely, in the song "Everything's Alright" from *Jesus Christ Superstar*.

Jesus isn't dismissing the importance of helping the poor. He's just recognizing the significance of the occasion—the woman's act of devotion as he prepares for his death. His words aren't a dismissal of the fight against poverty, but an acknowledgment of its ongoing nature. He's likely alluding to Deuteronomy 15:11, where God demands consistent help for the poor:

"There will always be poor people in the land. Therefore, I command you to be openhanded toward your fellow Israelites who are poor and needy in your land."

The Deuteronomy passage calls for ongoing *generosity and action* to alleviate poverty, not apathy and resignation. By invoking this scripture, Jesus reinforces the idea that caring for the poor is a perpetual moral duty. He wasn't saying "look away and get used to it"—he was reminding us that the fight against poverty never ends.

For many Christians, it hasn't even started yet.

GOD'S TOTALLY WOKE TAKE ON POVERTY

God repeatedly commands His people to care for the poor, the oppressed, and the marginalized. The Hebrew prophets frequently spoke out against injustice and called for social and economic reforms to address the plight of the poor. Isaiah 1:17 says, "Learn to do right; seek justice. Defend the oppressed. Take up the cause of the fatherless; plead the case of the widow."

Here are a few examples of how God views poverty, long before Jesus, and long before televangelists. These are not, generally, the Old Testament verses your racist cousin likes to quote.

- In Deuteronomy 15:7–11, God demands consistent help for the poor: "If among you, one of your brothers should become poor, in any of your towns within your land that the Lord your God is giving you, you shall not harden your heart or shut your hand against your poor brother, but you shall open your hand to him and lend him sufficient for his need, whatever it may be" (ESV).

- Leviticus 19:9–10: God commands landowners to leave a portion of their harvest for the poor and the foreigner, demonstrating a societal responsibility to care for those in need: "When you reap the harvest of your land, do not reap to the very edges of your field or gather the gleanings of your harvest. Do not go over your vineyard a second time or pick up the grapes that have fallen. Leave them for the poor and the foreigner."
- Then there's Proverbs, which doesn't leave a lot of wiggle room for interpretation:
  - Proverbs 14:31: "Whoever oppresses the poor shows contempt for their Maker, but whoever is kind to the needy honors God."
  - Proverbs 31:8–9: "Speak up for those who cannot speak for themselves, for the rights of all who are destitute. Speak up and judge fairly; defend the rights of the poor and needy."
  - Proverbs 22:22–23 warns, "Do not exploit the poor because they are poor and do not crush the needy in court, for the Lord will take up their case and will exact life for life."
  - Proverbs 19:17: "Whoever is kind to the poor lends to the Lord, and he will reward them for what they have done."

JESUS, AND HIS FAVORITE ISSUE

In every one of Jesus's live appearances, talking about poverty was like his "Layla." His ministry expressed constant solidarity with the poor, the oppressed, and the marginalized.

He does not mention welfare queens or cutting the capital gains tax:

- In the Beatitudes (Matthew 5:3–12), he specifically blesses the poor, the meek, and those who hunger for righteousness, emphasizing God's preference for the struggling.
- In Luke 4:18–19, he declares that he has come to bring good news

to the poor, to proclaim release to the captives, and to let the oppressed go free.

- In Luke 6:20–21, he says, "Blessed are you who are poor, for yours is the kingdom of God. Blessed are you who hunger now, for you will be satisfied."
- In Matthew 6:2–4, Jesus instructs his followers on the proper discreet way to give to the needy, emphasizing humility over public recognition.
- Luke 12:33–34: "Sell your possessions and give to the poor. Provide purses for yourselves that will not wear out, a treasure in heaven that will never fail."
- In the parable of the workers in the vineyard (Matthew 20:1–16), Jesus suggests that all workers deserve a fair wage, regardless of the hours worked, prioritizing economic justice and equity.

Jesus also knows it's not cool for respectable members of society to be seen with the poor and homeless, so he commands you to invite them over. In Luke 14:12–14, JC says to the host who'd invited him, "When you give a luncheon or dinner, do not invite your friends, your brothers or sisters, your relatives, or your rich neighbors; if you do, they may invite you back and so you will be repaid. But when you give a banquet, invite the poor, the crippled, the lame, the blind, and you will be blessed. Although they cannot repay you, you will be repaid at the resurrection of the righteous."

And Jesus prefers the poor, as well. In Mark 12:41–44, he sits down opposite the treasury, a specific area in the Second Temple in Jerusalem, where people would deposit their monetary offerings to support the temple and its services. Several rich people put in large sums, but a poor widow appeared and put in two small copper coins, worth about a penny. Jesus calls his disciples and says "Truly I tell you, this poor widow has put more into the treasury than all the others. They all gave out of their wealth; but she, out of her poverty, put in everything—all she had to live on."

He's not so impressed by a flat tax, or by easy philanthropy that never feels a pinch.

ABOUT THAT TEMPLE FREAKOUT

> "Indebtedness was a cruel reality in the Ancient Near East that kept people in poverty. Debt jubilee is found in the Torah in Leviticus 25:1–55 and in Deuteronomy 15:1–2, which certainly influenced Jesus's teachings. The latter says that debt is to be forgiven every seventh year."
>
> Dillon Naber Cruz

Jesus driving the money changers from the temple in Jerusalem is one of the most dramatic and symbolic actions in the Gospels. The cleansing of the temple is described in all four Gospels (Matthew 21:12–13; Mark 11:15–18; Luke 19:45–46; John 2:13–16). It's usually a dramatic high point in every Jesus movie.

We've seen how Jesus challenged many of the old laws, but there's one practice clearly forbidden by both the OT and Jesus, and that's usury, lending money at very high interest rates to gouge the poor. Because some ancient traditions never go out of style.

The Bible is clearly opposed to people who take advantage of the poor or needy—and on many occasions expressly forbids us to lend money on interest.

- Exodus 22:25: "If you lend money to one of my people among you who is needy, do not treat it like a business deal; charge no interest."
- Leviticus 25:35–37: "If any of your fellow Israelites become poor and are unable to support themselves among you, help them as you would a foreigner and stranger, so they can continue to live among you. Do not take interest or any profit from them, but fear your God, so that they may continue to live among you. You must not lend them money at interest or sell them food at a profit."
- Deuteronomy 23:19–20: "Do not charge a fellow Israelite interest, whether on money or food or anything else that may earn interest."

Jesus keeps this rally going, rejecting the exploitative nature of charging interest on the poor, as that can make it impossible to climb out of poverty.

- Luke 6:34–35: "And if you lend to those from whom you expect repayment, what credit is that to you? Even sinners lend to sinners, expecting to be repaid in full. But love your enemies, do good to them, and lend to them without expecting to get anything back."

The cleansing occurs on Holy Monday, after Jesus arrives in Jerusalem on Palm Sunday. Jews would come from all different regions to observe Passover, and they'd all bring their various different currencies. They'd need to convert their currency to the special temple currency so they could pay the temple tax and purchase sacrificial animals. Y'know, like we all used to do with Grandma, at the holidays.

The money changers were the guys who'd exchange foreign monies for the temple currency. They generally exploited the pilgrims by charging exorbitant exchange rates and fees, which nowadays we call random surge pricing. This price gouging was especially hard on the poor, and Jesus was rightfully angered that a house of worship had been turned into a profit center.

- John 2:14–16: "In the temple courts he found people selling cattle, sheep, and doves, and others sitting at tables exchanging money. So he made a whip out of cords, and drove all from the temple courts, both sheep and cattle; he scattered the coins of the money changers and overturned their tables. To those who sold doves he said, 'Get these out of here! Stop turning my Father's house into a market!'"
- In Matthew 21:13, he quotes Isaiah 56:7 and Jeremiah 7:11, saying, "It is written, 'My house will be called a house of prayer,' but you are making it 'a den of robbers.'"

Jesus drove the profiteers out of the temple, in full view of religious authorities and the occupying Romans, who enjoyed crucifying Jews for less. It was an incredibly symbolic act of authority—from a guy who *officially* didn't have any.

Three nights later, the story tells us, he was arrested.

RAGING SOCIALIST JESUS AND THE OG HOLY LAND CREW

Back when Bernie Sanders was running for president, people across the political spectrum expressed doubts that Americans would ever vote for a socialist Jew. I'd like to remind those people that we celebrate the *birthday* of a socialist Jew every December 25. We even take the day off.

Many clergy, academics, and theologians argue that the Gospel teachings of Jesus Christ share more in common with socialist principles than with capitalist ones. There's absolutely no reason to believe this, beyond the fact that it's correct.

Jesus's ministry focuses on communal support for the marginalized and calling out the rich. I know, we've all shared a long car drive at some point with some undergrad guy who's exactly like this.

But this is not the soft caricature so many try to dismiss as Hippie Jesus. The Gospels present him as a revolutionary, who challenged the status quo and advocated for the liberation of the oppressed.

Now, I'm not going to push that argument too hard, as I don't wish to get any family members excommunicated. But critique of economic injustice and exploitation, concern for the oppressed and marginalized, solidarity with the poor—all these calls for justice and social transformation are concepts that predate our modern economic dodgeball teams.

Jesus calls out the spiritual failing of materialism, as in the story of the rich fool (Luke 12:16–21) and with his warning that one cannot serve both God and money (Matthew 6:24). In Luke 6:24, he says, "But woe to you who are rich, for you have already received your comfort." His critique of wealth accumulation and focus on fair distribution of resources is just a bit more in line with socialist ideologies than some of my comedian friends working over at the Fox Business channel.

By this time, the fundamentalist who's still reading this for the purpose of a scathing review on Amazon is likely hissing about socialism in a full-throated Ayn Randian snit. But you tell me what's more in the spirit of Christ—"From each according to his ability, to each according to his needs" or "Greed is good"?

Jesus was a nonprofit prophet, but was he really a socialist? The short answer's no, because socialism didn't exist yet. But let's point out:

- He never owned property.
- He said, "It's easier for a camel to pass through the eye of a needle than for a rich man to enter the kingdom of heaven."
- He told people to pay their taxes.
- He never healed the blind and then billed them.
- He never gave anyone a mandatory drug test before dispensing some loaves and fishes.

I'll never say Jesus was a socialist. But I will say if he were alive now and preaching the exact same message, right-wing Christians would call him one.

Capital worshippers will be dismayed to know Jesus's early followers were not free market devotees of privatization and wealth accumulation.

Wait until your commie-hating fundamentalists get a load of this passage from Acts of the Apostles: "All who believed were together and held everything in common, and they began selling their property and possessions and distributing the proceeds to everyone, as anyone had need" (Acts 2:44–45 NET).

This sinister theme is reiterated in Acts of the Apostles 4:32–35: "Now the multitude of those who believed were of one heart and one soul; neither did anyone say that any of the things he possessed was his own, but they had all things in common . . . Nor was there anyone among them who lacked; for all who were possessors of lands or houses sold them, and brought the proceeds of the things that were sold, and laid them at the apostles' feet; and they distributed to each as anyone had need"(NKJV).

So the first believers "had all things in common" and sold their possessions to distribute to those in need—an early Christian model of resource distribution, shared ownership, and community support. It should be noted that this sinister communal living was a voluntary system, and there was no requirement to participate. Everyone took care of each other, so no one was left wanting.

And you thought *Judas* was evil.

Later comes the Epistle of James, attributed to the brother of Jesus. James powerfully addresses poverty, wealth, and social justice; condemns the exploitation of the poor and favoritism of the rich; and clearly seems to share some DNA with his more divine brother.

James 1:27: "Religion that God our Father accepts as pure and faultless is this: to look after orphans and widows in their distress and to keep oneself from being polluted by the world."

James 2:2–4: "Suppose a man comes into your meeting wearing a gold ring and fine clothes, and a poor man in filthy old clothes also comes in. If you show special attention to the man wearing fine clothes and say, 'Here's a good seat for you,' but say to the poor man, 'You stand there' or 'Sit on the floor by my feet,' have you not discriminated among yourselves and become judges with evil thoughts?"

Something, Something, Camel, Needle

In Matthew 19:23–24 Jesus uses a striking metaphor to illustrate the difficulty of entering the kingdom of God for those who are preoccupied with wealth.

THE SCRIPTURE: "Truly I tell you; it is hard for someone who is rich to enter the kingdom of heaven. Again, I tell you, it is easier for a camel to go through the eye of a needle than for someone who is rich to enter the kingdom of God."

THE CLAIM: A somewhat popular argument attempts to reinterpret Jesus's very direct message by asserting that there was a smallish gate in Jerusalem known as the "Eye of the Needle," which was *so narrow* that camels had to be unloaded and kneel just to pass through. So hey—it could be tricky, but it could be done! Proponents argue that Jesus was metaphorically using this gate to illustrate the difficulty, but not *impossibility*, of the rich entering heaven.

There are, alas, two problems with this theory. First, there's no historical evidence of such a gate ever existing in Jerusalem during Jesus's time. Second, this claim undermines the rest of Jesus's teachings by arguing that Jesus was just really sloppy at metaphors.

I mean, in Luke 12:15, Jesus says, "Watch out! Be on your guard against all kinds of greed; life does not consist in an abundance of possessions." The camel-and-needle metaphor is consistent with these broader teachings on wealth and spirituality.

As Jesus said in Luke 6:24–25, "Woe to you who are rich, for you have already received your comfort. Woe to you who are well fed now, for you will go hungry. Woe to you who laugh now, for you will mourn and weep."

Does he sound ambiguous to you?

PRAYER AGAINST CARE

After Theodore Roosevelt quit the Republican Party, he ran for president in 1912 as a progressive reformer advocating universal healthcare. Ninety-eight years later—in spite of the furious efforts of TR's former party—the Democrats passed a healthcare bill called the Patient Protection and Affordable Care Act, also known as "Obamacare."

I was never a fan of the name; I always thought if we're going to call the ACA "Obamacare," then it's only right to call Social Security "FDR-care," Medicare "LBJ-care," and trying to defund all three "Trump-care."

At a time when forty-five thousand Americans were dying each year due to lack of health insurance coverage, the number-one cause of bankruptcy in the US was inability to pay medical costs. In 2000 the World Health Organization had ranked America number thirty-seven out of 191 countries in the world in terms of health system performance. And while the ACA brought improvements, it wasn't a "reform" of our healthcare system.

Obamacare had no universal coverage, nor a public option allowing Medicare for whoever needed it. Uninsured Americans would still be required to purchase the same private insurance plans Democrats had previously railed against. Liberals who'd wanted single-payer healthcare, the same "socialist" coverage enjoyed by 100 percent of our capitalist allies, were dismayed when it passed, arguing that the act was more watered down than a keg of O'Doul's.

But if you think the lefties were upset, you cannot imagine the rage of fundamentalists when they discovered that poor and struggling Americans might get some help with health insurance. The Christian right immediately launched a yearslong assault against the ACA.

The Christian Coalition opposed the ACA on economic grounds, arguing that it would lead to higher taxes and increased government spending. Christian nationalist congresswoman Michelle Bachman, in a 2013 WorldNetDaily interview, said "I think the reason is because President Obama can't wait to get Americans addicted to the crack cocaine of dependency on more government healthcare." Subtle, I know.

Congressmembers assailed the ACA as socialism, because there's nothing funnier than senators with socialized healthcare warning the rest of us about the evils of socialized healthcare.

But Obamacare was the opposite of socialism—it forced people to buy private, for-profit plans. The status quo that the right-wing folks were defending—making local taxpayers foot the bill when uninsured folks show up in emergency rooms—now, that sounds like socialism.

And the conservative Christians of America should've been leading the charge. Because reform—including universal healthcare—that saves American lives represents the core values they claim to believe in.

The ACA wasn't a cure; it was harm reduction. It didn't solve America's healthcare problems. But it was a start.

Within ten years of passage, thirty-nine states and the District of Columbia had adopted new Medicaid expansion, providing more coverage to millions of low-income Americans. A 2019 study published in *Health Affairs* estimated that the ACA's Medicaid expansion alone saved an estimated 19,200 lives over four years (2014–2017).

The US uninsured rate dropped from 16 percent in 2010 to 8.6 percent in 2020. Insurance companies were prohibited from denying coverage or charging higher premiums to individuals with preexisting conditions, crucial for many Americans with chronic illnesses.

Which you'd think would be impressive to "pro-life" people.

THE CLAIM: "Sure, Jesus told us to help the sick, but he never said the government should force us to do it."

THE REALITY: This spiritually flimsy comeback has become a moral loophole to help some believers sleep at night while their uninsured neighbors suffer. The Jesus our right-wing friends claim to follow dispensed healthcare freely and never seeks to profit from it.

In Matthew 10:8, he commands his followers to cure the sick.

In Matthew 25:36, he teaches that caring for the sick is akin to caring for him.

In Luke 4:40, he heals more people than can be counted.

And don't forget that the Good Samaritan paid a stranger's medical bills, out of pocket.

Christ followers have an inherent obligation to help the sick and suffering. That's why, once upon a time, the church built so many hospitals—to follow Jesus's marching orders.

Jesus never experienced democracy like America, where we the people are the government. We hire the leaders, for better or worse. Our morality and values dictate our choice of elected policymakers. So if Christians believe in following the actual teachings of Christ, why not vote for those who'll care for the least of us, since it's literally what he commanded?

Why not have a society like France, Germany, the UK, Sweden, Japan, South Korea, Australia, New Zealand, Canada, Brazil, and Israel all enjoy, where citizens pay for healthcare at tax time, and neighbors aren't sentenced to death or bankruptcy for lack of coverage.

Proverbs 31:8–9: The Bible calls on believers to "speak up for those who cannot speak for themselves, for the rights of all who are destitute." Ensuring access to healthcare for all, regardless of financial status, is the biblical point of view.

Matthew 9:35: "Jesus went through all the towns and villages, teaching in their synagogues, proclaiming the good news of the kingdom and healing every disease and sickness."

Access to healthcare for all is consistent with Jesus's entire operation, and Medicaid is exactly the kind of community social action that he'd be proud of. Fans of Jesus should applaud the fact that our country has such a system, that covers over ninety million of us.

Author and theologian Dillon Naber Cruz, a military vet known online as "the Tattooed Theologian," suggests we "Imagine the positive benefits of applying the Golden Rule (Matthew 7:12; Luke 6:31) to healthcare in America. No one would choose to have life-altering medical situations lead to being crippled by debt. No one would willfully choose to skip treatment or to not buy medication because it is too expensive. Applying the Matthean Golden Rule caveat 'in everything you do' to healthcare would mean that we enact a robust universal healthcare system in which no person is left to the malicious whims of healthcare profiteers whose money is made from human suffering. Jesus wanted to alleviate suffering and would definitely be against his ostensible followers profiting from it."

And if you're still against universal healthcare because of your devotion to Almighty Capitalism, please remember what COVID-19 taught us—providing coverage to as many as possible amid a deadly airborne pandemic is better for all American businesses. A strong economy requires a healthy labor force.

Decades of research from organizations like Blue Cross Blue Shield, the American Medical Association, and the Harvard T.H. Chan School of Public Health bear this out. Keeping citizens from serious illness, permanent disability, or being unable to work at full capacity is crucial to America's economic well-being. Even if you don't care about poor people, think of the poor money.

As Pastor John Pavlovitz told me, "Throughout the Gospels, we see Jesus healing a disparate collection of those he came into contact with: a bleeding woman, a despised leper, a man born blind. The commonality was the need. The only shared prerequisite was pain. There was no inventory of dating history, voting record, or religious affiliation, no moral screening done to decide who was worthy to be healed. Their suffering and Jesus's compassion made them worthy.

"If we want to perpetuate the life and teachings of Christ, we need to create a system that allows every sick and injured human being to have unimpeded access to care; that there are no spiritual litmus tests that would include or disqualify them."

TRICKLE-DOWN VS. SOCIAL SAFETY NET, WITH JESUS AS REF

In this corner, Social Security, providing financial support to retirees, disabled individuals, and survivors, ensuring a basic level of income for those who can no longer work or who have lost a family breadwinner. Also, Medicare, offering health insurance to Americans sixty-five and older, as well as to younger individuals with disabilities, ensuring that they have access to necessary care.

And in this corner, trickle-down economics, also known as supply-side Reaganomics, with a record of forty years of promises that benefits for the super-rich will eventually, any day now, trickle down to the rest of society.

Your referee, Jesus of Nazareth, with three years' experience preaching compassion, care for the vulnerable, and off-putting talk of social justice.

Round 1—Direct Support vs. Indirect Benefits

In Matthew 25:35–36, Jesus commends those who provide direct assistance to those in need: "For I was hungry, and you gave me something to eat, I was thirsty and you gave me something to drink, I was a stranger and you invited me in, I needed clothes and you clothed me, I was sick and you looked after me."

- Social Security and Medicare provide *direct*, tangible support to those in need, aligning with Jesus's teachings about caring for the poor and vulnerable.
- Trickle-down economics relies on *indirect benefits* that go to the wealthiest first, and they'll enjoy that, and eventually they may buy enough things to juice the economy and help those in need, someday.

VERDICT: LBJ/FDR. Providing food, clothing, shelter, and care is a more direct way to meet the needs of the poor and marginalized than waiting for millionaires to passively stimulate local economies.

Round 2—Personal Responsibility to the Poor vs. Systemic Reliance on Wealth

- Jesus places the responsibility directly on both individuals *and society* to care for the needy in Matthew 25. Each person's actions or indifference toward the "least of these" are, for Jesus, a direct measure of their righteousness.
- Trickle-down economics relies on a system where the ever-increasing wealth of the rich is believed to benevolently benefit everyone else. This systemic reliance does nothing to directly help the poor; but does help believers dodge any sense of personal accountability over it, which can be priceless.

VERDICT: "Safety net" over "Meh, it'll all work out."

Round 3—Collective Responsibility

As Jesus says in Matthew 25, "Truly, I say to you, as you did it to one of the least of these my brothers, you did it to me." Social Security and Medicare embody a real societal commitment to ensuring that everyone, especially the most vulnerable, has access to basic necessities.

And trickle-down economics celebrates individual wealth creation, because who needs to get all depressed thinking about the dregs, am I right?

VERDICT: Matthew 25:41–43: "Then he will say to those on his left, 'Depart from me, you who are cursed, into the eternal fire prepared for the devil and his angels. For I was hungry, and you gave me nothing to eat, I was thirsty, and you gave me nothing to drink."

For those who believe the Bible, this is Jesus condemning the individuals and nations who fail to help the needy. And he's not impressed by how much they hated socialists.

Thoughts and Prayers

Jesus tells his followers to feed the hungry and care for the sick—not to pray that someone else will do it.

Offering "thoughts and prayers" for the poor is typically done by politicians who don't think and don't pray. It's a convenient substitute for tangible help or systemic solutions. Prayer is supposed to be a way to seek guidance, not an excuse for inaction.

Jesus's brother nails why faith without works doesn't work in James 2:15–17: "Suppose a brother or sister is without clothes and daily food. If one of you says to them, 'Go in peace; keep warm and well fed,' but does nothing about their physical needs, what good is it? In the same way, faith by itself, if it is not accompanied by action, is dead."

1 John 3:17–18 calls for financially helping those in need as a demonstration of God's love. "If anyone has material possessions and sees a brother or sister in need but has no pity on them, how can the love of God be in that person? Dear children, let us not love with words or speech but with actions and in truth."

That's the Bible endorsing direct relief for the needy, and opposing "thoughts and prayers."

LIBERATION THEOLOGY VS. PROSPERITY GOSPEL

> "For many Christians, the real problem is not a compassion problem but a proximity problem. We have moved away from the places Jesus moved into. We've moved away from the pain and the suffering of the world."
>
> Shane Claiborne

Liberation theology argues that the church should actively work to alleviate poverty and oppression, and calls for structural changes to address systemic injustices and inequalities. It sees faith as a thing you *do.*

Many Christians consider liberation theology to be truest to the teachings of Jesus, because it uncomfortably places the needs and rights of the poor and oppressed at the center of its theology, much like, I don't know, the whole Bible.

LT advocates for a faith that's active and engaged in the world. It encourages Christians to get their hands dirty, take tangible steps to fight injustice, and directly aid those in need.

It is not, however, a philosophy that'll help you cash in with any decent for-profit megachurch.

Meanwhile . . .

THE CLAIM: The prosperity gospel, aka the "health and wealth gospel," is a religious belief among some Christians that material wealth and success—and continuing good health—are God's will to reward them for being so wonderful and awesome.

Popularized by Pastor Joel Osteen of the Lakewood megachurch in Houston, the prosperity gospel asserts that faith, positive speech, and donations to religious causes will increase your material wealth and success. It preaches that wealth and health are true signs that God likes you and tends to associate generous donations with divine returns. Followers are encouraged to give generously, often to the ministries of prosperity preachers, with smiling promises that God will return their gifts, multiplied.

THE SCRIPTURE: These verses are often cited to suggest that wealth is a sign that God's a fan of you.

Deuteronomy 8:18 (God gives wealth): "But remember the Lord your God, for it is he who gives you the ability to produce wealth."

Proverbs 10:22 (the blessing of wealth): "The blessing of the Lord brings wealth, without painful toil for it."

THE REBUTTAL: It's all awfully cute. It's also the opposite of pretty much everything taught in the New Testament. Nowhere does Jesus ever promise wealth to anyone, for any reason. Jesus taught humility, self-denial, and service to others, often warning against the dangers of wealth and materialism:

Matthew 6:19–21: "Do not store up for yourselves treasures on earth. . . . But store up for yourselves treasures in heaven. . . . For where your treasure is, there your heart will be also."

Jesus is *very* specific that his movement is about what you *do*, not what you get. And yes, according to the Bible, God's blessings can include material provision. But Jesus emphasizes a life of sacrifice, announcing that following him would involve more hardship than material comfort:

Luke 9:23: "Whoever wants to be my disciple must deny themselves and take up their cross daily and follow me."

John 16:33: "In this world you will have trouble. But take heart! I have overcome the world."

Hey, Paul, while we're on the subject, do you want to weigh in?

1 Timothy 6:9–10: "Those who want to get rich fall into temptation and a trap and into many foolish and harmful desires that plunge people into ruin and destruction. For the love of money is a root of all kinds of evil."

Thanks, Paul. You don't get enough credit for that line.

Of course, this kind of "God wants *you* to be rich—call now!" ministry is nothing new. And Joel Osteen is not a bigoted fundamentalist demagogue; his ministry isn't constantly attacking the marginalized. I must also say the prosperity gospel is not Christian nationalism, and it's not about hate.

But the prosperity gospel is dangerous, victim-blaming junk theology that has nothing to do with Jesus's teachings on humility and service over wealth and comfort. If you're going to preach that material riches are proof of faithfulness and righteousness, then you're also messaging that failure and hard times are signs of personal sin or spiritual inadequacy. It's the same old ugly idea Falwell pushed—that your poverty is your fault because of some moral deficiency—but it's all dressed up with a smile and quality hair products.

Prosperity-gospel thinking is designed to avoid tackling the root causes of poverty and inequality. I know—"understanding institutionalized poverty" and "social reproduction of marginalized classes" aren't great for filling up the megachurch baskets.

What the Bible Really Thinks of Rich People

It's not great.

- Proverbs 23:4: "Do not wear yourself out to get rich; do not trust your own cleverness."
- Ecclesiastes 5:10: "Whoever loves money never has enough; whoever loves wealth is never satisfied with their income. This too is meaningless."
- James, brother of Jesus, 5:1–6: "Now listen, you rich people, weep and wail because of the misery that is coming on you. . . . You have hoarded wealth in the last days. Look! The wages you failed to pay the workers who mowed your fields are crying out against you. The cries of the harvesters have reached the ears of the Lord Almighty. You have lived on earth in luxury and self-indulgence. You have fattened yourselves in the day of slaughter. You have condemned and murdered the innocent one, who was not opposing you."

Let's post *this* verse on public school walls.

THOU SHALT LET GO OF THY SEX HANG-UPS

"But among you there must not be even a hint of sexual immorality, or of any kind of impurity, or of greed, because these are improper for God's holy people."

St. Paul, Ephesians 5:3

"Human sexuality is a divine gift, forming part of the complex union of body, mind and spirit which is our humanity."

Quaker Faith and Practice 22.11

THE AWKWARD, UNFORTUNATE TALE OF ONAN

One of my favorite Bible stories appears in Genesis 38, about a guy named Onan. And whether you've heard of him or not, I can guarantee that his story has, at some point, touched you. He's inadventently one of the most influential characters in the whole Bible.

Back in the day, old Judah had two grown sons—Onan and his older brother, Er. And Er was an evil man, "wicked in the eyes of the Lord," possibly with unresolved anger over being named Er. But God doesn't like him.

So, one day, God smites Er. That's how God solves His problems; it's how we know He's a man.

Old Judah runs to Er's younger brother saying "Onan, your brother never had a child. God wants you to go in unto thy brother's wife and raise up offspring to continue his bloodline. You gotta follow our laws, kid. The tent's over there, impregnate her; that she might bear an heir for Er."

It's possible I'm paraphrasing a bit.

Needless to say, Er's widow had no say in any of this. (This was Tamar, celebrated in chapter 5.) Now we don't know how Onan went about setting the mood—candles, incense; these guys don't seem to have been terribly big on seduction. But we do know that Onan had reservations about impregnating his recently dead brother's widow. It does sound like a primitive white-trash sitcom—*My Name is Er*.

But you gotta do what the Lord and the law command, right?

So Onan performs his tribal duty, aka the Lord's work. But realizing that these wouldn't even be his kids—and it can't be fun for the widow—Onan creates the rhythm method as we know it and spills his seed on the ground. This infuriates the Lord—who, I guess, likes to watch—and God smites Onan. The End.

It's a classic, although you might not have heard it as a child. I've yet to see a Claymation Onan film for the kids.

But it got the point across. The sin of Onan was *obviously* that he spilled his seed. He failed to make a baby.

And so this charming anecdote became one of the original reasons behind the church's beliefs that:

1. Any non-procreative sex was a sin.
2. Hence, all birth control is a sin (even if you're poor).
3. Hence, same-sex relationships are sin.
4. Hence masturbation is a sin, against the will of God.

In fact—to this day, the clinical term for touching yourself? Onanism. Which the poor guy didn't even do. Imagine not wanting to impregnate your dead brother's wife, having God kill you for it, then having that particular activity nicknamed after you?

Imagine the confusion of millions of teenagers if they ever found out we got "masturbation is a sin" from *this* story. Adam and Eve in the garden was the origin of guilt, but Onan might just be the origin of shame.

And even if you're the kind of person who believes every word of the Bible is absolute, literal fact, you must agree we're looking at thousands of years of useless shame, confusion, and guilt because somebody got the story wrong. When you actually read the context, it's clear that Onan's sin wasn't spilling his seed—it was disobeying a direct order from the commander in chief.

But that didn't stop the shame from flowing. The Catholic Church long loved this story. Puritans have lived by it. This crucial misinterpretation of an ancient tale proves that most personal sexual shame doesn't come from God, and it doesn't come from you.

It originates from the hang-ups of dead guys.

The Bible is not against birth control, it doesn't ban masturbation, and Jesus never technically comes out against premarital sex. Yet generations of men and women have been programmed with shame for the filthy, unholy passions God designed for them.

Traditionally, the church hasn't exactly encouraged open dialogue about sexuality, leading to widespread ignorance, endless guilt, an expensive lack of comprehensive sex education, and way too many people making unhealthy choices due to unprocessed traumas or suppressed emotions.

For centuries, shame-based Christianity taught that all sexual urges were evil and dirty, and that God obviously hardwired humans to enjoy the mating process this much because He's quite appalled by the mating process He created.

This chapter will explore how the church developed some serious sexual hang-ups, and how none of them came from Jesus.

THY DIRTY PARTS

> "Sex is all about how we relate to God and to each other. Yet, sexuality also reveals our longing for connection with God and other humans."
>
> Richard Rohr, Franciscan priest and author, 2018

The conservative Christian ideal of sexuality—existing exclusively between one man and one woman, within one heterosexual marriage—is a lovely and iconic concept. It's also not for everybody, nor realistic for everybody. And the guilt that can come from not conforming to this ideal has made many people miserable across many generations.

Entire movements within Christianity have used the Bible to shame premarital sex, emphasizing virginity as the primary marker of moral worth, especially for women.

> Genesis 3:6–7 (the Fall of Adam and Eve): "Then the eyes of both of them were opened, and they realized they were naked; so they sewed fig leaves together and made coverings for themselves."

Right off the bat, nakedness is associated with sin and shame, fostering a perception of sexuality as inherently corrupt. We should always remember that body shame belongs in the media, not the church.

The Bible often portrays sexual desire as a red screaming hazard light of temptation and sin. Levitical law featured many purity code regulations related to sexual activity, including incest, bestiality, adultery, and relations with those fearsome menstruating women.

Deuteronomy 22:20–21 discusses the consequences for a woman who's found to not be a virgin on her wedding night: "If, however, the charge is true and no proof of the young woman's virginity can be found, she shall be brought to the door of her father's house and there the men of her town shall stone her to death. She has done an outrageous thing in Israel by being promiscuous while still in her father's house. You must purge the evil from among you."

The violent penalty for the man who took said virginity goes unmentioned.

St. Augustine (354–430 AD) really helped set the tone in shaping Western Christian attitudes toward sexuality, like his book *On Marriage and Concupisence*: "It is, however, one thing for married persons to have intercourse only for the wish to beget children, which is not sinful: it is another thing for them to desire carnal pleasure in cohabitation, but with the spouse only, which involves venial sin."

Augustine associated original sin with sexual desire, even though the Bible doesn't. But Augustine suggested that sexual desire only existed because of the disordered state of humanity after the Fall. We weren't bad because of desire; we had desire because we were bad. Augustine taught that sex was inherently linked to sinfulness, so it was only to exist for procreation within marriage. And even then, it was still sin.

Got that? God wants you to feel very bad for the biological impulses He hath imposed on thee.

Early Christian monastic movements, such as those led by St. Anthony the Great and St. Benedict, also emphasized celibacy and asceticism. Monks and nuns often took vows of chastity, seeing sexual activity as a distraction from spiritual devotion. But this association between holiness and abstinence cemented the broader Christian cultural attitude that viewed sex as something nasty and wrong, and only enjoyed by very bad, albeit relaxed and markedly happier, people.

Of course, one could also argue that God should've provided a more mundane means of reproduction. But the church has used the fear of eternal damnation for centuries to regulate behavior, including sexual conduct. Teaching that sexual sins lead to divine punishment can instill deep fear and shame in any believers, or populations, you might want to control.

EVERYTHING JESUS EVER SAID ABOUT PREMARITAL SEX, BIRTH CONTROL, GAY SEX, ANY FORM OF SODOMY, AND/OR MASTURBATION

"Do not judge, or you too will be judged. For in the same way you judge others, you will be judged, and with the measure you use, it will be measured to you."

Matthew 7:1–2

PREMARITAL SEX

> "Sexuality and shame have been used since the very beginning of Christianity by men who were terrified that women so readily responded to Jesus' message of full equality and freedom."
>
> Diana Butler Bass, author of *A People's History of Christianity*

Both testaments famously emphasize sexual purity and prohibit sex outside of marriage. Adultery is condemned in the Ten Commandments (Exodus 20:14) and fornication is frequently denounced by St. Paul (e.g., 1 Corinthians 6:18–20). Which has fostered centuries of shaming sex before marriage, as well.

And I don't really need to say this, but the shame of sex before marriage is generally concentrated on one gender just a bit more than another.

Jesus doesn't talk much about sex before marriage, as it wasn't a major issue. Nor was it an option. First-century Jews got married shortly after puberty, around thirteen or fourteen for girls like the Virgin Mary.

Sex *outside* of marriage, of course, is consistently condemned. And being married off by your parents as a child, often to a stranger, isn't always as fun or sexy as it sounds. It was actually a recipe for deeply unhappy marriages, historically not great for fidelity.

The Bible does, however, have plenty of polygamy and concubinage, especially for patriarchs and kings.

Abraham had two wives, Sarah and Hagar, and later had children with Keturah in Genesis 16:1–4; 25:1–2.

Jacob married Leah and Rachel AND had kids with their maidservants, Bilhah and Zilpah, in Genesis 29:15–30; 30:1–13.

David had lots of wives, including Michal, Abigail, and Bathsheba, in 2 Samuel 5:13 and 1 Samuel 25:42–43.

And Solomon, with seven hundred wives and three hundred concubines in 1 Kings 11:3, appears to be directly competing with Zeus.

Deuteronomy 21:15–17 goes into detail on the inheritance rights of a man's children from different wives, which proves that polygamy was recognized and regulated under the laws of Moses. Which means plural marriages are a form of "traditional biblical marriage." Shout-out to all you old-school polyamorous Christian folk.

Concubines were women who had a recognized relationship with a man but didn't have the same status or rights as a wife. They provided men a means of having extra offspring, and this particular "sex outside of marriage" was totally allowed and regulated in Exodus 21:7–11.

The New Testament, however, promotes monogamy as the only alternative to celibacy, as in 1 Timothy 3:2, influencing centuries of belief that monogamous relationships, that last for life, are the only relationships with value.

And while Jesus doesn't endorse a lot of sexual activity, he does talk about humility and self-awareness, not casting the first stone, and removing the plank from one's own eye before addressing the speck in another's (Matthew 7:3–5). He's never even slightly judgmental when it comes to sexuality, something for libertines and prudes to keep in mind.

BEATING THE BISHOP

> "As far as the east is from the west, so far has He removed our transgressions from us."
>
> Psalm 103:12

To reiterate, the Onan story isn't about masturbation, even though his name became synonymous with it. But Christians have long been taught that masturbation is contrary to the principles of sexual purity, self-control, and the sanctity of the body. Sexual activity should be reserved for marriage, we are told, and any sexual expression outside of heterosexual marriage—even on one's own, in private—is drenched in sin.

The Catholic Church officially teaches that masturbation is morally wrong, viewing it as a violation of chastity and an improper use of sexuality. Some evangelical groups view masturbation as sinful due to its inherent connection with "lustful thoughts," which I suppose are a prerequisite for masturbation.

And when have Catholic or evangelical leaders ever gone wrong when it comes to sex?

Early Christian writers like Augustine and Thomas Aquinas viewed masturbation as sinful, as sexuality exists only for procreation within marriage. These men, being unmarried celibates, could never have understood how many marriages might one day be saved by masturbation.

And not all Christians believe that masturbation is inherently sinful. Views among Protestant denominations vary, with many seeing it as a matter of personal conscience, self-awareness, and healthy sexual expression, just don't do it at the bus stop.

Perhaps self-pleasure really does enrage the God who gifted humans with arms just long enough. But it's still never specifically forbidden in the Bible.

BIRTH CONTROL

> "Unlike plagues of the dark ages or contemporary diseases we do not yet understand, the modern plague of overpopulation is soluble by means we have discovered and with resources we possess. What is lacking is not sufficient knowledge of the solution but universal consciousness of the gravity of the problem and education of the billions who are its victims."
>
> Rev. Dr. Martin Luther King Jr., from May 5, 1966, speech delivered by Coretta Scott King, accepting an award on his behalf from the Planned Parenthood Federation

Years ago I helped pay my way through college by working at a terrific Catholic residential home for developmentally delayed youth. During the summer, I was a camp counselor; during the school year I'd work overnight shifts in the boys' wing on my weekends. One of the highest priorities of overnight staff, understandably, was making sure that none of the boys ever made it out of the boys' wing over to the girls' wing during the late hours—and vice versa. Parents had entrusted their children to our care, and the implications of what could happen if any of us fell asleep on the job were tremendous for the families, and the liability of the church.

That sort of thing never happened that I know of, but during one long night, the on-duty nurse confided to me that the teenage girls who lived in the residence—all of them—were on birth control, "just in case." And this was a church-run facility.

I admit, it took me a few minutes to understand what I was being told.

The Catholic Church officially opposes artificial contraception based on natural law theory and the idea that each sexual act should be open to the possibility of procreation. The Vatican's always been famously anti–birth control, with pope after pope traveling the world and commanding impoverished believers to avoid family planning. Can't be devout unless you're pumping 'em out.

That the church would quietly prescribe birth control pills to every underage girl in the facility—to avoid potential embarrassment and cover itself legally—was a revelation to me. I've had relatives with very large families because this same church told their parents and grandparents that contraception was a sin.

Of course, if the pope is against birth control because the Bible commands us to "be fruitful and multiply," then why is the pope celibate?

The Catholic Church's celibacy rule didn't actually go into effect until 1138 AD. The first pope, St. Peter, was married, as were priests and popes for over a thousand years. Which means, technically, married priests are the conservative point of view.

Pope Innocent II put the sex ban in place because the church didn't want priests leaving land and wealth to their widows and kids. That's right—priests are celibate not because sex is bad, or because Jesus was a bachelor, but because the church was greedy. Way before *The Da Vinci Code.*

Contraception Is Christian

"I do not think it is correct to argue that birth control is sinful. It is a serious mistake to suppose that it is a religious act to allow nature to have its way in the sex life."

Dr. Martin Luther King Jr., *Advice for Living*, 1957

"Birth control is a matter of Christian liberty. Christians who thoughtfully and wisely practice birth control are being faithful to Christ.

Pastor Tom Hicks, "Is Birth Control Biblical?"

"Evangelical couples may, at times, choose to use contraceptives in order to plan their families and enjoy the pleasures of the marital bed."

Dr. R. Albert Mohler Jr., President of the Southern Baptist Theological Seminary, "Can Christians Use Birth Control?"

PRO-BIRTH CONTROL, PRO-FAMILY

Ladies, conservative men have decided your birth control isn't medicine—which it is—because the Bible's against birth control—which it's not.

The Affordable Care Act of 2010 mandated that most employers would have to cover contraception for women, as reproduction is a legitimate health concern. Some Catholics flipped out, as requiring church-run businesses to offer contraception to women was a blasphemous violation of their beliefs. Of course, Viagra for men is still very much covered.

Right-wing politicians screamed that such coverage was proof of President Obama's "war on religion," as the white Christian majority again framed itself as an oppressed minority. The media exploded with a clickbait narrative of Christianity under assault, and the White House caved. They caved so hard, miners were trapped inside. They granted exemptions for churches to deny contraceptive care for their female employees. In 2017, the Trump administration expanded exemptions, allowing even nonreligious employers with moral objections to refuse coverage.

I enjoy this debate, because anti–birth control politicians are traditionally the best argument *for* birth control. But the media never asked one simple question—where does the Bible specifically ban contraception?

The Bible never explicitly mentions birth control in modern terms, and interpretations vary widely. But progressive Christians taught me that the Bible also teaches principles of stewardship, which involve responsibly managing resources, both for individuals and families. Family planning and birth control can be viewed as exercising prudence and wisdom in preparing for the well-being of one's family, including the health and welfare of children.

Birth control can help couples plan families and space out pregnancies, which leads to greater family stability—and the ability to provide for children. At the risk of heresy, this seems to align pretty well with biblical teachings on maintaining a stable and nurturing family environment.

Access to birth control helps reduce poverty by allowing women and men to plan their families and still pursue educational and professional opportunities.

And reducing poverty is, according to the book, the Lord's work.

Tragically, many men still don't understand that birth control can be used for medical reasons beyond preventing pregnancy, such as regulating cycles, treating hormonal imbalances, and other matters that are none of our damn business. Sane Christians argue that the Bible encourages caring for one's health, and modern medicine is a tool to fulfill this.

Jesus talked about banning birth control exactly as much as he talked about monster trucks. In fact, at no point in the Bible does anyone ever say "Thou shalt not wear a jimmy hat." And yet for thousands of years, poor people have been taught that family planning is an unpardonable sin, often by celibates.

Friends, if the earth revolving around the sun proves anything, it's that popes can be wrong. The church, like Onan's tribe, is really just keeping their numbers up.

And I know some of you are thinking, "But hey, the Bible says to be fruitful and multiply." And that's true. A short six thousand to ten thousand years ago, when we're told there were but two people, God said, "Be fruitful and multiply."

Now, there's eight billion of us. Mission accomplished, multiplication complete.

"Be fruitful and multiply," meet "Be prudent and moderate."

THE MAN WHO TAUGHT CHRISTIANITY TO HATE SEX

Paul, again.

St. Paul wrote the book on New Testament attitudes toward sexuality, literally. Whatever Paul was, sex-positive he was not, and his rants against sexuality prompted centuries of stringent moral codes regarding sexual behavior, contributing to generations of fear, acting out, abuse, and shame:

"Flee from sexual immorality. All other sins a person commits are outside the body, but whoever sins sexually, sins against their own body. Do you not know that your bodies are temples of the Holy Spirit, who is in you, whom you have received from God? You are not your own; you were bought at a price. Therefore, honor God with your bodies" (1 Corinthians 6:18–20).

If Jesus ever married, the scriptures don't want us to know about it, so he's always just been presumed to have been celibate. Paul, on the other hand, relentlessly preaches total sexual abstinence, more than some Paul-quoters might realize.

In 1 Corinthians 7:1–9, he suggests that it is better to remain unmarried and celibate, as he is, because it allows one to devote oneself more fully to the Lord. However, he acknowledges that not everyone can do celibacy as awesomely as he can, so he begrudgingly permits marriage to avoid sexual immorality:

"Now concerning the matters about which you wrote: 'It is good for a man not to have sexual relations with a woman.' But because of the temptation to sexual immorality, each man should have his own wife and each woman her own husband" (1 Corinthians 7:1–2).

He also advises those who are married to remain married, but emphasizes that it's way better to remain sexlessly single:

"Are you bound to a wife? Do not seek to be free. Are you free from a wife? Do not seek a wife. But if you do marry, you have not sinned, and if a betrothed woman marries, she has not sinned. Yet those who marry will have worldly troubles, and I would spare you that" (1 Corinthians 7:27–28 ESV).

And as we've seen, if your religious sect enforces celibacy for enough centuries, all kinds of unpleasant things can happen. Am I right, Catholics?

Paul's advice on marriage is partly influenced by his belief in the imminent end of the world. He believed that the return of Christ and the end of the current age were very near:

"What I mean, brothers and sisters, is that the time is short. From now on those who have wives should live as if they do not. . . . For this world in its present form is passing away." (1 Corinthians 7:29–31)

Paul's teachings on marriage are *his personal bits of advice,* tailored to the circumstances of his time. But these teachings led to a toxic dichotomy in Christian thought—celibacy is a higher, more spiritual state, while marriage is an unfortunate but necessary concession for inferior primitives who can't control their debased libidos.

And that's the binary choice the founder of modern Christianity gave the world. Be close to God and deny the body He gave you, or enjoy the body God gave you and deny Him.

Naughty Bits

The Bible contains an abundance of sexually provocative and deeply creative passages not suitable for Sunday school. Passages filled with love, desire, and sexuality, both explicit and implicit. When you get past all the rape and exploitation, some of it's quite beautifully written.

1. Song of Solomon (Song of Songs)

The Song of Solomon is a poetic sensual dialogue between lovers. Many interpret the book as an allegory for God's love for Israel, or perhaps Jesus's love for the church. Whatever it represents, it was not written by someone uptight over sexuality and physical desire:

- Song of Solomon 4:5–7: "Your breasts are like two fawns, like twin fawns of a gazelle that browse among the lilies. Until the day breaks and the shadows flee, I will go to the mountain of myrrh and to the hill of incense. You are altogether beautiful, my darling; there is no flaw in you."
- Song of Solomon 7:7–8: "Your stature is like that of the palm, and your breasts like clusters of fruit. I said, 'I will climb the palm tree; I will take hold of its fruit.' May your breasts be like clusters of grapes on the vine, the fragrance of your breath like apples."
- Song of Solomon 1:13: "My beloved is to me a sachet of myrrh resting between my breasts."

2. Ezekiel 23

We cover this in the feminism chapter as well; it contains a parable about two sisters, Oholah and Oholibah, who represent the cities of Samaria and Jerusalem. It uses highly graphic sexual imagery to metaphorically slut-shame both towns for their infidelity and idolatry.

- Ezekiel 23:3: "They became prostitutes in Egypt; engaging in prostitution from their youth. Their breasts were fondled and their virgin bosoms caressed."
- Ezekiel 23:8: "She did not give up the prostitution she began in Egypt, when during her youth men slept with her, caressed her virgin bosom, and poured out their lust upon her."

I mean, it's misogyny, sure. But somebody put a lot of thought into that imagery.

3. Genesis 19:30–38

Don't forget the delightful story of Lot and his daughters after the destruction of Sodom and Gomorrah. Believing they're the last people on earth, Lot's daughters get Dad drunk and have relations with him to preserve their family line.

- Genesis 19:33–35: "That night they got their father to drink wine, and the older daughter went in and slept with him. He was not aware of it when she lay down or when she got up. The next day the older daughter said to the younger, 'Last night I slept with my father. Let's get him to drink wine again tonight, and you go in and sleep with him so we can preserve our family line through our father.' So they got their father to drink wine that night also, and the younger daughter went in and slept with him. Again he was not aware of it when she lay down or when she got up."

Folks who want to believe Sodom and Gomorrah was about consensual same-sex relations get to defend this part as normal.

4. Proverbs

This chapter describes the seductive tactics of an adulterous woman; I'm sad to say, she sounds simply spectacular.

- Proverbs 7:16–18: "I have covered my bed with colored linens from Egypt. I have perfumed my bed with myrrh, aloes and cinnamon. Come, let's drink deeply of love till morning; let's enjoy ourselves with love!"
- Also, Proverbs 5:3: "For the lips of an adulteress drip honey, and her speech is smoother than oil."

5. Hosea 1:2–3: The Marriage of Hosea and Gomer

The story of the prophet Hosea, who is commanded by God to marry a prostitute named Gomer as a symbol of God's relationship with Israel. The imagery of marital infidelity and prostitution is used metaphorically to shame Israel's spiritual unfaithfulness. Noticing a pattern yet, ladies?

"When the Lord began to speak through Hosea, the Lord said to him, 'Go, marry a promiscuous woman and have children with her, for like an adulterous wife this land is guilty of unfaithfulness to the Lord.'"

Women who enjoy sex—always a reliable go-to when you need an easy villain.

6. Ezekiel 16:25

This verse uses graphic language to describe the metaphorical unfaithfulness of Jerusalem to God, using sexual imagery to convey spiritual infidelity. If it seems misogynist, just remember—it's actually the entire nation of Israel being called a dirty harlot.

"At every street corner you built your lofty shrines and degraded your beauty, spreading your legs with increasing promiscuity to anyone who passed by."

Again we see that if you're looking to shame an entire population, you'll never go wrong with whore-talk.

SEX-POSITIVE CHRISTIANITY—NOT AN OXYMORON

> "Because true belonging only happens when we present our authentic, imperfect selves to the world, our sense of belonging can never be greater than our level of self-acceptance."
>
> Brené Brown, *Daring Greatly*

Sex-positive Christianity is a theological and cultural perspective within the faith that challenges the religious narratives that promote sexual shame, guilt, and stigma—because none of them come from Jesus. It seeks a world where nice honest people, believers and otherwise, can explore and embrace their sexuality free from judgment, condemnation, or fear of punishment. People may make mistakes, and they may get hurt and grow from it, but what consenting adults do is generally none of our business, right?

Sex-positive Christians affirm that sexuality is a gift from God and an essential aspect of human identity and relationships. They reject the ancient hang-ups that equate sex with sin, or view it merely as a means of reproduction; instead, they recognize its potential for pleasure, intimacy, mutual fulfillment, and yes, spiritual growth.

Sex-positive Christianity can be a force of healing for survivors of sexual abuse. Shame can distort our perceptions of ourselves for years, and push us to act in ways we don't actually really want to behave, to self-medicate from trauma. There are many resources and communities that can help replace fear and shame with healing and empowerment.

Sex-positive Christianity (say it with me, people) affirms the inherent goodness of sexuality, whether it comes from God or not.

And if more Jesus followers realized that Jesus never said anything about premarital sex, homosexuality, bisexuality, birth control, touching oneself, etc., more right-wing Christians might be able to enjoy one of God's greatest gifts for themselves and stop viewing it as a sin.

Because if anybody needs it, it's the right-wing Christians.

After all, if God didn't like sex, He wouldn't make us cry out His name when it's especially hot.

THOU SHALT NOT KILL PEOPLE WHO KILL PEOPLE TO PROVE KILLING PEOPLE IS WRONG

"The profound moral question is not, 'Do they deserve to die?' but 'Do we deserve to kill them?'"

Sister Helen Prejean

Welcome to the chapter where I lose some of the liberals and moderates.

George Carlin famously pointed out that America began as a nation of slave owners who wanted to be free. I'd humbly add a second great founding hypocrisy—that one can only become president of the USA if they're a follower of Jesus who also believes in governments murdering sinners. As of this publication, twenty-one US states still kill their prisoners.

While every US president has professed themselves to be Christian, only one has cited Christ to oppose the death penalty: our thirty-ninth president, Jimmy Carter. Joe Biden ran on abolishing the federal death penalty in 2020, but that policy was never actually, er, executed. In 2024, Biden did commute the sentences of most federal death row inmates to life in prison.

It's almost impossible to imagine a death penalty abolitionist being elected to our nation's highest office. And yet capital punishment is one of the most directly anti-Jesus policies any government could enforce.

Now, this may shock you, but everybody's favorite radical long-haired nonviolent homeless revolutionary Jew never said, "Forgive us our trespasses as we lethally inject those who trespass against us."

THE CLAIM: "The Bible totally supports the death penalty."

THE SCRIPTURE: It's "eye for an eye" time.

- Exodus 21:23–25

  "But if there is serious injury, you are to take life for life, eye for eye, tooth for tooth, hand for hand, foot for foot, burn for burn, wound for wound, bruise for bruise."
- Leviticus 24:19–20

  "Anyone who injures their neighbor is to be injured in the same manner: fracture for fracture, eye for eye, tooth for tooth. The one who has inflicted the injury must suffer the same injury."
- Deuteronomy 19:21

  "Show no pity: life for life, eye for eye, tooth for tooth, hand for hand, foot for foot."

The problem is that these verses were part of the Mosaic Law, given to the Israelites during their time in the wilderness.

THE FACTS: Jesus overturns "eye for an eye" in his very first sermon. That one on the mount, that the Christian nationalists never quote, ever.

He begins with something everyone can agree on:

"Blessed are the merciful, for they will be shown mercy" (Matthew 5:7).

Which is very pleasant, catchy, and true. But this is New Covenant time, and the carpenter's here to explicitly reject the concept of retribution. He tells the crowd that the time has come for nonviolence and forgiveness.

> You have heard that it was said, "Eye for eye, and tooth for tooth." But I tell you, do not resist an evil person. If anyone slaps you on the right cheek, turn to them the other cheek also."
>
> Matthew 5:38–39, 43

As discussed in chapter 1, this was Jesus's way of changing the law by fulfilling the law. The "eye for an eye" principle was foundational in early law for fair justice, but Jesus expands it to advocate for forgiveness, a transition from strict legalism to a spirit of mercy and reconciliation. He completely rejects the principle of retributive justice.

And he literally announces he's changing it. "It *was* said, an eye for an eye."

Many Hebrews looking for a Messiah who would drive out the Romans didn't know what to make of this Nazarene advocating non-retaliation and turning the other cheek. This commandment to forgive those who hurt you was a radical call to break all cycles of violence, and to deliberately reject righteous vengeance. By preaching love for our enemies, Jesus further dispels any justification for violence—including legal executions.

The Rev. Dr. Jeff Hood is a spiritual advisor to death row inmates throughout the US. He's helped many condemned men through their final days, and when I asked him about Christians citing "eye for an eye," he didn't hold back: "There is no such thing as an actual Christian that believes such bullshit. You cannot follow Jesus and be in the eye or tooth-snatching business. I've also called these people self-righteous eye molesters. They think they can go after whatever eyes they want . . . but never consider why their own eyes might not be so safe."

BELOVED BIBLE RULES THAT COULD GET YOU KILLED

In Genesis 4:15, after Cain slays his brother Abel, God puts a mark on Cain so that he will be protected. Which means *the first-ever murderer got a pardon from God Himself.*

After this, however, Jehovah commands folks to kill each other in many different ways, for many different reasons.

THE CLAIM: "God commands the death penalty multiple times."

Oh yes, He does. And most likely, you don't agree with them. The Bible contains numerous laws prescribing death for a variety of offenses, reflecting the legal and moral codes of ancient Israelite society, which some folks in this century might describe as "harsh."

THE SCRIPTURE: The most straightforward and widely accepted basis for the death penalty in the OT is murder. "Whoever strikes a man so that he dies shall be put to death" (Exodus 21:12). But many other offenses could also get one righteously stoned by a mob of their peers. And while it wasn't the greatest strategy for keeping the tribe's numbers up, they certainly got creative:

- Worshiping other gods: Deuteronomy 17:2–5

  "If a man or woman living among you . . . has worshiped other gods, bowing down to them or to the sun or the moon or the stars in the sky . . . take the man or woman . . . and stone that person to death."
- Disrespectful kids were fit for death: Exodus 21:17

  "Anyone who curses their father or mother is to be put to death."
- Criticizing God: Leviticus 24:16

  "Anyone who blasphemes the name of the Lord is to be put to death. The entire assembly must stone them." This included cursing or speaking irreverently about God.
- Working on the Sabbath: Exodus 31:14

That's Saturday, sports fans. "Anyone who desecrates it is to be put to death; those who do any work on that day must be cut off from their people." In Numbers 15:32–36, we learn the story of some poor fellow, stoned to death for gathering wood on the Sabbath.

- Magic and witchcraft were lethally frowned upon: Exodus 22:18

  "Do not allow a sorceress to live." Sorry, psychic friends.

- Adultery: Leviticus 20:10

  "If a man commits adultery with another man's wife—with the wife of his neighbor—both the adulterer and the adulteress are to be put to death." We'll keep referencing this one for all y'all Trump Christians out there.

- Disobedience to parents: Deuteronomy 21:18–21

  It could earn you a public execution, young man. If a stubborn and rebellious son refused to obey his parents, the community was obliged to stone him to death. It's nice to remember when folks actually did things with their neighbors, before we were all obsessed with screens.

Again, a primary focus for the Israelites in the wilderness was increased procreation, which puts many of these capital offenses into context. We don't know how severely these laws were enforced versus how much they were there to keep people faithful and reproducing. And again, *none of these laws apply to New Covenant Christianity.*

AMERICA, SLAYING AT SLAYING

> "The reality is that capital punishment in America is a lottery. It is a punishment that is shaped by the constraints of poverty, race, geography, and local politics."
>
> Bryan Stevenson, Equal Justice Initiative

With over 1,570 executions in the past five decades, the US is a proud shining outlier among our developed allies; more than 70 percent of nations globally have banned the practice, according to the Death Penalty Information Center. According to the center, in 2020 only five other countries executed more of their citizens than the US: China, Iran, Egypt, Iraq, and Saudi Arabia.

When you factor in the costs of a capital punishment trial, including appeals, the costs of maintaining death rows, and the costs of actual executions, it's considerably more expensive to murder a prisoner than to incarcerate them for life without parole. Reports from the state of North Carolina (2011), the Kansas Judicial Council (2014), the Nevada Supreme Court (2015), the California Legislative Analyst's Office (2021), and Florida's 2010 Commission on Capital Cases have all confirmed the higher fiscal impacts associated with the death penalty compared to life imprisonment. States that have had moratoriums or bans on the death penalty, including Illinois, Ohio, Colorado, and New Mexico, have all cited cost savings as a justification, in addition to it not actually being a deterrent.

In recent years we've seen 150 death row inmates freed by DNA evidence or recanted testimony, some after decades in prison, all appeals exhausted.

It's impossible to say how many innocent prisoners have been killed. A 2014 study in the *Proceedings of the National Academy of Sciences* estimated that at least 4.1 percent of condemned inmates were falsely convicted.

And let's not forget the well-documented tradition of horrifically botched executions. Sometimes, killing guys on the taxpayer dime doesn't go as smoothly as everyone would hope.

Most executions in America are still carried out via lethal injection. But the first American executed in 2024, Alabama death row inmate and convicted killer Kenneth Eugene Smith, also became the first person in the world to be executed by the experimental torture of nitrogen hypoxia.

Fifty-eight-year-old Smith had already spent decades on death row for his 1988 crime. In 2022, he'd survived a botched execution by intravenous injection that lasted hours and reportedly amounted to torture. Two years later, Smith was strapped to a table, fitted with a mask, and forced to breathe only nitrogen gas, causing asphyxiation.

Rev. Jeff Hood was there. He described the nitrogen execution of Smith as the worst thing he'd ever witnessed on death row:

> Then, the nitrogen started to flow. I watched as Kenny's head turned redder and redder. His body began to pump adrenaline ferociously. Ants seemed to be running underneath every part of his skin. It looked as if his head was going to explode—perhaps even his whole body. We were told that Kenny would go unconscious in seconds. Then, seconds started to turn into minutes. Kenny began to heave. Each time he rose, mucus, saliva, and other fluids shot from his mouth and out the front of the mask. The liquids began to drizzle down like a waterfall. His eyeballs were bulging out. Back and forth over and over, everything, everywhere moving all at once. Like a fish out of water being stepped on until they flop no more. What type of assholes would devise a way to watch someone suffocate to death? The "Christian" leaders of one of the most "Christian" states in the United States.

The United Nations condemned the execution, stating, "Alabama's use of Kenneth Smith as a human guinea pig to test a new method of execution amounted to unethical human experimentation and was nothing short of State-sanctioned torture."

A month later, Turning Point USA founder, MLK hater, and Christian nationalist bamboozler Charlie Kirk said on his *Thoughtcrime* podcast that he wanted to see corporate-sponsored TV executions of Donald Trump's political opponents: "It should be public. It should be quick. It should be televised.... You could sell, you could fund the government. You could have like, 'brought to you by Coca-Cola.'"

Kirk suggested that children should be made to watch public murder, and that such executions "should be taken in a holy way."

Antisemitic child-man podcaster Nick Fuentes announced that under his America First movement, all non-Christians would be executed: "When we take power, they need to be given the death penalty. . . . They must be absolutely annihilated when we take power."

I'm not pretending that the majority of Americans don't support capital punishment, although that number has steadily declined for years. But did you ever notice how so many Americans who warn of the perils of "big government" want that same government to have the power to strap a citizen to a table and fill them with poison until they die? Does it get more "big government" than that?

And every year on Good Friday, when pro-death-penalty Christians mark the execution of anti-death-penalty Jesus, do they ever sense the irony?

Or is "irony" too polite a term?

I COULD TELL YOU THE REASONS

> "With every cell of my being and with every fiber of my memory I oppose the death penalty in all forms. I do not believe any civilized society should be at the service of death. I don't think it's human to become an agent of the angel of death."
>
> Elie Wiesel

- I could remind you that research has consistently shown that having a death penalty does not deter crime in any state more effectively than life imprisonment. And crime hasn't gone up in states that have dropped capital punishment. It's not a deterrent; it just helps lazy politicians get elected.
- We should also mention the not-unpersuasive argument that the

death penalty should be viewed as a form of cruel and unusual punishment, which is prohibited by the Eighth Amendment of the US Constitution, if you're into that sort of thing.

- There are those who might be moved by the fact that a significant number of people on death row suffer from severe mental illness, which often contributed to what got them convicted in the first place. Death row inmates often spend years, if not decades, in solitary confinement, which has been shown to have severe psychological effects on these people at the absolute lowest rung of society—those locked in cages, waiting to die. Ethical concerns about killing mentally ill prisoners aren't everybody's cup of tea, I acknowledge.

I could give you all these reasons. But at the end of the day, these stats and facts won't move our Christian brothers and sisters, so I have to put my faith in a higher power. Jesus, take the wheel.

BUT THEN THERE'S JESUS

> "What you do to these men [on death row], you do to God."
>
> Mother Teresa

Again, Jesus wastes no time overturning all death penalty laws at the very beginning of his public ministry. After he overturns "eye for an eye" in that sermon on that mount, he rolls out the Golden Rule: "Do to others what you would have them do to you" (Matthew 7:12). This compassionate reciprocity is to be extended to all, including the worst of us.

THE CLAIM: "Jesus was literally just talking about slaps when he said, 'Turn the other cheek.' That doesn't mean he opposed executing criminals."

THE SCRIPTURE: Jesus challenges the use of legally sanctioned capital punishment in John 8:1–11. This is, of course, the story where he intervenes in the case of a woman caught in adultery; it's Jesus's most direct rejection of executions in the Bible.

A few Pharisees present Jesus with the adulteress (again, the adulterous guy isn't in trouble). The law demanded that she be stoned to death. Jesus famously shuts this down without breaking a sweat: "Let any one of you who is without sin be the first to throw a stone at her."

This moment is essential to Jesus's entire ministry. He deliberately ignores the required punishment for violating the seventh commandment, thou shalt not commit adultery.

But he isn't just rejecting a punitive approach to justice. By announcing that only people who've never sinned have the moral authority to pass any kind of lethal judgment, Jesus proclaims the universality of sinning—and the need for humility and self-reflection when we judge others. He's reforming it all into his new legal system that promotes mercy—and the possibility for redemption—over harsh punishment.

In the end, Jesus never approves of the woman's sin, but he offers her forgiveness and a fresh start, because he's all about repentance and transformation, not judgment.

THE CLAIM: "Yes but we're talking about horrible people who deserve to die!"

THE JESUS PARTS: There's Matthew 18:21–22, where Peter comes up to Jesus and asks, "Lord, how many times shall I forgive my brother or sister who sins against me? Up to seven times?"

Jesus replies, "I tell you, not seven times, but seventy-seven times."

Again, Matthew 5:7: "Blessed are the merciful, for they shall receive mercy."

And don't forget the Our Father, Jesus's most iconic bit of prose: "Forgive us our trespasses, as we forgive those who trespass against us" (Matthew 6:12–14).

His approach is always redemption and reconciliation, rather than convincing oneself that it's not murder if the condemned guy really deserves it.

"BUT, ABORTION!"

THE CLAIM: "How can you hypocrites be proabortion for the unborn, but pro-life for evil murderers who deserve to die?"

THE RESPONSE: As covered in chapter 7, Jesus never mentions terminating pregnancies and the Bible never bans the practice. But he does consistently stand up for the absolute worst of us. In Matthew 9:13, he announces: "But go and learn what this means: 'I desire mercy, not sacrifice.' For I have not come to call the righteous, but sinners." Jesus worked these themes into his storytelling, too.

In Luke 15:1–7, Jesus tells the very beautiful parable of the lost sheep, which illustrates that God, good shepherd that He is, cares for every last individual and considers them all of equal importance, including the ones written off as "lost."

In Luke 15:11–32, we get the parable of the prodigal son, which also highlights JC's theme of forgiveness and restoration over punishment. The father welcomes back his irresponsible screwup kid with open arms and celebrates his ability to mend his ways, rather than condemning him for his failings.

In Matthew 18:21–35, Jesus tells the parable of the servant who was forgiven a large debt by his master, but then coldly refused to forgive a smaller debt owed to him by another servant. Once again, he highlights the hypocrisy of refusing to forgive while receiving mercy yourself.

Why, it's almost like he's warning the smug, assured people about something.

THE WORLD'S MOST FAMOUS VICTIM OF THE DEATH PENALTY

Crucifixion is one of the most brutal and humiliating methods any government has ever devised to kill its prisoners. It was a form of execution reserved for the most despised criminals, and the act of carrying one's own cross was meant to add to the shame and suffering.

And even in the face of this extreme violence—bleeding to death and slowly suffocating, while people are laughing at him—Jesus never calls on God for any kind of vengeance: "Father, forgive them, for they do not know what they are doing" (Luke 23:34). His dying words literally emphasize mercy and forgiveness over punishment.

Ya Want More?

James 4:12 says God's the only one who can take a life in the name of justice: "There is only one Lawgiver and Judge, the one who is able to save and destroy. But you—who are you to judge your neighbor?"

In James 1:20, Jesus's brother reiterates: "For the wrath of man worketh not the righteousness of God" (KJV).

In Romans 12:19, Paul warns against answering evil with evil, and reminds us that it's God who takes care of payback—and He does it in the afterlife: "Avenge not yourselves, but rather give place unto wrath: for it is written, Vengeance is mine; I will repay, saith the Lord" (KJV).

LAST WORDS

"I object to my government killing people because my government is meant to be me, and I object to me killing people."

Steve Earle, songwriter

Here I get to praise the Catholic Church.

Over the years, the Vatican has voiced opposition to capital punishment through official statements, declarations, and the teachings of popes. In a 1999 homily in St. Louis, Pope John Paul II said, "Modern society has the means of protecting itself, without definitively denying criminals the chance to reform. I renew the appeal . . . for a consensus to end the death penalty, which is both cruel and unnecessary."

In August 2018, Pope Francis approved a revision to the *Catechism of the Catholic Church,* explicitly stating the church's opposition to the death penalty in all circumstances. The revised section of the *Catechism,* paragraph 2267, states: "The Church teaches, in the light of the Gospel, that 'the death penalty is inadmissible because it is an attack on the inviolability and dignity of the person,' and she works with determination for its abolition worldwide."

I asked Rev. Jeff Hood what people who've never been on death row should know about legal executions, and what it says about the society that allows them. Hood reflects, "The State executes someone in the name of its citizens. We become murderers. Just because you're not in the chamber does not absolve you of guilt. The execution is being carried out in your name.

"You are strapping the person down. You are ignoring their cries. You are reading the death warrant. You are denying mercy. You are pronouncing the sentence. You are setting yourself in a position of judgment."

Central to Jesus's message is his whole idea of redemption, and the always present possibility of forgiveness for everybody, even those of us who have committed the most horrible of crimes. The death penalty, quite permanent and irreversible, rejects the possibility of repentance and change that Jesus keeps talking about.

It's a lot to take in, I know. Just remember, right-wing friends: If you support government murder of sinners, you can stop pretending you believe "all life is sacred."

THOU SHALT NOT HATE GUN CONTROL OR WORSHIP WARRIOR BRO-DUDE JESUS

"Our faith compels us to protect the sanctity of human life. We are called to reject a culture of fear and self-protection that fuels a cycle of violence."

United Methodist Church, "Take Action: United Methodist Call to End Gun Violence," 2021

"Our faith calls us to act on behalf of those who are most vulnerable. This includes advocating for gun control laws that will help reduce the epidemic of gun violence in our society."

Presbyterian Church (USA)

"We utterly deny all outward wars and strife and fightings with outward weapons, for any end, or under any pretence whatsoever; and this is our testimony to the whole world."

Quaker Peace Testimony

The right to bear arms, enshrined in the Second Amendment of the US Constitution, is at present worshiped by much of right-wing US Christianity. The anti-violence teachings of Jesus, however, are not.

We live in a world where Christian nationalists maintain a proud tradition of re-creating Jesus in their own image. And it turns out, their Christ isn't the nonviolent bearer of compassion who demands we turn the other cheek.

When it comes to war, torture, the death penalty, and gun proliferation, some of Jesus's locked-and-loaded fans have overlooked his teachings, like they overlook the words "well-regulated militia" in the Second Amendment.

Right-wing US Christian groups consistently oppose popular gun-safety measures that don't involve confiscation, such as background checks, assault weapon bans, and restrictions on high-capacity magazines. Such measures, we are told, infringe upon sacred ideals of "individual rights" and "personal freedom."

Also, regulating guns pre-massacre requires more work than offering "thoughts and prayers" post-massacre.

Christianity has a long history of violence, and it's mutated into this twenty-first-century sacrament of enabling more violence, most of it preventable, all in the sacred name of personal freedom.

In the seventies and eighties, televangelists and organizations like the Moral Majority relentlessly preached from the pulpit that gun ownership wasn't merely a constitutional right, but a *God-given one*, and an essential aspect of American freedom and Christian identity. They framed any policies that might make it harder for criminals to get guns—or any legislation to keep legal guns from becoming illegal guns—as an atheistic overreach of government power. And grievance, as we have learned, is good for business.

By the late twentieth and early twenty-first centuries, the rise of the religious right in the US had blended Christian identity with an aggressive political and cultural militancy. Some evangelical groups started taking a more combative stance, interpreting "spiritual warfare" as actual warfare. Jesus came to be frequently depicted as a militaristic defender of traditional values, aggressively willing to battle, well, whoever. "It's in the Bible."

This has allowed generations of Christians to read Jesus's words about love and nonviolence, while simultaneously being taught by mortal men that sometimes violence is just what the Messiah ordered.

Within a few decades, the US had the highest rate of gun ownership in the world, an estimated 393 million guns owned by civilians. That's approximately 120 guns per 100 people. The next highest country, Yemen, has about 52 guns per 100 people. And they've been in a state of violent civil war for over ten years.

This elite status has allowed the US to be number one in many other exclusive categories.

- As of this writing, the US has approximately 49,000 gun-related deaths a year, about 134 per day, according to Small Arms Survey. The American Medical Association has declared gun violence a public health crisis.
- America experiences more mass shootings than any other country, and we have a higher rate of police officers being killed by firearms than most developed nations. According to the National Law Enforcement Officers Memorial Fund, guns were the leading cause of law enforcement officer deaths in the US in 2022, accounting for about 60 percent of the total.
- In 2020, firearm-related injuries surpassed motor vehicle crashes to become the leading cause of death among US children and adolescents aged one to nineteen.

Are you feeling safe yet?

Guns don't kill people, but NRA people who own congresspeople make it easier for deranged people to be heavily armed people who kill innocent people.

It's the sort of situation that almost seems designed for the members of a peaceful religion to come and save us from.

But as you probably know, right-wing Christians defiantly refuse to do anything that might help drive these fatality numbers down. Those Christians who boast so proudly of "pro-life" convictions are also fighting for emotionally unstable twentysomething males to have easy access to AR-15s.

And let me say, dear reader, that I'm not anti-gun or anti–gun ownership. My Southern grandmother always had a shotgun in the corner by the front door and I've always respected firearms (if not all the people who worship them). I've got nothing against hunting for food; I also believe most guns and ammunition should be legal and free for most women.

And having fired guns in my life, I've long understood the appeal. I can appreciate how attached some can get to the experience.

But an AR-15 for civilian use is not your "God-given right"; it's your goddamn entertainment.

Christian nationalists aren't interested in the nonviolent Jesus of the Gospels. They worship a right-wing warrior Jesus, Lord of the Strapped, Ragingly Heterosexual Bro-Dudes.

ALL ABOUT LUKE 22

These days, armed Christians have some shiny new ammo in the fight to prove you can be a follower of Jesus while *also* enjoying machines designed to kill lots of people, real fast.

And it's quickly become a mantra for fun-loving, gun-loving, Father-and-the-Son-loving Christians.

THE CLAIM: "Jesus tells us to sell our cloak and buy a sword."

THE SCRIPTURE: It's Luke 22:36: "He said to them, 'But now if you have a purse, take it, and also a bag; and if you don't have a sword, sell your cloak and buy one.'"

Now, this may surprise some of you who don't remember that part in the Bible when Jesus turns water into whup-ass. But apparently, out of all four books that tell the story of Jesus, this one little line is proof that Christians are obligated to stockpile automatic weapons, while apparently getting a waiver on turn-the-other-cheek.

Whether you believe in Jesus in any literal, metaphorical, or spiritual way, you may encounter this talking point. In fact, take a step away and search "Luke 22:36" on social media for a few minutes.

Tons of right-wing guys are citing it to argue that Jesus was totally pro-gun, and down with heavily armed self-defense. The Gun Owners of America website proudly announces, "Truth #1: Jesus *wanted* His disciples to get swords."

Some Christian gun owners have even had "Luke 22:36" inscribed on their firearms, so they never forget how much Jesus digs their piece.

But sadly, Luke 22 devotees have taken one line of text—a line that makes them very, very happy—out of context.

Because what Jesus is really doing in the story is talking about prophecy—and being a criminal. Here's the backstory the NRA doesn't bother with.

THE RATHER IMPORTANT CONTEXT: Part of Luke's account of what happened to Jesus just before he was arrested and executed, the story takes place on Holy Thursday, the night Jesus is taken into custody. After the Last Supper but before he goes to pray in the garden, Jesus explains to his apostles that his fate is part of a prophecy from Isaiah—and he warns them about the struggles that will be coming.

Jesus asks, "When I sent you without purse, bag, or sandals, did you lack any thing?"

They reply, "Nothing."

Note there's no mention of a weapon, or of ever needing one. He's never told them to arm themselves before. But Jesus throws down the line about how now it's time:

"But now if you have a purse, take it, and also a bag; and if you don't have a sword, sell your cloak and buy one."

In the next lines—which are never cited—Jesus explains that the only reason the disciples need swords is because Isaiah's prophecy says they're supposed to be criminals, and they need to look the part: "It is written: 'And he was numbered with the transgressors'; and I tell you that this must be fulfilled in me. Yes, what is written about me is reaching its fulfillment."

There's that word again—"fulfillment." Jesus is referencing Isaiah 53:12, which prophesied: "Therefore, I will give him a portion among the great, and he will divide the spoils with the strong, because he poured out his life unto death, and was numbered with the transgressors. For he bore the sin of many, and made intercession for the transgressors."

As you may have noticed, Jesus is in no way talking about armed self-defense. He's talking about having a sword *as a prop* so he can get arrested. And in the very next line, the apostles say, "Hey, Jesus, we've already got two swords here with us."

Jesus replies, "That's enough."

And that's it. They've got what they need to get arrested. They drop the subject of swords and move on. Nobody actually goes out to buy late-night swords at the Jerusalem Walmart. And later, when the jackbooted guards swoop in to deprive him of his sacred liberty, Jesus does not exercise his right to self-defense; it's Peter who draws his sword, cutting off the ear of the high priest's servant. Does Jesus join the fight? No.

Instead, in Matthew 26:52's account, Jesus immediately rebukes Peter for taking up arms. He heals the wounded man (who came to help arrest him) and tells his followers, "Put your sword back into its place. For all who draw the sword will die by the sword."

His literal last words to his apostles: reminding them how much he disapproves of violence, even in self-defense. And you really don't need to search how many guys inscribe "Matthew 26:52" on their guns.

Note that Jesus never comes out against *owning* swords. He never vilifies swords, or calls for them to be banned. I would never claim that Jesus is anti–sword ownership.

But he seriously comes out against ever *using* them on people.

You'd think our Christian nationalist friends might understand that Jesus's ministry is one of peace, love, and faith in God, not Glocks. Believing this one line to be a literal commandment from Christ to literally buy swords for impending armed conflict is only possible *if one has never read the actual story.*

Jesus often spoke in figurative language and parables. Some theologians think his instruction to "buy a sword" was a metaphor for being prepared for the violence that's about to come, not a literal call to arms.

But Luke 22:36 proves that the best weapon for refuting the Bible-thumpers is usually the Bible itself. Because the only way you can cling equally to both a Bible and a gun is by skipping the Jesus parts.

ALPHA-BRO CHRIST

The concept of a "warrior Jesus" has been invoked by quite a few individuals and movements throughout history. You'd think it might be blasphemous to blend Christ's image with your own militant agenda, but testosterone is a strange and fragile thing.

From the Crusades to our modern gundamentalists, portraying Jesus as some kind of battle-ready soldier has often helped justify violence in the name of power. Blending the Prince of Peace with your own hypermasculine combat fantasies can be quite a studly upgrade from all that yammering about peace and non-retaliation.

Pope Urban II's call for the First Crusade in 1095 framed the mission as a holy war, endorsed by a more militant image of Jesus than the actual Bible provides. In the American Civil War, both sides used Christian imagery to justify their causes, and in a 1922 speech, Hitler famously said, "My feelings as a Christian points me to my Lord and Savior as a fighter."

In modern political discourse, particularly among extreme right-wing and nationalist groups, Jesus is often depicted as a jacked-up, long-haired, battle-ready Lord of the Bench Press who brings good tidings of gun rights, homogenous communities, and aggressive opposition to whoever you think deserves it.

More and more right-wing pastors stress Jesus's masculinity over his message, deeming any depiction of a compassionate Jesus as weak or "hippie."

Witness, please, these big bad butch believers, selling Macho Jesus to insecure men who appreciate the spiritual benefits of phallocentric piety. I apologize if any of this gets a little homoerotic.

> "Jesus wasn't an effeminate hippie . . . Jesus Christo gets pitched as some unisexual, religious, gluten-free Gucci model who might confuse us in regards to his actual gender."
>
> Evangelical Pastor Doug Giles

> "God, at a physiological level, sent His Son Jesus into the world with a male, testosterone-producing body that equipped Him with the masculine attributes required to fulfill His physical duties as Messiah . . . He was wonderfully and perfectly masculine."
>
> Dale Partridge, relearn.org, 2022

> "In Revelation, Jesus is a pride fighter with a tattoo down his leg, a sword in his hand, and the commitment to make someone bleed. That is a guy I can worship. I cannot worship the hippie, diaper, halo Christ because I cannot worship a guy I can beat up."
>
> Pastor Mark Driscoll, RelevantMagazine.com

For some Christians, masculinity is synonymous with dominance, violence, and trying way too hard, bro. Fetishizing a chest-thumping, militarized Rambo Christ says more about one's own insecurities than about the carpenter who frequented the poor neighborhoods of Galilee.

Kristin Du Mez's *Jesus and John Wayne* is a definitive read on this issue. She explained to me, "'This militarized version became popular during the early Cold War era, when 'Christian America' needed strong men to defend against communism. Christian leaders were quite explicit that this defense was a military one, but it also entailed exercising patriarchal authority in their own families and churches. A strong nation required a strong moral foundation, and patriarchal authority would ensure that. Masculine strength was thus essential to defend faith, family, and nation.

"Evangelicals enjoyed cultural and political power at this time, but this came to a crashing halt in the 1960s. The civil rights movement, the feminist movement, and the anti-war movement all threatened the power of white men, in one way or another. Now, fellow Americans became the enemies, and the assertion of white patriarchal authority was the way to right these wrongs, to restore American greatness, and restore their understanding of 'true Christianity'—one that was compatible with Cold War militarism, and with free enterprise capitalism."

The hypermasculine rhetoric of the pious Warrior Dude-Bros doesn't align much with the cheek-turning carpenter of the Gospels. Their Jesus is a Rebel without a Cross.

As Du Mez added, "Toxic masculinity revolves around exercising power and resenting anyone who threatens that power. The Jesus of the gospels divested himself of power and offered himself up on the cross to save sinners. He uplifted the lowly, blessed the meek, and at every turn refused earthly power and told his followers to do the same."

That's why certain guys prefer the more militant Book-of-Revelation Jesus, as vividly described by a guy named John (who's probably not John the Apostle), writing down visions that sound like Doors lyrics.

This Jesus is a ketamine seizure Carpenter of Carnage in a heavy-metal video filmed at the gun show. In Revelation 19:12–16, "His eyes are like blazing fire, and on his head are many crowns. He has a name written on him that no one knows but he himself. He is dressed in a robe dipped in blood, and his name is the Word of God. The armies of heaven were following him, riding on white horses and dressed in fine linen, white and clean. Coming out of his mouth is a sharp sword with which to strike down the nations."

This Messiah doesn't ask you to welcome the stranger or be nice to women or care about the poor. This is the Jesus the Christian nationalists truly follow—John's NyQuil hallucination of Apocalyptic Alpha Christ.

They like him angry. A grievous Jesus frees us.

Conservative media and religious leaders have, over decades, inflamed tensions to such an extent that every now and then, some armed feverish true believer who hates abortion clinics, religious minorities, or LGBTQ people decides that God's given him a pass on the rule of law—and His own commandments.

Look at the Colorado Springs shooting of November 27, 2015, when a fifty-seven-year-old white male gunman used a semiautomatic rifle to murder three people and injure nine more at a Planned Parenthood clinic. In a divorce document, his ex-wife had testified, "He claims to be a Christian and is extremely evangelistic, but does not follow the Bible in his actions.

He says that as long as he believes he will be saved, he can do whatever he pleases. He is obsessed with the world coming to an end."

Christian nationalism already promotes a dangerously exclusionary vision of the US as a fundamentally "Christian" nation. Their rhetoric thrives on militaristic imagery and language, framing political or cultural conflicts not as societal problems we should all try to solve, but as "spiritual warfare." Constant flex-talk desensitizes followers to the use of violence in defense of their beliefs; because after all, they're on God's side and you're not. So how could God not approve?

THE LOW-T ADVENTURES OF ACTUAL NONVIOLENT JESUS

> "The gospel is clear: we are called to love our neighbors as ourselves, which includes taking action to protect them from violence. Our faith compels us to advocate for common-sense gun safety laws that reduce the risk of harm to our communities."
>
> Rev. Dr. William Barber II

Jesus was a member of an oppressed people, occupied by a foreign empire. There were many brave Jews who violently resisted the Romans, but Jesus chose to not join any armed rebellions. He instead preached love for those who persecute you, and kept rejecting the concept of earthly power.

After Jesus fed the multitudes with the miracle of the loaves and fishes in John 6:15, the crowd wanted to make him their king, by force. Consistently, power was not Jesus's priority, and he withdrew instead to a solitary place.

If it's not obvious this far into the book, Jesus's whole thing was about putting the well-being of others over individual desires. While self-defense is of course permissible, Christians are specifically encouraged by Jesus to pursue boring, emasculated, nonviolent solutions to our disputes.

By refusing to accept—or even consider—modest regulations like universal background checks or limits on high-capacity magazines, right-wing

Christians have declared their spiritual preference for personal convenience and self-interest over the lives of others. The communal aspects of faith, the call to love and serve others, all crushed by a theology of ME ME ME ME ME ME.

If you're elevating yourself above others based on your belief in Jesus, then you don't even believe Jesus. His movement's 100 percent about humility.

Prioritizing civilian access to mass-kill weaponry—instead of measures that could protect lives—isn't really in Jesus's sacred wheelhouse.

The deeply silly portrayal of Christ as a warrior figure has always been a product of male insecurity and/or political agendas; it's designed to ruggedly sidestep those tough-sell commandments of love, forgiveness, and reconciliation.

Also, if you need an AR-15 for hunting, you're not a Second Amendment champion; you're a guy who sucks at hunting.

GUNS IN CHURCHES, BECAUSE OF COURSE

In late 2023, a three-judge appeals court panel overturned a New York law that prohibited the carrying of firearms into churches. With this ruling, New York involuntarily joined over a dozen US states that permit, in some capacity, loaded weapons to be brought into houses of worship.

My first thought when I heard this was, "Great—if anyone deserves the right to protect themselves, it's the altar boys."

Then I was told these laws allow pretty much *anyone* to bring concealed handguns into God's house. Now some might disagree, but I will always fight for people of faith to prove to the rest of us that they don't have any faith. For yea, though I walk through the Valley of the Shadow of Church, I will fear no evil; my Glock and dwindling testosterone shall comfort me.

And maybe that's the whole problem with Christianity—they let a nonviolent long-haired martyr run the startup. Some Christians don't want the Prince of Peace; they want a prince who packs a piece.

So I guess I've finally come to believe that guns *should* be allowed in church. It's the people who'd want to bring guns into church who shouldn't be allowed in church.

And again, most Christians don't oppose gun control—many denominations actively support stricter regulations that don't involve confiscation: expanding background checks, registering all guns like cars, and banning high-capacity magazines, which makes it easier to tackle mass shooters when they're inconveniently forced to reload mid-massacre.

Of course, if Jesus had had an AR-15, he could've just mowed down the Romans, avoided crucifixion, and never had a religion named for him. But then none of us would ever know who Jerry Falwell was.

THE CLAIM: "Jesus said he came to bring a sword so I get to ignore that hippie stuff."

THE SCRIPTURE: Matthew 10:34: "Do not suppose that I have come to bring peace to the earth. I did not come to bring peace, but a sword."

The "sword" here isn't a literal blade for the shedding of blood. It's a symbol of the division the ideas of radical love, justice, and equality could cause in society structured around patriarchy, conservative religious legalism, and imperial oppression. Yes, it's Jesus bein' all metaphorical again.

It's not a call to violence or an endorsement of it. But taken out of context, this verse has been weaponized by extremists to justify violence, aggression, and the belief that Jesus brings peace through superior firepower.

The messages the Nazarene brought—of the first being last, of loving enemies, of caring for the poor, of breaking down walls between insiders and outsiders—threatened the entire system. He's warning of social upheaval that comes from embracing this narrow way of radical reform.

It's a message that's true in any culture. Choosing to stand for the vulnerable and challenge injustice will sometimes mean being rejected by people close to us. Jesus is brutally honest that living by these principles will sometimes cost something.

Sorry, guys—he's still not pro-weapon. His story literally ends with him choosing to endure violence instead of inflicting it.

WHEN THE PIOUS ATTACK

Jesus was, in fact, extremely masculine—but not in the way these modern Christian nationalists define it. His strength wasn't measured by how many enemies he could crush but by how he used his power to protect, uplift, and care for those worse off than him. Which is a terrific feminine trait, as well.

Strength is measured by who you protect, not who you attack. Jesus modeled the strength to care for those on the bottom rungs, not pick on them. Homeless people. Immigrants and foreigners. Convicted criminals. The sick, disabled, and those born different. Slut-shamed women and those outside the sexual mainstream. He didn't just tolerate these people; he loved, defended, and prioritized them.

You learn a lot about a person by who they choose to ridicule, scorn, or scapegoat. Jesus saved his harshest words for the powerful who loved their own authority and/or piety over using their power to help others.

There's a growing plague of politicians, preachers, and influencers who wrap themselves in religious language while attacking anti-discrimination policies, women, immigrants, the poor and struggling, LGBTQ people, and anyone else on society's margins.

It's the oldest grift in toxic religion: cruelty in piety drag. Sneering at the homeless, mocking migrants fleeing violence, persecuting queer kids, and demeaning anyone who doesn't fit one's definition of acceptable.

It's a weak masculinity, one that seeks to make ableism great again in the form of grown men casually normalizing "retarded" as a slur. Because basic respect and dignity for developmentally different kids has apparently become woke.

And these same guys—some of them celebrity billionaires, by the way—would never have the guts to use that word at the Special Olympics. Not because they respect the athletes, but because deep down, they know that using a slur for those born differently is an unmanly, punk-ass choice. Sorry, Jesus . . .

If you want to know who's walking the way of Jesus, don't just listen to what they preach—watch who they attack. There's one rule that consistently applies to both Christianity and comedy—don't punch down.

13

THOU SHALT NOT HATE JEWS, MUSLIMS, OR EVEN ATHEISTS

"I have other sheep that are not of this fold."

Jesus (John 10:16, ESV)

No baby comes out a religious bigot; it usually takes a village of religious bigots to help the little ones along. And history has shown that the easiest way to mass-produce more bigots is to justify any prejudice as divinely ordained by God.

Young people, born in the shadow of the religious violence of 9/11, have grown up to witness armed and unstable men, mostly white Christian nationalists, commit mass murder against Jews at a synagogue in Pittsburgh, against Muslims at a mosque in New Zealand, against Latinos at a Walmart in El Paso, against African Americans at a supermarket in Buffalo and a church in Charleston, and against gay people at a nightclub in Orlando.

Scapegoating entire groups works, because it provides certain folks with magically simplistic solutions to complex problems, while *also* validating a prejudice. It never helps resolve any of those "underlying causes of societal problems" the irritating woke folk keep talking about. But scapegoating can help a certain kind of politician—or religious figure—obtain power.

We recognize, now, that European Jews being blamed for various societal issues led to widespread anti-Semitism—and widespread acceptance of their persecution. African Americans were (and are) blamed for violence and poverty, which has historically been used to justify discriminatory laws, abusive policing, segregation, and redlining. Immigrants of every generation are perpetually blamed for job shortages or crime rates, despite a lack of evidence.

Scapegoating lets us project our frustrations and fears onto a certain vulnerable group. And every now and then, the right charismatic demagogue shows up to explain how some acceptable-to-hate minority group poses an existential threat to our way of life—and *only he* can save us from this threat.

Scapegoating is how prejudice and discrimination become normalized within societies. It's very easy to get caught up in what your culture considers to be normal, and most of us raised subjectively within a cultural prejudice generally don't realize it.

If one's Christianity is a clique, rather than a calling, prejudice against other religions is always a quick and easy path. And you'll always be able to find religious leaders willing to justify or exploit somebody's hatred of an entire group.

Scapegoating: It's in the Bible

In Exodus 26:33–34, we learn about the construction of the Holy of Holies in the tabernacle, the portable sanctuary used by the Israelites during their journey through the wilderness. The Holy of Holies was the innermost and most sacred area of the tabernacle (and later the temple), where the Ark of the Covenant was kept, separated from the rest of the tabernacle by a veil or curtain for a little extra privacy.

Only the high priest could pass behind the curtain and enter the Holy of Holies, and that was Moses's brother Aaron. But even as high priest, Aaron could only enter it once a year, on the Day of Atonement (Yom Kippur), as directed in Leviticus 16:2.

"The Lord said to Moses: 'Tell your brother Aaron that he is not to come whenever he chooses into the Most Holy Place behind the curtain in front of the atonement cover on the ark, or else he will die. For I will appear in the cloud over the atonement cover.'"

Now, that would've been enough for me to never set foot behind that curtain. Then again, I've seen the end of *Raiders of the Lost Ark*, so I have that over Aaron.

But Aaron had a habit of standing behind that set of curtains near ark *a little too often*, and it didn't take long for the Lord to become quite annoyed with Moses's brother.

As atonement, God orders Aaron to present offerings, including two goats. One goat was to be sacrificed, the good old-fashioned way, but the second was to be kept alive. The high priest would then lay his hands on this goat and confess over it all the sins of the Israelites, thereby symbolically transferring all their transgressions onto this, the "scapegoat."

"But the goat chosen by lot as the scapegoat shall be presented alive before the Lord to be used for making atonement by sending it into the wilderness as a scapegoat" (Leviticus 16:10).

The extremely innocent scapegoat was then sent off on its own into the wilderness, carrying the sins of the people with it. And the term is used to this day to describe any innocent person—or group—who takes the blame for the sins of others.

ANTI-SEMITISM: FOR FANS OF A JEW, WHO CAN'T STAND THE JEWS

In July 2010, an under-medicated Glenn Beck argued on his Fox News broadcast that Jesus was "not a victim" when he was crucified. Fair enough, as Yeshua offered himself up willingly and never put up a fight—even though his armed friends were there, ready to stand back or stand by.

But then Glenn had to go say the quiet part out loud: "If he was a victim, and this theology was true, then Jesus would've come back from the dead and made the Jews pay for what they did."

The most effective way of slandering Judaism—a religion Jesus was born into, sought to reform from within, and never renounced or quit—is to collectively blame "the Jews" for Jesus's execution. It's evil, it's dishonest, and it works—and not just in German.

Historically, blaming Jews for Jesus's death—charmingly known as "deicide" or "Christ killing"—has been used to justify centuries of persecution, discrimination, forced conversion, and violence, culminating in horrors like the Holocaust.

THE CLAIM: "The Jews killed Jesus."

The Gospels do depict a group of the authoritarian Pharisees playing a role in Jesus's arrest. In Matthew 26:3–4, some of the chief priests and elders plot to deliver him to the Roman Empire, and John 19:14–15 presents the narrative where a local crowd calls for Jesus's crucifixion.

These texts have historically been interpreted by non-Jews in a way that assigns collective guilt to the Jewish people for Jesus's death, with many generations of churches happy to reinforce the talking point.

THE SCRIPTURE: The Bible *does* directly tell us which people were primarily responsible for Jesus's death, and they just so happen to be the only characters in the book who might contemporaneously be called "white": the Romans.

- Jesus was given to Roman authorities, held in a Roman jail, and had a trial overseen by a Roman governor.
- Roman soldiers tortured and scourged him; Romans twisted together a crown of thorns and forced it on him, along with a purple robe, to mock him.
- Roman soldiers forced him to carry his Roman cross to the Roman-chosen site of Rome's crucifixions, Golgotha.
- Romans, and only Romans, drove nails through his wrists and feet, to maximize his pain and prolong his death.

- Romans ridiculed him by hanging a sign above his dying body announcing, "This is the King of the Jews," as they pierced his side.
- Or, if you're Glenn Beck, "killed by the Jews."

Friends, two thousand years ago the Roman Empire dominated the Mediterranean region, including the areas Jesus lived. While a few Jewish leaders played a role in the story of Jesus's arrest and trial, it was the Roman authorities who did the dirty work.

The Jews did not control the Romans, and they didn't have the power to force the Romans to kill anybody.

As Rabbi Danya Ruttenberg told me, "The Romans had the power, the Romans had the military force, and the Romans levied the taxes."

And after the Romans killed Jesus, they took over his operation, and eventually the Holy Roman Empire rewrote the Jews as the real bad guys. And you've probably never heard anyone try to blame the Italians for killing Jesus. And they shouldn't. I've got relatives who would have heart attacks.

The truth behind the story of Jesus's death is that there were many different participants in his killing—the government, the military, some of the religious bosses, the citizens—even his own friends who denied him and sold him out.

I've always thought the death of Jesus was like a spiritual game of blackjack. When the hand came down, the Romans hit, Judas doubled his bet, Jesus surrendered, the apostles just stood, and Peter split.

The point of the story is that *everyone* killed Jesus; all of them. And then Jesus comes back and forgives everyone.

ROME TO PITTSBURGH, A LONG AND WINDING ANTI-SEMITIC ROAD

Under imperial Christianity, Jews faced increasing legal restrictions, like prohibitions against new synagogues or holding certain offices. By the early Middle Ages, various church councils passed laws that restricted Jews' rights and segregated them from Christians. The Fourth Lateran Council in 1215 required Jews to wear distinctive clothing and to live in separate neighborhoods, which we would now call ghettos. Jews were often barred by Christians from owning land, holding public office, and participating in various careers.

During the Crusades, Jewish communities were attacked in Europe en route to the Holy Land, resulting in widespread massacres. The First Crusade of 1096 saw brutal attacks on Jewish communities in the Rhineland, now Germany. In cities like Worms, Mainz, and Cologne, Crusaders decimated Jewish communities, motivated by religious fervor and the spiritual joys of zealotry and plunder.

The twelfth century brought us the myth of blood libel, accusing Jews of murdering Christian children to use their blood in religious rituals. Certain Christians, all too happy to believe and spread the lie, righteously justified pogroms and massacres.

Throughout the Middle Ages and into the Renaissance, Jews faced expulsions from many European Christian countries: evicted from England in 1290, France in 1306 and 1394, and Spain in 1492. The Spanish Inquisition (1478–1834) even targeted Jews who had converted to Christianity, accusing them of secretly practicing Judaism, leading to more torture and execution.

Then Martin Luther comes along in the sixteenth century. Father of the Protestant Reformation, he's famously outraged at the hypocrisy and corruption of the church, and hailed as one of the great reformers of Christianity. He's also one of the most raging Jew-haters of all time.

Luther initially expressed hope of "reform" that would coerce Jews to convert to Christianity. When they didn't bite, he wrote venomously anti-Jewish tracts, such as the delicately titled *On the Jews and Their Lies* (1543), which called for harsh measures including the destruction of synagogues and the expulsion of Jews:

> Therefore, be on your guard against the Jews, knowing that wherever they have their synagogues, nothing is found but a den of devils in which sheer self-glory, conceit, lies, blasphemy, and defaming of God

> and men are practiced most maliciously and veheming his eyes on them. . . .
>
> But what will happen even if we do burn down the Jews' synagogues and forbid them publicly to praise God, to pray, to teach, to utter God's name? They will still keep doing it in secret. If we know that they are doing this in secret, it is the same as if they were doing it publicly, for our knowledge of their secret doings and our toleration of them implies that they are not secret after all and thus our conscience is encumbered with it before God."

It's easy to persecute when you're convinced an angry God will punish you for not persecuting.

By 1936, as European Jewish hatred began to reach its apex, the Nazis published a version of the Gospel of John designed exclusively to demonize Jews. German Bishop Weidemann wrote in the preface, "Lest sticklers become annoyed with us, we desire to help him who searches for truth. The German of the Third Reich must know what Christ, Whom the Jews nailed to the cross, means."

The prevailing Nazi belief was (and is) that Judaism was the enemy of Jesus, and that it was therefore *inconceivable* that Jesus could have been of Jewish blood. This conviction, along with centuries of religiously sanctioned hatred, facilitated the Shoah, with over six million souls exterminated by a Christian nationalist society.

Back in the States, Christian anti-Semitism was normalized by figures like Charles Coughlin, Catholic priest and vastly popular radio personality. Coughlin built a tremendous fan base in the early days of radio with coast-to-coast broadcasts that taught Christians to blame Jews for economic troubles, and promoted conspiracy theories about Jewish control of banking and government.

He also frequently linked Jews to communism, which is, of course, a thing these guys still do. They'll tell you Jews hoard all the money, *and they're also communists.*

Coughlin went on to claim that fascism was an appropriate response to the threat of communism and Jewish influence. In December 1938, following the Kristallnacht pogrom in Nazi Germany, the celebrity priest declared that Jewish refugees should not be allowed to enter the US, saying in 1938, "When we get through with the Jews of America, they'll think the treatment they received in Germany was nothing."

Henry Ford, founder of Ford Motor Company and one of America's most acclaimed industrialists, famously published a series of anti-Semitic articles in his newspaper, *The Dearborn Independent*, featuring bits of homespun wisdom like "Jews are the scavengers of the world. Wherever there's anything wrong with a country, you'll find the Jews." Ford collected his essays in the subtly titled *The International Jew: The World's Foremost Problem*.

After World War II ended and the horrors of the Holocaust were revealed, many Christian denominations began to reassess their bigoted and deeply stupid beliefs. The Catholic Church's Second Vatican Council (1962–1965) produced the *Nostra Aetate*, a document that repudiated the charge of deicide against Jews once and for all, at least for those who took the time to find and read it.

Ford Motor Company has apologized extensively, over years, for its founder's words, and even Glenn Beck apologized for his Christ-killing smears (although never on his TV show, it should be noted).

But anti-Semitism doesn't go away, it just assumes different forms.

Today, you'll find many right-wing Christians who hold on to certain anti-Semitic beliefs while still openly supporting the nation of Israel—but not because they care about Israelis.

THE CLAIM: "I can't possibly be anti-Semitic if I support the government of Israel."

THE AWKWARD REALITY: And as you've probably figured out, many Christian nationalists don't "stand up for Israel" because they have a genuine affinity for Jewish people or their well-being, but because of their interpretation of the prophecies related to the rapture.

Some of our fundamentalist friends with a premillennial dispensationalist bent believe that a literal rapture will occur, where true Christians are taken to heaven, and remaining humans will face the tribulations. Just like the Book of Revelation, except for how the word "rapture" never appears in the Bible.

They believe that once the tribulations begin, Jews will either face violent death from an angry God, or have the chance to be coerced into converting to Christianity. They love the Jews *that much*.

Pastor John Hagee touts himself as founder of Christians United for Israel, but he's not particularly fond of Jewish people. He tipped his hand to NPR in 2006 when he revealed, "It was the disobedience and rebellion of the Jews, God's chosen people, that gave us the Holocaust."

For master-race Christians, Israel is merely necessary to help fulfill a prophecy that whisks them to heaven while violently disposing of all the folks they don't much care for. The fate of the modern state of Israel is a necessary puzzle piece for these End Times elitists, so certain of their own Get-Out-of-Apocalypse-Free status.

Exclusionary Christianity

THE CLAIM: "Jesus is the only way to salvation, so other religions are false and inferior."

THE SCRIPTURE: "No one comes to the Father except through me" (John 14:6).

THE REBUTTAL: Many Christians interpret this one as a call to share their faith rather than to demean others. But when someone cites John 14:6 to condemn all non-Christians, the first thing I like to ask is "How exactly do we go *through* Jesus?"

I mean, if "no one comes to the Father except *through* him," do we have to physically pass through his body? His chest, rib cage, etc.?

If the answer is a disgusted "No, of course not," then congratulate your debate partner for realizing that Jesus spoke in parable and metaphor. He did *not* mean to literally pass through him.

Rather, Jesus means that no one "comes to the Father" unless they live by his teachings, believe in his divinity, or both. And if Jesus is love, is living by his teachings not enough of an access pass?

For fundamentalists, it doesn't matter how Jesus-like someone is—if they weren't born into the right religion, it's hellfire for all eternity—right there with the Jews, Buddhists, Muslims, atheists, Hindus, Zoroastrians, Wiccans, pagans, all the Native Americans, and probably the Scientologists, too. Theirs is an extremely homogeneous heaven.

But let's say someone actively worships Jesus—like, oh I don't know, the Nazis—but does the *opposite* of his commandments. Ask your exclusionary Christian friend, "Can a Nazi still get to heaven by belief alone? Or is it about following Jesus's teachings? Does a Nazi Christian score higher than a Christlike-non-Christian?"

Many Christians believe in a loving God who recognizes the sincerity of one's heart and actions, regardless of religious affiliation. Many Christians believe that sincere seekers of truth, regardless of their label, may still be part of God's big plan, whatever that winds up being. Many Christians believe in not being complete dicks to people.

Jesus, as we've seen, showed compassion to people outside his faith, which suggests a broader understanding of God's love that's not confined to just one club.

In John 14:2, part of Jesus's farewell to his disciples, he says, "In my Father's house are many mansions: if it were not so, I would have told you. I go to prepare a place for you" (KJV).

"Many mansions" can be seen as a metaphor for the diversity of ways people can relate to God, emphasizing that God's universe is wide enough to accommodate different faith traditions and personal journeys. And it could be seen as a promise of God's inclusivity, offering space for all people, reflecting the very Jesus-like idea that God's kingdom is not limited.

But that won't stop people who believe God judges humans based on their religious affiliation, rather than for their hearts and actions. And if you're elevating yourself above others based on your belief in Jesus, then you don't actually believe in Jesus. His movement's 100 percent about humility.

ISLAM: A WHOLE RELIGION FUNDAMENTALISTS GET TO HATE!

When a 2017 Pew Research Center survey showed that nearly three-quarters of white evangelicals believed there to be a natural conflict between Islam and democracy, many expressed shock that 25 percent of white evangelicals *didn't* feel that way.

Islamophobia is one of many bigotries available to Christians who don't much care for DEI commandments against judgment and condemnation of others.

When I was a teenager, my family was unexpectedly blessed when my beautiful Italian American cousin Debbie from New Jersey married an Egyptian doctor. I had never been to a cross-cultural wedding before; getting unreasonably attractive and brilliant mixed-race cousins could only benefit my gene pool.

When my father first began having health problems, it was our Egyptian American cousin who helped get him into Sloan Kettering for treatment. So we were seriously not allowed to ever be unkind toward Muslims.

Islam is the third largest religion in the US, right after Christianity and Judaism. Compared with 70.6 percent of Americans who follow Christianity, Muslims comprise 0.9 percent of the population, but their numbers are growing. Islam is also one of the most racially diverse religions in the US.

During the Crusades (eleventh to thirteenth centuries), Christian religious zeal was supercharged by a desire to reclaim the Holy Land from Muslim control. The rhetoric surrounding these military campaigns pushed biblical justification for violence against Muslims, portraying them as enemies of Christendom. This set a historic precedent for despising all of Islam, a narrative that's persisted in various charming forms.

After 9/11, frenzied Christians openly demonized every Muslim who had ever drawn breath. Innocent people victimized by the Islamophobic rage included not only Muslims, but also Hindus, Sikhs, and Christians—especially if they were nonwhite and/or wore different-looking clothes. America got a front-row seat to a right-wing Christianity that seemed sanctioned by God to burn in searing hatred for an entire faith.

Stereotyping based on the actions of a minority contradicts the biblical call to love one's neighbor and not favor one group over another (James 2:1). It's no different from claiming all Christians are Nazis based on the ones who committed the Holocaust, or that all Catholic priests are . . . well, you know.

No Love Like Christian Hate, Muslim Edition

Of the many bigotries wallowed in by Christian nationalist nepo-baby Franklin Graham, his hatred of Muslims stands out: "The God of Islam is not the same God . . . I believe it is a very evil and wicked religion."

Rev. Pat Robertson preached in 2002, "[Islam] is not a peaceful religion that wants to coexist. They want to coexist until they can control, dominate and then, if need be, destroy."

Chip off the ol' bigot Jerry Falwell Jr. asserted, "If more good people had concealed carry permits, then we could end those Muslims before they walked in."

Southern Baptist pastor and prominent Trump supporter Robert Jeffress teaches us that "Islam is wrong. It is a heresy from the pit of hell."

THE CLAIM: "Islam worships a false God."

In 2003, Lt. Gen. William Boykin, deputy undersecretary of defense for intelligence, made some remarks while in uniform to a group of fundamentalists. While recounting a Muslim terror suspect he'd been hunting, Boykin said, "I knew that my God was bigger than his. I knew that my God was a real God, and his was an idol."

THE FACTS: It's the same God, folks.

What the good general and so many fail to realize is that both Christians and Muslims believe in a single, omnipotent, and transcendent deity. Allah is a contraction for *al-ilāh,* "the-God," in Arabic. Back in the seventh century, the first Muslims described God with basically the same name the Hebrews used, "eloh" or "elohim." Abraham is considered the founder of all three religions. Sorry, bros.

THE CLAIM: "Islam hates Christianity."

THE FACTS: Muslims revere Jesus as a great prophet, and the Virgin Mary is mentioned more in the Quran than in the Bible.

Islam teaches that the Quran is the final revelation from God, and earlier prophets, including Jesus and Moses, received revelations from the same God. They view Muhammad as the final messenger, meant to complete the monotheism trilogy.

The Mormons went their own way post–New Testament; the Muslims took their own Part Three in another direction.

NO, CHRISTIANS CAN'T HATE MUSLIMS AND STILL BE CHRISTIAN

Belief in Jesus doesn't mandate hatred or discrimination against different faiths; the teachings of Jesus forbid it. Islamophobia requires division and conflict, rather than peace and reconciliation.

"Love your neighbor as yourself" (Matthew 22:39). Note the lack of an asterisk on this commandment, which sadly means it applies to all humanity, without regard to said neighbor's religion, race, or background.

So if you hate Muslims or Jews because "they reject Jesus," then it's actually *you* who's rejecting Jesus. Real followers of the Nazarene are required to love both Palestinians and Israelis equally. Try that line at the cookout.

GIVE ME A CHRISTLIKE ATHEIST OVER A FRAUD CHRISTIAN ANY DAY.

I love many atheists. I like to say that I believe in them, but my nonbeliever friends get tired of that joke.

I also love many people of different faiths. And all my life, I've watched atheist and believer friends fight each other, often abrasively. Which honestly always seemed strange, because both groups have one crucial thing in common—nobody actually knows anything.

Belief in God is great. Hey—you've got to blame somebody. But I also believe that the nonbelievers who champion reason, science, and common sense, and all the non-Christians who value love over fear and superstition, will find a special place in heaven. Should there be one.

And I can say this because some of the most Christlike people I've known have been atheists, and some of the most unholy heathens I've met call themselves "Christian."

But our friends in right-wing media would disagree, and atheist-bashing is always solid and acceptable ratings bait for a cable news audience.

And yes, hatred of atheists is fundamentally against the teachings of Jesus.

They Know Not What They Meme

THE CLAIM: "Atheists are bad people we should look down on."

THE SCRIPTURE: "The fool says in his heart, 'There is no God'" (Psalm 14:1).

THE CONTEXT: This verse is often cited to label atheists as "fools" and to suggest that denying God's existence is inherently irrational or dumb. The problem is, there really wasn't an atheist movement as we know it in the ancient Holy Land, so these scriptures aren't about nonbelievers. In the biblical context, the term "fool" (Hebrew: *nabal*) often refers to someone who is morally corrupt, rather than someone who lacks belief in God.

The context of this psalm is more about a specific moral or spiritual failing and is in no way a blanket condemnation of all nonbelievers.

THE CLAIM: "Yeah, but Jesus says it, too."

THE SCRIPTURE: "Whoever does not believe will be condemned" (Mark 16:16).

THE CONTEXT: Again, this verse doesn't justify any animosity toward atheists, or anyone else who doesn't share the same beliefs. The verse focuses on the relationship between faith and salvation, highlighting personal accountability in a spiritual sense—it doesn't prescribe how Christians should treat nonbelievers.

The Great Commission (Matthew 28:19–20) calls for spreading the gospel through teaching and example, not through coercion, hatred, or hostility. In Christian theology, judgment and condemnation are roles reserved for God. Passages such as Romans 12:19 assert: "Do not take revenge, my dear friends, but leave room for God's wrath, for it is written: 'It is mine to avenge; I will repay,' says the Lord."

Christians are called to witness and serve their faith, not to judge or condemn others for their beliefs or lack thereof. If actual Christians really believed that atheists were condemned to eternal suffering, they'd go *out of their way* to be kind to these poor damned souls.

Which brings us to that surprising friend of the nonbeliever, Pope Francis.

In 2013 Francis was still new on the job, so things were a little shaky. Maybe he resented that Pope Emeritus Benedict still got to hang around the Vatican and make him wear that "trainee" badge.

But the new pope really upset the papal routine when he did something that popes almost never do—something cool. Francis said that *everyone* can be redeemed through good deeds, even atheists.

Using scripture from the Gospel of Mark, Francis explained how Jesus's disciples were upset that someone apart from their group was doing good. In other words, Jesus was preaching that those outside of one's exclusive spiritual club can still be good people.

Francis emphasized the importance of "doing good" as a principle that unites all humanity. "They complain," the Pope said in his homily, "'If he is not one of us, he cannot do good. If he is not of our party, he cannot do good.' And Jesus corrects them: 'Do not hinder him,' he says, 'let him do good.'"

The disciples, Pope Francis explained, "were a little intolerant," closed off by the idea of owning the truth, convinced that "those who do not have the truth, cannot do good."

I guess that's why there are no scenes in the Bible of Jesus in high school. If you think he was hassled as an adult, just imagine how the jocks at Nazareth High would've reacted to his anti-clique message.

Francis went on to say, "All of us have this commandment at heart: do good and do not do evil. All of us. 'But, Father, this is not Catholic! He cannot do good.' Yes, he can . . . The Lord has redeemed all of us, all of us . . . not just Catholics. Everyone! 'Father, atheists?' Even atheists. Everyone! We must meet one another doing good. 'But I don't believe, Father, I am an atheist!' But do good: we will meet one another there."

Then Francis broke out his acoustic guitar and sang a rousing chorus of "Get Together" backed up by the Vatican's Swiss Guard Jesse Colin Young tribute band.

Not surprisingly, the elders of the church flipped out. A pope who says atheists go to heaven? Won't that upset all those dead misunderstood pedophiles who still got to heaven anyway?

Of course, this compassion and common sense expressed by the pope was soon met with a "correction" from the Vatican. Francis was only the pope, so it's not like he's qualified to speak for all Catholics.

The Vatican quickly issued a statement asserting that despite what Francis had said, non-Catholics are still going to hell. You know, like Gandhi, the Dalai Lama, Malcolm X, Golda Meir, MLK, and Pocahontas.

Those who refuse to join the Catholic Church, a Vatican spokesman said, "cannot be saved." In other words, go ahead and do all the good you want, folks; help your fellow human and be a giving, moral person. But if you don't buy this one organization's specific set of beliefs, all your good deeds and service to humankind count for nothing, and you win an eternity of pointlessly burning in agonizing unending damnation. Amen.

THOU SHALT NOT BE, OR DEFEND, A WHITE SUPREMACIST

"Anyone who claims to be in the light but hates a brother or sister is still in the darkness."

1 John 2:9

"We have abundant reason to rejoice that in this Land the light of truth and reason has triumphed over the power of bigotry and superstition, and that every person here may worship God according to the dictates of his own heart. In this enlightened Age and in this Land of equal liberty it is our boast that a man's religious tenets will not forfeit the protection of the Laws, nor deprive him of the right of attaining and holding the highest Offices that are known in the United States."

George Washington, who owned people

I'd like to begin and end this chapter on Christian prejudice by telling you a bit about my paternal grandfather.

My grandfather was named Leonard, and sometimes went by Lenny. He was a real old-school Brooklyn guy, with an accent you only hear nowadays in old movies. He said things like "cock-a-roach," and pronounced Broadway "Broad-WAY." He was a house painter who had painted the homes of both General Douglas MacArthur and Bob Keeshan (aka Captain Kangaroo). This impressed me deeply as a child, and honestly it still does.

As my grandmother's health declined, my grandparents moved out near us on Long Island and became a regular part of our lives. Leonard was kind and warm, and he dutifully cared for my grandmother through several brutal years of declining health.

He was also a rather prejudiced working-class white guy from Brooklyn and bigoted toward many, many types of people. It was from him that I first learned:

"Da Blacks cause all da crime."

"Da Jews killed Jesus Christ."

"Da Pawta Rickens take all da jobs."

My mother, who loved and cared for her father-in-law, would politely refer to him as "Archie Bunker" when he wasn't around.

He was also a devout Catholic who never missed Mass. But even at church, my grandpa found ways to discriminate. He would only receive Communion wafers from an actual priest, and staunchly refused to take bread and wine from any plainclothes eucharistic ministers—including my dad. If we were in line for Communion, and Grandpa could see a civilian, not a priest, dispensing the host to his line, he'd abruptly switch lines to make sure he only received from the real deal. "I only take da holy Eucharist from a Cat-lick priest," he'd tell me.

I swear, in my memory he called it "the holy Uterus," but I'm sure that's not the case.

My mother would later share stories of harrowing arguments my dad had with his own father over dinner, shouting fights about civil rights, Nixon, and the Vietnam War. But for years, I was too young to know I had a prejudiced grandpa; he was always very friendly, even if he constantly smoked in the house.

Before I had the vocabulary to put such confusion into words, I'd notice how tense Mom and Dad got every time Emmanuel Lewis would pop up on TV in a Burger King commercial, and Grandpa would call him "Da little colored kid." And that was one of the more benign comments.

Many of us have had family like this; many of us have loved family like this; and many of us have struggled with the impression that prejudice and Christianity seem to be a package deal.

Modern white supremacy exists on a broad, and expanding, spectrum. From the KKK, neo-Nazis, and armed militias to bloviating public intellectuals lending credibility to white replacement theory, from dog-whistle politicians and media to smiling church folk who oppose every racial justice movement, generations of white Christians have resisted any changes to a racially exclusive status quo.

Some of the most heinous acts of white supremacist violence have been carried out by individuals or groups who claimed to serve Christian values, from the 16th Street Baptist Church bombing of 1963 to the Charleston church massacre of 2015 and the 2017 Unite the Right rally in Charlottesville.

But white supremacy is a system that can't merely be reduced to its most violent expressions. Supremacists don't all necessarily *hate* anyone; it's often easier to just stay pleasantly indifferent to racial injustices and talk vaguely about "traditional demographics" and "heritage."

But all forms of white supremacy—belief in the superiority of white people over others—stand in direct contradiction to the life and teachings of Jesus, who consistently commanded love for all people, especially the persecuted or marginalized. Jesus was about humbling oneself, not exalting one's own group. White supremacy divides humanity into superior and inferior groups, giving a pasty middle finger to Jesus's message of radical unity.

Christian theology teaches that every person is made in the *Imago Dei*—the image of God (Genesis 1:27). White supremacy rejects this by implying that some humans look more like that image than others.

In Luke 4:24–27, Jesus enraged his own townspeople by reminding them that God could bless despised outsiders like Phoenicians and Syrians while Israelites suffer. He totally lost the crowd by dismantling the kind of exclusion that supremacist ideology requires.

When white supremacists chant *"You will not replace us"* or desperately claim that they must protect "white heritage" through cultural domination, they're aligning themselves with the rich fool who hoards treasures on earth (Luke 12:13–21), not with Jesus.

And don't tell your racist cousin, but placing racial preference above Jesus's commandments to love technically counts as idolatry. Jesus said that God's kingdom is not of this world (John 18:36) and our earthly divisions should not dictate spiritual truths.

No one can serve both Christ and white supremacy. It's not merely un-Christian; it is anti-Christian.

SLAVERY, WITH HAM

America is the only nation on earth where Christianity has been historically entwined with white supremacy from its beginning. Slavery, and the succeeding years of segregation and institutionalized racism in America, endured for one reason—Christian leaders consistently validated it.

From precolonial days, US Christians who defended owning, raping, beating, and selling other humans used biblical interpretations to justify an economic and moral evil that some Christians still won't acknowledge. They cited passages that seemed to condone slavery, or at least punishment for Black people. The fact that these arguments weren't from Jesus never seemed to matter, nor did the fact that these arguments were absolute moral sewage.

As they did with the Native peoples, slaveholders and their defenders claimed that converting enslaved Africans to Christianity was actually a benevolent act, since it would obviously save their souls and improve their moral character, as they were gradually worked to death. It was an unholy pretext for maintaining control over enslaved humans *and* reinforcing their subservience. Being "saved" didn't save them.

The granddaddy of psychotic theological fraud was "the Curse of Ham," used for *centuries* to justify the superiority of some races and the enslavement of nonwhite peoples. I first learned this one when I took an Old Testament as Literature course in college, and I still have a hard time believing this is something America used.

THE CLAIM: "God sanctioned slavery for Black people because of Noah's son."

THE SCRIPTURE: Genesis 9: 20–24.

The story appears in the Genesis account of Noah, and it is some seriously ridiculous and deeply unholy bullshit.

Ham was one of Noah's three sons, all of whom came off the ark post-flood. One day, Noah was happily enjoying the fruits of his vineyard when he got so drunk he passed out naked in his tent. Ham accidentally walked in, and I'll let Genesis explain the rest:

"Ham, the father of Canaan, saw his father naked and told his two brothers outside. But Shem and Japheth took a garment and laid it across their shoulders; then they walked in backward and covered their father's naked body. Their faces were turned the other way so that they would not see their father naked. When Noah awoke from his wine and found out what his youngest son had done to him, he said, 'Cursed be Canaan! The lowest of slaves will he be to his brothers.'"

Now, this curse was directed at Canaan, Ham's son, and it was prophesied that Canaan's descendants would be "servants" to the descendants of Shem and Japheth, who didn't commit the sin of seeing their drunk naked dad, because Ham had thoughtfully warned them first.

Some might say this story was a sign that Noah needed to go to a meeting, but for centuries of theologians, it meant slavery got to be on the menu. Ham is cited as the father of Canaan, Put, Egypt, and Cush, which sometimes, for some, referred to Africa. Many Christians were duly instructed that

1. Noah cursed Ham,
2. Ham's brown-skinned descendants went on to populate Africa, and,

3. logically, this meant God wanted African people to always be servants.

You got that? A five-hundred- to six-hundred-year-old man gets so sloshed he passes out buck naked, his kid is forced to witness this, and that's why slavery's okay.

It's so manipulative, so evil, so stupid, and it was more than enough.

THE DEBUNKING: Where to begin?

Noah cursed Canaan, Ham's son, who wasn't even there. Why? Some scholars have speculated it's a storytelling device, as the Canaanites would later be mortal enemies to the Jewish people. Others theorize that young Canaan was actually the one who saw the old man naked. But if Ham's descendants were meant to be slaves, and Ham was also the "Father of Egypt," then why was Egypt the nation famous for taking slaves?

It probably won't surprise you to learn that the Bible never mentions the race of Ham or his descendants. The text simply states that Canaan would be a *servant* to his relatives. There was never any biblical basis for linking this "curse" to *any* specific race or ethnic group. Nonetheless, for centuries Black people were known as "the sons of Ham," and the "Curse of Ham" theology gave a green light to white supremacy and black subordination.

Christian slavery defenders never doubted their piety, knowing their human property was sanctioned by the Almighty. The penalty for the dad who gets drunk and passes out naked in front of the kids, however, remains unrevealed.

Both Mormon church founder Joseph Smith and his famous successor Brigham Young taught that Black people were under the Curse of Ham, as well as the Curse of Cain. Recall that after Cain kills his brother and God banishes him from the garden, God puts a mark on Cain so that no one can harm him.

The Mormons believed that the "Mark of Cain" meant black skin, leading them to forbid Black people from entering the Mormon priesthood. In 1978, when Christian president Jimmy Carter threatened to revoke their tax-exempt status over this racism, God suddenly revealed that they were finally allowed to let dark-skinned men—only men—become priests.

The Curse of Ham would eventually be fully debunked by scholars as a misapplication of scripture, but centuries of damage had been done.

We should be very clear—there is no possible way to follow the teachings of Jesus and engage in or defend the practice of slavery. Christians who own slaves aren't Christian, no matter how brutally they force their slaves to convert.

Jesus lays down the Golden Rule in both Matthew 7:12 and Luke 6:31 when he says, "Do to others as you would have them do to you." Unless you're enslaving someone because you yourself would like someone to do it to you, this one's pretty airtight. Raping, mutilating, and owning people are in no way covered under this policy.

Defending monuments and flags that celebrate white supremacists who slaughtered US troops to keep innocent people enslaved isn't really covered by Jesus, either.

Once slavery was officially ended, a century of American apartheid began. And it probably won't surprise you to learn that under Jim Crow, Christians on the right argued that racial segregation was just part of God's natural order.

Sure, slavery was wrong, and we get that now (as we put up statues glorifying the guys who fought for it). But segregation, they preached, was a holy and sacred way to preserve the purity of each race, which was seen as a moral duty. They claimed that God created distinct races, and that mingling or mixing them was against His divine plan; the Bible justified separate racial nations with God-ordained boundaries, which proves that God would hate integration.

Four years after the federal desegregation mandates following *Brown v. Board of Education*, Southern Baptist pastor Rev. Jerry Falwell sermonized, "If Chief Justice [Earl] Warren and his associates had known God's Word and had desired to do the Lord's will, I am quite confident that the 1954 decision would never have been made. . . . When God has drawn a line of distinction, we should not attempt to cross that line."

Rev. Bob Jones Sr. gave a radio address on Easter Sunday 1960 titled "Is Segregation Scriptural?" where he cited Acts of the Apostles: "From one man he made all the nations, that they should inhabit the whole earth; and he marked out their appointed times in history and the boundaries of their lands" (Acts 17:26).

This was proof, said Jones Sr., "that God Almighty fixed the bounds of their habitation. That is as clear as anything that was ever said."

Except "nations" doesn't mean "races." Also, the verse clearly focuses on the unity of all humanity as descendants of *one ancestor* (Adam), highlighting our shared origin. This actually signifies equality and cancels out any claim of racial superiority.

Jesus *never* condemns interracial or interethnic relationships. His focus is always on the human heart, breaking down barriers, and one's relationship with God, never external attributes like race or ethnicity. White supremacists don't read the book.

It was only in 1967 that the Supreme Court's decision in *Loving v. Virginia* struck down state laws banning interracial marriage, declaring them unconstitutional. And for decades, nobody ever had to worry that a future Supreme Court might revisit it.

WHITE PEOPLE, TIRED OF TAKING IT FROM THE MAN

A core element of Christian nationalism is the myth that America was founded as a deeply Christian nation, and yeah, we may have dabbled in a little ethnic cleansing, some random occasional slavery, and some barely there segregation, but that doesn't matter in our golden imagined past.

I hope I'm not spoiling anything here, but most Christian racists don't think their views are problematic. They'll tell you that white Christians built the US, all on their own, and anyone who uses woke race-baiting terms like "slavery" or "genocide" or "systemic" probably hates white people, and that's why we need prayer in schools.

For all of our lives—and our parents' and grandparents'—white Christians have dominated society and influence in the US. In the 1970s and

1980s, white Christians (including both Protestants and Catholics) made up a majority of the population, accounting for nearly two-thirds of Americans.

But by the early 2020s, this figure had dropped to about 40 percent. White evangelical Protestants, a significant subgroup, have also experienced decline, shrinking to roughly 14 percent of the population as of 2022.

Today, a large segment of the Republican Party base believes whites are the true victims of racism, and that Christians are under attack. Which makes a lot of sense when you consider that our most popular religion has always been Christianity, whites are still our largest racial group, and white Christians still dominate elected office at all levels, as well as the judiciary, corporate America, land ownership, media control, and Renaissance Faires.

In a 2020 poll from the Public Religion Research Institute (PRRI), more than seven in ten Fox News Republicans said that there's a lot of discrimination against Christians, and 58 percent claimed there's a lot toward white people. Only around *one-third or less* say that Black people (36 percent), Hispanic people (34 percent), or Asian people (27 percent) face discrimination like white folks must endure.

In PRRI's 2023 survey, asked whether they agreed or disagreed with the statement "immigrants are invading our country and replacing our cultural and ethnic background," 81 percent of Christian nationalist adherents agreed.

The creeping panic of no longer being the majority has led some of our friends and neighbors to see Christian nationalism as the only way to get a lost nation back on track. It's all about power and domination. The movement is growing, and it doesn't have to be huge to be dangerous. Quite a few of these racists are armed, delusional, and in the process of completely freaking out.

DENIAL, A RIVER IN AMERICA

In a 2018 PRRI survey, 86 percent of white evangelical Protestants and 70 percent of both white mainline Protestants and Catholics said that the "Confederate flag is more a symbol of Southern pride than of racism."

Ten states—all in the South—observe both Martin Luther King Jr. Day and at least one Confederate holiday. In 2000, when South Carolina became one of the last states to honor MLK with a state holiday, the legislature also voted to create "Confederate Memorial Day." Florida doesn't celebrate Juneteenth, but maintains multiple state holidays honoring white supremacist Confederates.

When my parents first retired down south, they adjusted to church calendars that listed MLK Day as "Jackson-Lee-King Day." Martin Luther King's federal holiday had been piggybacked with the names of two white supremacists who'd taken up arms against the US to guarantee Dr. King would be born a white man's property. In the twenty-first century, there are Christians who put all three of those men on the same moral level.

I asked theologian and author Dillon Naber Cruz about Christians who also engage in, or defend, white supremacy: "Jesus did not qualify his command 'to love as I have loved' (John 13:34) by saying 'only if you understand them and their lived experience.' He likewise did not qualify 'love your neighbor as yourself' with any statements about whether or not someone arrived in a country legally or not, whether they follow the same faith as you or not, whether or not they speak the language, or any other qualification that racists, bigots, and Christian supremacists do.

"Christians should strive to be like Daryl Davis, the Black man who befriends KKK members and gets them to leave the Klan behind. That is radical. That is Christlike. I hope that one day soon I can be more like Daryl Davis than I currently am because I do struggle to find love and compassion for people who espouse hatred towards others."

When the Natives Are More Christlike Than the Colonizers

When the Wampanoag fed the Pilgrims on that first mythic Thanksgiving, they had no idea they'd just invented a social safety net for undocumented immigrants.

But without ever hearing of Jesus, they welcomed the stranger and fed the hungry. You tell me who was closer to Christ—those Indigenous people, or the Christians who took their land?

Community and Generosity

- Jesus taught his followers to care for one another, saying, "Give to everyone who asks of you" (Luke 6:30). The early Christian community shared everything in common (Acts 2:44–45).
- Indigenous nations often prioritize the group over the individual. Resources are shared to ensure collective well-being, rather than individual accumulation of wealth. Potlatch ceremonies among Northwest Coast tribes are a way of redistributing wealth and honoring generosity.

Peacemaking and Forgiveness

- Jesus blessed the peacemakers (Matthew 5:9), forgave his enemies, even on the cross (Luke 23:34), and taught his followers to turn the other cheek (Matthew 5:39).
- Many Indigenous practices emphasize resolving conflict through council meetings and restorative justice over punishment. The Iroquois Confederacy's Great Law of Peace influenced democratic peacemaking principles.

Respect for the Marginalized

- Jesus consistently uplifted the poor, sick, and outcasts: "Whatever you did for one of the least of these . . . you did for me" (Matthew 25:40).

- Elders, children, and those in need hold special respect in many Native cultures. The Lakota value of *Wóohola* (respect) calls for honoring *every* member of the community.

Leadership as Service

- Jesus defined leadership as servanthood, teaching, "Whoever wants to become great among you must be your servant" (Mark 10:43).
- Native tribal leaders are often expected to serve their communities selflessly. The concept of the "servant leader" is deeply rooted in Indigenous governance.

Big Humble

- Jesus embodied humility, from birth in a manger to washing his disciples' feet (John 13:12–17). He taught that "the first will be last" (Matthew 20:16) and blessed the "poor in spirit" (Matthew 5:3).
- Humility is a cornerstone of many Native cultures, seen as essential for living in harmony with the Creator and community. The Navajo tradition teaches individuals to "walk in beauty" with humility.

Given the extremely clear ethical teachings of Jesus, white supremacy must be called out as not only a social evil but also a theological heresy. In Dr. Anthea Butler's essential *White Evangelical Racism: The Politics of Morality* in America, she writes, "Because of racism, evangelical decency was lost, and evangelicals' resentments grew."

I asked her, is there even a way to "fix" the movement?

She replied, "Evangelicals will have to become more accepting of others, willing to let go of racism, and actually pay attention to the Red-Letter words of Jesus. Right now, I don't think there is any way to fix the movement unless it has a crushing, decisive defeat at its quest to make America a theocracy."

We're presently witnessing US white supremacists finally realizing they're about to become a minority. They're not going to go gracefully.

According to the US Census Bureau and various studies based on trends in birth rates, immigration, and changing racial and ethnic identification, white folks are projected to become a minority (meaning less than 50 percent of the total population) around the year 2045.

So, if you know a Christian who's afraid of one day becoming a minority, this might be a perfect time to be more Christian to minorities.

Let me end this chapter on prejudice where I began, with my grandfather, Lenny the house painter from Brooklyn.

When I was fourteen, Lenny's wife died after long, agonizing years of illness; he subsequently came to live with us. He'd been caring for her for years, all the while ignoring his own lung cancer from decades of heavy smoking.

My brothers were both down south that summer, and I was doing Long Island regional theater every night. During the day, I'd watch Mets games with my grandfather. As a lifelong Brooklynite who'd never recovered from the Dodgers leaving for California, his greatest bigotry was for the Bronx. "I only watch da Mets. Dat's it. No Yankees. If da Mets aren't on, I'll watch da Yankees and root for them ta lose."

Each night I'd get home late after a rehearsal or show, and my grandfather would be sitting at the kitchen table, in too much discomfort to sleep, smoking. I'd sit with him every single night and talk until I could no longer stay awake; often I'd just sit there with him in silence.

I loved him so much. I was painfully inarticulate and knew he was dying, and I had come to see his many prejudices by then. I couldn't understand how this particular man had raised a son like my father, who was such a staunch anti-racist before that term even existed.

But I do understand, as so many do, how you can love a family member in spite of their racism, anti-Semitism, xenophobia, homophobia, or misogyny, or in the case of my grandfather, all of the above. I also understand that sometimes love is the only thing that can ever draw them away from their prejudices, hang-ups, and hate.

A few months later, my grandfather took a bad fall and was rushed to Stony Brook University Hospital, where it became clear that the end was near.

As my grandfather lingered, still conscious, my dad called his local parish to request a priest to come perform the last rites. But when he arrived, my parents were alarmed that the church had dispatched a *Filipino* priest to pray with my grandfather.

The sadness and dread in my parents' faces was something I'll never forget. They actually asked me to wait in the hospital corridor at first, as they didn't want my last memory of the old man to be one of racism, a racism that repels the very love that seeks to heal it.

But in the end, my grandfather was past all that. He warmly received a nonwhite priest. They prayed together and held hands, the last rites were administered, and my grandfather thanked the priest, who embraced him in his hospital bed.

I was holding my grandfather's hand when he died. But my enduring memory of the whole experience was the gratitude in my parents' faces. At the end of an old Catholic man's life, he was able to overcome a curse, a curse that had been placed within him, and embrace someone of a different race with love and gratitude. One of the saddest days of my father's life was also one of his happiest.

THE CHRISTIANS AND THE CHRIST FOLLOWERS

"The Christian ideal has not been tried and found wanting. It has been found difficult; and left untried."

G. K. Chesterton

"Not everything that is faced can be changed, but nothing can be changed until it is faced."

James Baldwin

Now perhaps you're thinking—so what? You've made it to the end of all this and you've decided to just let the right-wingers have Christianity. Let it rot. It's responsible for incalculable suffering, oppression, torture, injustice, and terrible music. Lots of great symphonies and gospel music, sure, but also a pestilence of Christian rock bands violating the commandment "Thou shalt not suck."

And I can't disagree with all the harm Christianity's been used to inflict. Apparently, Jesus died for our sins so we could commit all new ones, with brutal creativity. There's no way to accurately measure the pain that's been inflicted in Jesus's name, cloaked in all the respectability of organized religion.

But the flip side to this argument is why faith has continued to sustain and evolve. Organized religion and individual spirituality are not the same.

And there's no way to measure the amount of good that has come through all kinds of spiritual *and* religious people. History and media don't record the everyday acts of individual love and kindness by Christians, Jews, Muslims, and all believers of good faith.

I'd like to think the media will get it together and stop letting these mean frauds hide behind religion. Imagine a news culture where fundamentalist preachers and politicians are asked follow-up questions about what their holy books actually say.

THE YIN AND YANG OF CHRISTIANITY

If there's one thing Martin Luther King Jr. showed history, it's that liberal Christians—and their conservative and non-Christian allies—have the power to stand up to an authoritarian Christian establishment and call it out on its own terms. And for every grifting fundamentalist preacher, there have always been real Jesus followers who walk the walk.

The fundamentalists' and nationalists' Holy War has never been for Jesus, and it's never been against Satan. It's always just been a struggle for their own power.

Maybe we just need to acknowledge, as a culture, that there are "Christians," and there are "Christ followers," and that those two groups are not always necessarily the same.

I know. You're so close to the end, and I'm playing with semantics. But "Christians" and "Christ followers" can reflect a stark divergence in beliefs, values, and actions.

Christian nationalists have always wielded faith as a tool of control and exclusion, prioritizing power and cultural preference over the words of Jesus. But Christ followers have always resisted these abuses and aligned themselves with the call to justice, mercy, and love.

Christian nationalists have always sought cultural dominance through legislation and suppression of dissent. But the Christ followers have always stood against oppression, embodying Jesus's teachings of justice and compassion.

Authentic Christianity puts the well-being of others first; it defends the persecuted, and serves rather than rules.

When colonizing Christians began their slaughter, Christ followers like Bartolomé de Las Casas shamed them with a Bible.

When Crusader Christians justified violence, Christ followers like St. Francis used nonviolence and scripture to demand peace.

When Confederate Christians justified human enslavement, Christ followers like Frederick Douglass, Harriet Tubman, and the Quakers called out slavery as a moral abomination and resisted.

When authoritarian Christians enforced segregation, Christ followers like MLK, Howard Thurman, Fannie Lou Hamer, and James Lawson took to the streets and took down systemic evil without violence.

In the late-nineteenth and early-twentieth centuries, certain Christian capitalists aligned with industrialists to oppose labor reforms, justifying greed and exploitation. And Christ followers like Dorothy Day and the Catholic Worker Movement championed the Biblical rights of laborers.

When Christian nationalists have pushed anti-LGBTQ legislation and bigotry, Christ followers like Gene Robinson, the first openly gay bishop in the Episcopal Church, and the Reverend Troy Perry, founder of the Metropolitan Community Church, have embraced LGBTQ individuals as beloved children of God.

Some of the best humans I've known have been Christ followers, and they weren't all Christian.

The world we share is changing. As of this writing, two-thirds of American adults identify as Christian. Back in the nineties, it was still 90 percent. If right-wing evangelicals and Catholics really want to slow the exodus of Americans from organized religion, this would be the perfect time to drop the hate, xenophobia, and Christian supremacy and build a movement that inspires people.

Standing up for the marginalized, conserving the planet and its resources, fighting injustice and poverty, and not judging people's private lives are all deeply popular ideas that align quite nicely with Jesus. Sure, they'd alienate some older bigoted demographics, and for many churches, they still fill the pews. But that demographic's already going away.

In a world of division and power struggles, the only authentic path forward for Christianity is reclaiming the essence of Jesus's teachings—challenging systems of injustice, caring for the struggling, and embodying love in word, deed, and policy.

I wrote this book because I was tired of fundamentalists distorting the Bible, tired of watching the faith of my parents used as cover for meanness. Everyone reading this probably knows someone who's a captive of toxic Christianity. For many of us, these aren't faceless crazed zealots and nationalists; they're our neighbors, coworkers, old friends, family members. We can't despise them back. We just can't.

We're called to be compassionate to these folks, to never give up on love, empathy, or critical thinking to reach them. Maybe you've witnessed a fundamentalist who grows beyond what they were programmed to be. It can be scary and wonderful. And growth is not to be answered with smug liberal "I told ya so's."

We can't hate them. But in a democracy, we must beat them.

This struggle against hypocrisy and spiritual thuggery won't be fought by politicians. It'll be won by ordinary people, calmly proving that hate is not a Christian value—at their jobs, over the family dinner table, and on social media.

If you want to trigger and enrage Christian nationalists, Jesus will show the way. Stand up for the oppressed, welcome the stranger, love your enemy, fight poverty and injustice, resist violence, and choose compassion.

Or just ask them which Jesus teachings justify their politics.

In Rian Johnson's film *The Last Jedi*, an aged Luke Skywalker says, "The Jedi don't own the Force."

It's almost a throwaway line, beautifully delivered by Mark Hamill. But it urgently speaks to the reality of toxic fundamentalism, a religion with many faces, all believing they own religion and faith itself.

But religious authorities don't own God, they don't own Jesus, they don't own the Bible, they don't own America, and they don't own you.

Ask your fundamentalist or Christian nationalist to read the Sermon on the Mount and then look at what their church fights for. Is their faith community working for the stuff Jesus talked about, or is he just a mascot for a mean little club that preaches superiority over service?

Authentic Christianity doesn't seek dominance, but transformation. Jesus of the Bible is constantly telling you to go *beyond your religion's rules* into a deeper kind of love.

This love is not merely a form of affection, or some passive, permissive state. It's an action-verb love, with all its challenges, discipline, and healing.

And finally, I'm not really here because two people once "broke a promise to God."

My father always told me that the same love that led him into the Franciscan order eventually led him *beyond* it: to marriage, family, a paycheck, and a house, to paying all those bills and taking all those extra shifts, hoping that maybe you'll leave the world a little bit better, since that's our part of the deal.

I'm only able to take up your time here because both of my parents once gave their lives to their church—their names, their freedom, their chastity, their obedience. For years. And then, they had a new spiritual calling.

Sometimes, changing your mind about religion is the most spiritual thing you can do.

My parents chose love over religion, because love is the only religion that always works.

Acknowledgments

This book was written in Florida, California, and New York; and in over two dozen hotel rooms across the United States.

With gratitude to my family; to Charmien LaFramenta for years of support, being my toughest living critic and sending me into isolation when I needed it. Thank you to Henry Jack Fugelsang for your patience, love, and brilliant humor. Thanks to my beloved brothers, Brian and Paul, two of the most complicated and brilliant people I know.

Deepest thanks to everyone at Simon & Schuster and Avid Reader Press, including Mr. Jofie Ferrari-Adler and my wonderful, wise, deeply tolerant editor, Carolyn Kelly.

Thank you so much to Dave Kass and to Eva Kerins, too. Thank you to everyone in production, including Allison Green, Annalea Manalili, Jessica Chin, Ruth Lee-Mui, and Hana Handzija. Thank you to Meredith Vilarello, Kayla Dee, and Emily Lewis in the marketing department; and to Alison Forner, Clay Smith, and Sydney Newman in the art department.

Thanks to my original editor, Julianna Haubner, who graciously received an early draft nearly twice the length of the book you're holding now.

Thanks to Bob LaFramenta, for his many years of kindness.

There's no adequate way to thank Julie Francella for the never-ending support and care given to me and my family throughout this process and beyond. Thank you for inspiring me.

Thanks to the amazing and tireless Ron Hartenbaum; and to George Vasilopoulos, Wendy King, Beowulf Rochlen, Kacey Evans, Sue Freund, and everyone at WYD Media and Political Voices Network.

Thanks to my wonderful producers at SiriusXM, Chris Hauselt and Thea Harper; and to my wonderful producers Neil Golub, Xorje Olivares, and Tatiana Zamis.

Thank you, Troy Conrad.

Thank you, Wayne Kabak, for being the finest William Morris agent who ever got me.

With gratitude to all the experts and authors quoted herein, including Dr. Anthea Butler, Rev. Barry Lynn, Kristin Kobes Du Mez, Keith Giles, Rev. John Pavlovitz, Pastor Desimber Rose, Dillon Naber Cruz, Rev. Dr. Susan Thistlethwaite, Rabbi Danya Ruttenberg, Rev. Jeff Hood, and Diana Butler Bass.

Thank you to my aunt Maureen Manacle; my aunt Dot Majewski; my uncle Bob Shank; my aunt Kathy Fugelsang; my mother-in-law, Joanne LaFramenta; and all my many cousins. Special thanks to my uncle and godfather Louis Fugelsang.

Thank you to Geoff Cheddy, who I love very much. Endless thanks to Neil Marks and Becca Parides.

Thank you, Frank Conniff, for being an inspiration, mentor, collaborator, and friend, for showing me how to make some of these matters funny, and for trusting me to sneak two cats onto a red-eye.

Profound thanks to Pam Mackinnon, Jim Nicola, Linda Chapman, and everyone at New York Theatre Workshop.

Thanks to the mighty Stephanie Miller; as well as Chris Lavoie, Jody Hamilton, Travis Bone, Jim Ward, Hal Sparks, Carlos Alazraqui, Frances Callier, Angela V. Shelton, Sean Comiskey, and Isabella Gerenscer.

Thank you, Lewis Black, Alan Zweibel, Judy Gold, Wanda Sykes, Rhonda Hansome, Margaret Cho, Dean Obeidallah, Travon Free, DL Hughley, Debra Wilson, Greg Proops, W. Kamau Bell, Negin Farsad, Alonzo Bodden, Dick Gregory, Rosie O'Donnell, Ahmed Ahmed, David Feldman, Paul Provenza, Darrell Hammond, Teresa Strasser, and Jim Gaffigan.

Thank you, Rick Overton, for your friendship and genius.

Thanks to Soledad O'Brian, Pete Dominick, Joy Reid, Ed Schultz, Rev. Michael Eric Dyson, Bill Maher, Scott Carter, Chris Hayes, Joy Behar, Don

Lemon, Stephanie Ruhle, Allison Gill, Abby Phillip, Nicole Sandler, Bill Press, Ayman Mohyeldin, and Karen Hunter. And thanks to all those nice conservative shows that have been kind and welcoming.

Thank you, Kelly Carlin. Your dad changed my life, but you made me better.

With gratitude to David Bohrman, Terry Baker, Shelley Lewis, Aaron Volkmann, Ron Zech, Jess Mabli, Katy Ramirez-Karp, Robert Lilly, David Sarosi, Matt Passett, Joanna Breen, Jennifer Granholm, Al Gore, and everyone who allowed these kinds of ideas at Current TV.

Thank you, Kate Schroeder.

Thank you, Steve Sadicario, Adam Liebner, Bill Clegg, JL Stermer, Mike August, Jennifer Craig, Chris Newman, Sandy Gallin, Gail Berman, and Bernie Brillstein for being so patient. Thanks, too, to Dave Gorab, Rory Belfi, and everyone at SiriusXM.

Thank you, David Crosby, for pushing me to do this, and for everything else.

Praise to Bishop John Shelby Spong, Sister Lilian Bouchard, Father Ray Rafferty, Rev. Jacqui Lewis, Professor Obery Hendricks, Father Richard Rohr, Marcus Borg, Karen Armstrong, Bart Ehrman, Rev. William Barber, Rev. Sandy Richards, Father Louis Reuss, Father Francis Pizzarelli, Reza Aslan, Dorothy Day, the *National Catholic Reporter*, Sister Helen Prejean, Hope House Ministries of Port Jefferson, Jemar Tisby, and the Catholic Center at NYU.

Thank you, Shane Killoran, for getting me to workshop parts of this in Beacon, NY; and for many other reasons.

Thanks, Budd Friedman, Jamie Masada, Estee Adoran, Barry Katz, Caroline Hirsch, Louis Faranda, Chris Mazzilli, Cary Hoffman, and far too many owners and bookers to name.

With gratitude to Alexandre Desplat, Nick Cave and Warren Ellis, James Horner, Hans Zimmer, Father John Misty, Bob Dylan, John Lennon, Kendrick Lamar, Gavin Greenaway, John Coltrane, The Velvet Underground, John Williams, Clint Mansel, Sister Rosetta Tharpe, PJ Harvey, Robbie Robertson, Johnny Greenwood, Neil Young, and Nina Simone.

Thanks to Jacki Schechner, Peter Ervolina, Marc Blanchenay, Scott

Rutkowsky, Ginny Reilly Drews, Sean Bertollo, Chely Wright, Sen. Gustavo Rivera, Keith Price, Barbara Barna Abel, Bill Flanagan, and Jeanne Heaton, the strongest person I know. Thank you, Paige Panzner, for many years of helping to figure it all out.

Thanks to Bill Van Horn, Bradlee and Marci Bing, Brent Earlanson, Vivian Koutrakous, Adrienne Grant, Carolyn Droskoski, and Theatre Three in Port Jefferson, NY.

Thank you to PBS, Roger Weisberg, and the entire crew of *Dream On*.

Jennifer Hegarty first began helping me compile the pieces that would become this book in 2015. In 2024 she helped me assemble a draft almost twice this length. I will always be grateful.

Thank you, Pier Paolo Pasolini, for *The Gospel According to St. Matthew*, which I saw at Cinema Village in NYC as a teenager and was never the same.

Thank you, The Duplex NYC, Our Lady of Perpetual Help Convent (Sound Beach, Long Island), Circle in the Square Theatre School, Boston University Theatre Institute, West Prep Academy (NYC), *The Nation*, Bill Bronner, Amelia David, The Young Turks, Terrie Silverman, Beth Lapides, Chuck D, Lily Tomlin, Jane Wagner, and Rob and Michelle Reiner.

I must also thank the many anonymous trolls I have debated or argued with on social media. I'm sorry for any times I gave in to anger, and I thank you for the lessons I learned from it. I also thank all the civil people who debate on social media, and they do exist.

Thanks to all the staff and tech crews at every theater, performing arts center, or club.

Finally, deepest thanks to all the listeners to our radio show and podcast, to all who've followed my curious path, and to everyone who comes to the live shows.

And thank you, George Harrison, for letting me ask you way too many questions about God. But that's another story.

About the Author

JOHN FUGELSANG is a comedian, actor, and broadcaster who hosts the acclaimed *Tell Me Everything* series on SiriusXM Progress, along with *The John Fugelsang Podcast*. He's been a regular on MSNBC, CNN, and FOX News, and hosted the live political talk show *Viewpoint* for Current TV. He retraced Alexis de Tocqueville's journey across the US for the PBS documentary *Dream On*, directed by Roger Weisberg and winner of the NYC Independent Film Festival award for Best Documentary. His Off-Broadway solo show, *All the Wrong Reasons*, directed by Tony Award–winner Pam MacKinnon and produced at New York Theatre Workshop, was nominated for the Drama League's Distinguished Performance Award. He's performed for US troops overseas, including the humanitarian mission to Haiti, and once interviewed George Harrison and Paul McCartney in different continents in the same week. His interview with George included several songs played impromptu on acoustic guitar; this proved to be George's final televised appearance and was broadcast on VH1 as "The Last Performance." Other credits include *CSI*, *Coyote Ugly*, *Maggie Black*, IFC's *The Onion News Network*, and the award-winning *Coexist Comedy Tour*. He's spoken on politics, comedy, and/or religion at nightclubs, universities, and the UK House of Commons. He lives with his family in New York City.